Women, Men and Politeness

Real Language Series

General Editors:
Jennifer Coates, Roehampton Institute, London
Jenny Cheshire, Universities of Fribourg and Neuchâtel,
and
Euan Reid, Institute of Education, University of London

Titles published in the series:

David Lee Competing Discourses: Perspective and
Ideology in Language
Norman Fairclough (Editor) Critical Language Awareness
James Milroy and Lesley Milroy (Editors) Real English: The
Grammar of English Dialects in the British Isles
Mark Sebba London Jamaican: Language Systems in Interaction
Ulrike H. Meinhof and Kay Richardson (Editors) Text, Discourse
and Context: Representations of Poverty in Britain
Janet Holmes Women, Men and Politeness
Ben Rampton Crossing: Language and Ethnicity Among Adolescents
Brian V. Street Social Literacies: Critical Approaches to Literacy in
Development, Ethnography and Education
Srikant Sarangi and Stefaan Slembrouck Language, Bureaucracy and
Social Control

Women, Men and Politeness

Janet Holmes

Longman
London and New York

Addison Wesley Longman Limited
Edinburgh Gate,
Harlow, Essex CM20 2JE, England
and Associated Companies throughout the world.

*Published in the United States of America
by Addison Wesley Longman Inc., New York*

First published 1995
Second impression 1996

ISBN 0 582 063620 CSD
ISBN 0 582 063612 PPR

British Library Cataloguing-in-Publication Data
A catalogue record for this book is
available from the British Library

Library of Congress Cataloging-in-Publication Data
Holmes, Janet.
   Women, men, and politeness / Janet Holmes.
      p. cm. - - (Real language series)
   Includes bibliographical references (p.   ) and index.
   ISBN 0 582-06362-0. -- ISBN 0-582-06361-2 (pbk.)
      1. Language and languages--Sex differences. 2. Courtesy.
   3. Sociolinguistics. I. Title. II. Series.
   P120.S48H64   1995
   306.4'4--dc20   94-28156
                                                        CIP

Set by 7 in 10/12 Sabon

Produced by Longman Singapore Publishers (Pte) Ltd.
Printed in Singapore

For David

Contents

Transcription conventions

I have generally transcribed utterances as simply as possible. Normal punctuation is used for examples which were noted down, but not recorded on tape or video. For recorded examples, no punctuation is imposed on the transcription, but I have used the following conventions to record features relevant to the particular examples.

Pause length is indicated by slashes: / indicates a short pause and // a slightly longer pause.

Pitch change is indicated above words where relevant: V indicates a fall-rise intonation; / marks rising intonation; \ indicates falling intonation.

Emphatic stress is indicated by capitals: e.g. CRAZY.

Turns: the relationship between speakers' turns is indicated visually: e.g. minimal feedback is placed at the point it occurs. Nell's *mm* occurs in the pause between Max's words *them* and *she's.*

Max: I mean I have no idea what story Pat had told them //
Nell: mm
Max: she's got a vivid imagination

Simultaneous speech is indicated with brackets:

Nell: mm/tricky/   did ⌈you ask her   ⌉
Max: ⌊I didn't know   ⌋ what to say

Unclear speech is indicated as follows: (......).

Acknowledgements

I would like to express my appreciation to the colleagues and friends who have helped me to write this book. In particular, I must thank Allan Bell, David Britain, and my editors, Jenny Cheshire and Jennifer Coates, all of whom read through this book in draft form and made many many helpful suggestions and comments. I must also thank Mike Bennett who helped me construct the figures and tables, and Meg Sloane who typed out many of the examples.

I must also express my thanks to Tony, Robbie and David Holmes who provided good company and support while this book was being written, as well as evidence that males can be linguistically polite when they put their minds to it!

The publishers are indebted to the following for permission to reproduce copyright material:

Dr David Britain for Figure 3.4 and Maria Stubbe for Figure 2.5.

1 *Sex, politeness and language*

Are women more polite than men? The question is deceptively simple. The answer, by contrast, is very complicated as this book will illustrate.

When a sociolinguist is asked this question her first reaction is to say 'it depends what you mean by politeness, and it depends which women and which men you are comparing, and it also depends on the context in which they are talking'. Considerations such as these mean that any answer needs to be hedged and qualified in all sorts of ways. But perhaps I should say right at the outset that, when all the necessary reservations and qualifications have been taken into account, I think the answer is 'yes, women are more polite than men'. This book explores some of the evidence for that conclusion.

Sex and language

There is certainly plenty of evidence of differences between women and men in the area of language. It is well established, for instance, that girls are verbally more precocious than boys (see Maccoby and Jacklin 1974; Chambers 1992).

> Over many years, women have demonstrated an advantage over men in tests of fluency, speaking, sentence complexity, analogy, listening, comprehension of both written and spoken material, vocabulary, and spelling.
>
> (Chambers 1992: 199)

By contrast

> men are more likely to stutter and to have reading disabilities. They are also much more likely to suffer aphasic speech disorders

after brain damage . . . Males are also four times more likely to
to suffer infantile autism and dyslexia than are females.

(Chambers 1992: 200)

Overall, females are clearly at an advantage in terms of verbal
skills, especially initially. But women and men also *use* language
differently, as we will see. And this is where differences in
politeness can be observed.

Most women enjoy talk and regard talking as an important
means of keeping in touch, especially with friends and intimates.
They use language to establish, nurture and develop personal
relationships. Men tend to see language more as a tool for
obtaining and conveying information. They see talk as a means to
an end, and the end can often be very precisely defined – a
decision reached, for instance, some information gained, or a
problem resolved. These different perceptions of the main
purpose of talk account for a wide variety of differences in the
way women and men use language, as the different chapters of
this book will illustrate.

Some of the patterns which will be described vary according to
the context. Men tend to dominate public talking time, for
instance, while women often have to work hard to get them to
talk in the privacy of their homes. Some of the differences reflect
different meanings attached to the same linguistic forms. Women
tend to use questions, and phrases such as *you know* to
encourage others to talk. Men tend to use such devices to qualify
the certainty or validity of the information they are asserting.
Men's reasons for talking often focus on the content of the talk
or its outcome, rather than on how it affects the feelings of
others. It is women who rather emphasise this aspect of talk.
Women compliment others more often than men do, and they
apologise more than men do too. All these patterns (and more)
will be explored and illustrated in the chapters that follow. They
certainly provide evidence that women and men use language
differently.

But if we are to assess whether one sex is more polite than the
other, we need to define what we mean by politeness. It is
important to begin with a clear understanding of what it means
to be linguistically polite.

What is politeness?

Example 1[1]
Wife lying in bed to husband who is getting dressed.
Amy: What time is it?
Carl: Almost seven o'clock.

Though language serves many functions, there are two – the referential and affective functions – which are particularly pervasive and basic (see Holmes 1982a, 1990a). The interaction in example 1 is primarily referential in its focus. Amy is seeking information which Carl supplies. On other occasions there could be other layers of meaning (e.g. a reproof for waking her so early), but in this case the only purpose of the question was to elicit the time. In other words it is clearly referential in its function.

Example 2
Young man, Alex, to friend contemplating a flat tyre.
What a bastard!

The utterance in example 2, by contrast, is primarily an expression of feelings. It expresses affective rather than referential meaning. No new information is conveyed that is not already apparent to the addressee. What the friend learns is how Alex feels about the situation they are observing. His utterance is clearly affective in its function.

The terminology differs, but this fundamental distinction has been repeatedly identified by linguists analysing many different features of language in a range of contexts (e.g. Brown 1977; Edmondson 1981; James 1983; Schiffrin 1987). The referential function of language is its function in conveying information, facts, or content. The affective function refers to the use of language to convey feelings and reflect social relationships. *Almost seven o'clock* is a predominantly informative utterance in response to *what time is it?*, whereas *What a bastard!* is an utterance with a predominantly affective message. Every utterance must express both functions, though one may be primary.

An utterance is always embedded in a social context which influences its form. The function of a greeting, an apology or a compliment will be predominantly affective or social. But even the form of a radio weather forecast which is predominantly referential in function, conveys information about the assumed social relationship between the presenter and the audience (Bell 1984, 1990). A great deal of the kind of conversation which is popularly labelled 'gossip' illustrates language serving both functions. Gossip conveys information – about people, events, attitudes – as well as serving the cohesive social function of emphasising membership of the in-group and reinforcing solidarity between contributors. In-group slang conveys a proposition (its referential meaning) as well as a social message in context (emphasising the boundaries of the group). Even the referentially orientated language of an exam paper reflects a particular (power-based) social relationship. Every utterance conveys social information about the relationship between the participants in the context in which it is uttered. The analysis of linguistic politeness focuses on this affective or social function of language.

Example 3
Young man knocks on a stranger's front door and says to the elderly man who opens the door.
I'm very sorry to bother you but our car has broken down. Could I possibly use your phone to ring the AA?

The young man in this example expresses himself very politely. He apologises for his intrusion, and his request for assistance is couched in very polite terms. Politeness is an expression of concern for the feelings of others. People may express concern for others' feelings in many ways, both linguistic and non-linguistic. Apologising for an intrusion, opening a door for another, inviting a new neighbour in for a cup of tea, using courtesy titles like *sir* and *madam*, and avoiding swear words in conversation with your grandmother could all be considered examples of polite behaviour.

In everyday usage the term 'politeness' describes behaviour which is somewhat formal and distancing, where the intention is not to intrude or impose, as illustrated in example 3 above. Being polite means expressing respect towards the person you are talking to and avoiding offending them. I will be using a broader definition of politeness. In this book 'politeness' will be used to refer to behaviour which actively expresses positive concern for others, as well as non-imposing distancing behaviour. In other words, politeness may take the form of an expression of good-will or camaraderie, as well as the more familiar non-intrusive behaviour which is labelled 'polite' in everyday usage.

This broader definition derives from the work of Goffman (1967) and Brown and Levinson (1987), which describe politeness as showing concern for people's 'face'. The term 'face' is a technical term in this approach. While it is based on the everyday usages 'losing face' and 'saving face', it goes further in treating almost every action (including utterances) as a potential threat to someone's face.

Everybody has *face needs* or basic wants, and people generally cooperate in maintaining each others' face, and partially satisfying each other's face needs. Politeness involves showing concern for two different kinds of face needs: first, negative face needs or the need not to be imposed upon; and secondly, positive face needs, the need to be liked and admired. Behaviour which avoids imposing on others (or avoids 'threatening their face') is described as evidence of *negative politeness*, while sociable behaviour expressing warmth towards an addressee is *positive politeness* behaviour (Brown and Levinson 1987). According to this approach, any utterance which could be interpreted as making a demand or intruding on another person's autonomy can be regarded as a potential *face-threatening act*. Even suggestions, advice and requests can be regarded as face-threatening acts, since they potentially impede the other person's freedom of action. Polite people avoid obvious face-threatening acts, such as insults and orders; they generally attempt to reduce the threat of unavoidable face-threatening acts such as requests or warnings by softening them, or expressing them indirectly; and they use positively polite utterances such as greetings and compliments where possible.

Using this definition, behaviour such as avoiding telephoning a colleague early on a Sunday morning or apologising for interrupting a speaker are expressions of negative politeness, while sending a birthday card to a friend, or calling a child *sweetie,* are expressions of positive politeness. As the examples suggest, politeness may be expressed both verbally and non-verbally, but in this book I will be focusing on *linguistic* politeness, or ways in which people express politeness through their use of language.

I suggested above that women tend to be more polite than men. More specifically, it will become clear in the following chapters that, in general, women are much more likely than men to express positive politeness or friendliness in the way they use language. Women's utterances show evidence of concern for the feelings of the people they are talking to more often and more explicitly than men's do.

> **Example 4**
> Helen and John were talking to their friend Harry who is a school principal. Harry was describing the problems that schools face in adjusting to the new competitive environment and describing the increase in stress this involved for teachers. In the course of the conversation he mentioned in passing some severe physical symptoms of stress that he had been experiencing. At this point Helen's attention was entirely directed to concern for his physical health, and as soon as there was an opportunity she asked, 'But are you OK now? Have you seen a doctor?'
>
> John's almost simultaneous comment continued the philosophical discussion about education policy: 'But this is a clear example of intensification of work – it's always the effect of pressure for increased efficiencies'. Harry's response to Helen's concern for his health was very brief and even a little impatient, suggesting her question was irrelevant, and this was reinforced as he picked up the discussion with John. When I questioned them later, both men remembered the incident and both argued that Helen's concern for Harry's health was inappropriate and distracting at that point in the discussion, even though they were all close friends.

This example suggests women and men may have different norms in this area. What each sex considers appropriate or polite in any particular context may differ quite markedly. Why should this be? Why do we find such differences in the way women and men use language?

Why do women and men interact differently?

A variety of explanations has been proposed for gender[2] differences in language use (see, for example, Henley and Kramarae 1991; Uchida 1992; Noller 1993). Some argue that innate biological differences account for sex-differentiated rates of language acquisition, for instance, as well as for differences in psychological orientation or temperament (e.g. Buffery and Gray 1972; McGlone 1980; McKeever 1987; Gottman and Levenson 1988). Psychological differences account for gender differences in orientation to others. Women are more concerned with making connections; they seek involvement and focus on the inter-dependencies between people (e.g. Chodorow 1974; Gilligan 1982; Boe 1987). Men are more concerned with autonomy and detachment; they seek independence and focus on hierarchical relationships. If one accepts this view, it is possible to see how such psychological differences might account for differences in the ways women and men use language. A preference for autonomy links more obviously with linguistic strategies that assert control, for example, while a focus on connection relates more obviously to linguistic devices that involve others and emphasise the interpersonal nature of talk.

Other researchers put a great deal of stress on socialisation as an explanatory factor (e.g. Maltz and Borker 1982; Tannen 1987). In many societies, girls and boys experience different patterns of socialisation and this, it is suggested, leads to different ways of using and interpreting language. In modern western societies, most girls and boys operate in single sex peer groups through an influential period of their childhood, during which they acquire and develop different styles of interaction. The boys' interaction tends to be more competitive and control-orientated, while the girls interact more cooperatively and focus on relative closeness. Gender differences in patterns of language use can be explained by the fact that girls and boys are socialised into different cultures. Each group learns appropriate ways of inter-acting from their same sex peers – including ways of interacting verbally.

A third explanation attributes gender-based differences in linguistic behaviour to the differential distribution of power in society. Men's greater social power allows them to define and control situations, and male norms predominate in interaction (Zimmerman and West 1975; West and Zimmerman 1987). It has also been suggested that those who are powerless must be polite (Deuchar 1988). So in communities where women are powerless members of a subordinate group, they are likely to be more linguistically polite than the men who are in control. An emphasis on in-group solidarity is a feature of oppressed groups (Brown and Levinson 1987); subordinate groups tend to stress the values and attitudes which distinguish them from those who dominate them. So this is another possible explanation for why women and men differ in the frequency with which they use some features of linguistic politeness.

How adequate are these explanations? Are they alternatives? Or does each have some contribution to make to our understanding of differences in women's and men's use of language? These are questions which will recur throughout the book as different examples of the way women and men use language are examined.

Analysing linguistic politeness

Linguistic devices expressing politeness

How can linguistic politeness be analysed and measured? What are the components of polite behaviour? These questions raise many interesting problems. Even restricting the focus to linguistic behaviour, there are potentially infinite means of expressing concern for the feelings of others. A greeting, a compliment, an apology, the use of hedges around a directive, giving encouraging feedback, using first names, using formal titles, adopting a gentle tone of voice, using emphatic stress to express enthusiasm . . . the list could go on and on. Languages provide infinite resources for expressing meaning, and linguistic politeness draws productively on these resources.

Different cultural and linguistic groups express politeness differently. Japanese linguistic politeness is more extensively expressed through the morphology of the language than is English linguistic politeness: Japanese verb forms, for example, are explicitly marked with suffixes selected for the degree of politeness they express as illustrated in example 5.

Example 5

(a) Sakai – ga   Suzuki-ni   chizu-o   kai – ta
    Sakai – Subject   Suzuki-for   map – Object   draw – past
          marker   marker   tense
    Sakai drew a map for Suzuki.

(b) Sakai – san   – ga   Suzuki – san – ni chizu-o
         respect   – Subject   respect   map – Object
         form   marker   form   marker

    kai – te   kudasai- mashti – ta
    draw – gerund   give   – polite – past
                        form   tense
    Mr Sakai gave Mr Suzuki the drawing of a map.

(Inoue 1979: 287–9).

The basic, straightforward, non-deferential utterance represented by (a) contrasts with the polite style used in (b) where the
polite verb ending *-mashti* is added to the verb *draw*. Moreover,
the speaker uses the respect form (or honorific) *-san* to express
respect for both the people mentioned, and the compound verb
form *kai-te kudasar-* showing deference to *Sakai*.

In Tzeltal, the language of a Mayan community, adverbial
particles which strengthen or weaken the force of speech acts
have been identified as important means of expressing politeness
(Brown 1980, discussed further in Chapter 3). Ochs's (1987)
research on Samoan suggests that variation in the frequency of
features such as case marking and word order may express
politeness among different groups. Though passing reference will
be made throughout this book to evidence such as this from other
languages and cultures, the focus will be on the way linguistic
politeness is expressed by women and men in English.

The linguistic means by which politeness is appropriately
conveyed in English are very varied. Lexical choice among
different words can be important in some contexts (e.g. slang
versus more formal vocabulary). An appropriate intonation can
reduce the apparent peremptoriness of a criticism, or convey
commitment to a compliment. Selecting the appropriate grammatical construction may convey greater or lesser politeness.
Modal verbs such as *would* and *could*, for instance, generally
soften directives, as illustrated in example 3 above and in
examples 6 and 7 below.

Different social groups use language very differently, and ways of being polite often contrast markedly. The use of slang among a group of young friends, for instance, reflects in-group membership, and so slang can express positive politeness or friendliness towards a new group member – it is an inclusive linguistic device. Swear words and insults may serve a similar purpose in other groups. Rugby players use insults such as *bastard, wanker* and the sexist *ugly girl* and *old woman* to express camaraderie: only members of the in-group are addressed in this way (Kuiper 1991). Within families, terms such as *dickhead* or *bitch* may be used as friendly insults between siblings, though they would not be used in the presence of non-family members.

Some groups use phrases such as *you know* and *sort of* more frequently than others as politeness devices. More frequent use of the tag *eh*, for instance (see Chapter 3) is a linguistic politeness device used more often by Maori than Pakeha New Zealanders (i.e. those of European origin). Though this book focuses on differences in the way women and men use politeness devices, it is important to bear in mind that gender is just one social variable which intersects with other social categories and groups that people belong to.

Form and function

Not only is there an infinite variety of ways of expressing linguistic politeness, it is also the case that the same linguistic devices can express different meanings in different contexts. There is nothing intrinsically polite about any linguistic form.

> **Examples 6 and 7**
> (6) Do you think it would be possible for you to contact Jean Thomas today?
>
> (7) Would it be a terrible imposition if I asked you to wash the dishes?

These utterances may appear extremely polite, but it is not possible to make such a judgement in a social vacuum. If utterance 6 is the first time this request has been made by the boss to the secretary, for instance, then it may well be accurately identified as a polite directive. It depends on the relationship between the two and their usual levels of social distance and formality. If they normally interact in a less formal style, and this is the second or third time the request has been made, then its formality may be an indirect expression of annoyance. The features which made it appear polite then function to express displeasure and irritation. Given the content of utterance 7, one might guess that rather than being genuinely polite, this utterance is sarcastic. If we know that it was addressed by a mother to her son, the likelihood that this interpretation is accurate is strengthened. The devices used to express the request politely exploit the usual signals of politeness between non-intimates (modal *would*, reference to the magnitude of the task, indirect strategy *if I asked you to wash the dishes* rather than direct *wash the dishes*). But these are inappropriate to such an intimate relationship – so in this context they function as indications of irony.

The meaning of the specific linguistic features used in both these utterances can only be interpreted accurately in the light of the relationship between the participants, and the particular context in which they were produced. In other words, analysing linguistic politeness involves attention to social context.

Social dimensions and linguistic analysis

There are a number of social dimensions which have proved useful in analysing linguistic politeness. I will briefly describe here the three dimensions which I will draw on most extensively in this book: (a) the solidarity-social distance dimension, (b) the power dimension, and (c) the formality dimension.

Solidarity-social distance

The relative social distance between the speaker and the addressee(s) is one of the most basic factors determining appropriate levels of politeness behaviour in most, if not all, societies. This is reflected in a wide range of sociolinguistic research over the last thirty years (see, for example, Geertz 1960; Brown and Gilman 1960; Bell 1984; Holmes 1992a). Theoretical models, such as those of Brown and Levinson (1987); Leech (1983) and Wolfson (1988), which have specifically addressed the issue of how to analyse linguistic politeness, all include consideration of social distance as a crucial factor.

Brown and Levinson (1987), for instance, identify relative social distance as a relevant social dimension in all cultures, though the precise factors which contribute to determining its importance in any community, and even in a particular interaction, will differ. Belonging to the same social group, sharing an occupation or common membership of a sports club or religious community, belonging to the same gender category, these are all factors which may be relevant in assessing the relative social distance or solidarity of particular relationships. But their importance must be assessed in context. Sometimes the fact that people work together, or the fact that they are all women, will contribute to their feeling more friendly towards one another. In other contexts, such factors may be irrelevant or may even increase social distance. Workmates may not be so friendly to each other when they are competing for promotion, for instance.

Frequency of interaction is another important factor to be considered in determining degree of solidarity. The social distance between two women who are both teachers at the same school and who see each other at the same squash club regularly, is likely to be less than the social distance between a female doctor and her male bus-driver patient whom she never sees except in the context of a medical consultation. Differences such as these are likely to be reflected in people's linguistic politeness behaviour.

Geoffrey Leech (1983: 126) also identifies social distance as a crucial factor in determining politeness behaviour or linguistic 'tact'. He points out that determining social distance involves considering the roles people are taking in relation to one another in a particular situation, as well as how well they know each other. So, a teacher might reasonably and legitimately say to a student *get that essay to me by next week*, but not *make me a cup of coffee* (Leech 1983: 126). The teacher's role confers authority over the student's academic behaviour, and so the imperative form, *get,* is justified in the former case. It is not normally part of a student's role to make coffee for a teacher, however, and a request of this kind would therefore need to be expressed with far more 'tact'. Politeness requires consideration of the rights appropriate to one's role.

One other model which puts a great deal of weight on social distance as a factor in accounting for differences in politeness behaviour is Nessa Wolfson's (1988) 'bulge' model of interaction. Wolfson suggests that, in general, speech behaviour tends to be most frequent and most elaborated between those who are acquaintances and casual friends, rather than between intimates or strangers. She writes

> when we examine the ways in which different speech acts are realised in actual everyday speech, and when we compare these behaviours in terms of the social relationships of the interlocuters, we find again and again that the two extremes of social distance – minimum and maximum – seem to call forth very similar behavior, while relationships which are more toward the center show marked differences.
>
> (Wolfson 1988: 32)

So at least in some respects we behave similarly to those at the two extremes of social distance, that is to people we do not know at all, on the one hand, and to intimates on the other. We do not bother to use a great deal of explicit linguistic politeness to people at either of these end-points on the social distance continuum.

People in between these extremes, however, namely acquaintances and friends, receive a great deal of attention in the form of linguistically polite interactions. We greet them more explicitly and profusely than strangers or intimates, we pay more compliments, issue more invitations, and apologise more frequently to people in the middle of the social distance dimension. In other words, as Figure 1.1 illustrates, there is a bulge in the amount of linguistic politeness that is paid to people who are neither in the category of complete strangers nor close and intimate friends.

Wolfson's model is based on the relative certainty of the relationships involved. She points out the two extreme points on the social distance axis which define *stable* relationships where people know what to expect (Wolfson 1988: 33). Strangers know where they stand with one another, as do intimates. There is little ambiguity in such clear-cut relationships, and similarly there is no need for ambiguity in speech behaviour. Relationships with casual friends are often much less certain and more ambiguous;

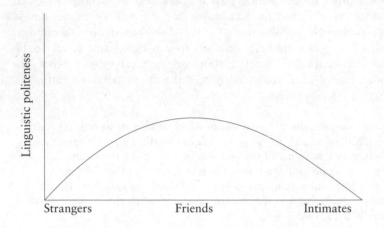

Figure 1.1 Wolfson's 'bulge' model. (Source: based on Wolfson 1988)

they are more 'dynamic and open to negotiation' (Wolfson 1988: 33), and in need of regular redefinition and reassurance. This is one of the functions of polite speech acts, and especially positively polite speech acts. Wolfson's model clearly treats relative social distance as a major factor in determining some aspects of linguistic politeness behaviour. In Chapters 4 and 5, we will see its usefulness in accounting for gender differences in patterns of compliments and apologies, in particular.

The specific way social distance or solidarity is expressed linguistically differs between different cultures (a point I will return to below). Generally, however, people express negative politeness more often to those it is appropriate to keep at a distance, and positive politeness more often to friends or potential friends. (Different cultures and social groups may, however, use very different criteria for placing people in such categories.) Positive politeness generally involves emphasising what people share, thus minimising the distance between them, while negative politeness avoids intruding, and so emphasises the social distance between people. For example, many English speakers use elaborated, qualified and sometimes very indirect ways of making requests to strangers or people they do not know well.

Examples 8–10
(8) *At a formal meeting.*
It's very hot in here. Would you mind if I opened a window.

(9) *On a plane.*
I'm sorry to disturb you but I think you may be in the wrong seat.

(10) *At a formal meeting.*
Excuse me, Dr Rubin, could you possibly pass the water.

In other words, in many contexts, as social distance increases so does negative politeness (see Figure 1.2).

Intimate ————————————————————— Distant
High solidarity   Low solidarity

POSITIVE POLITENESS	NEGATIVE POLITENESS

Figure 1.2 Solidarity-social distance dimension

By contrast, reduced social distance or high solidarity tends to result in the use of more positive politeness devices. Speakers are positively polite to friends and family with whom they get on well. The way such people greet each other, using informal linguistic features, compliments, and intimacy markers such as nicknames and endearments, illustrates this.

Examples 11–13
(11) *Wife and husband.*
W: Hi Rob – I'm home love.
H: Hooray dear – nice 'n early for once. Drink?

(12) *One friend to another.*
Alan: Miggles gidday – how y'doin'?
Margaret: Hi pal – great to see you. Wow you're looking good.

(13) *Mother to son.*
Bath-time Sonny-Jim.

Expressing the appropriate degree of politeness often involves assessing the social distance between speaker and addressee in a situation. The choice between first name (e.g. *Jean*) and title plus last name (e.g. *Dr Hall*), for instance, frequently reflects the relationship between participants on this dimension, and getting it wrong can cause offence (e.g. Brown and Ford 1961; Laver 1981). Nicknames (e.g. *Miggles, Sonny-Jim*), friendship terms (e.g. *pal, mate*), and endearment terms (e.g. *love*) are positive politeness devices which are appropriate to friends and family. More formal address terms such as title plus last name (*Mrs Thorne, Dr Rubin*) are examples of negative politeness devices which are appropriate for addressing people we know less well. In many European languages such as French, German and Italian, being linguistically polite involves a choice between T pronouns (such as French *tu*, German *du* and Italian *tu*) and V pronouns (such as French *vous*, German *Sie* and Italian *Lei*). One of the relevant factors in making this choice is the social distance or solidarity between the speaker and addressee (Brown and Gilman 1960). In multilingual communities the choice between different languages may reflect the same dimension. The choice of Shi, a tribal language, in the city of Bukavu in Zaire, for example, may express solidarity or positive politeness towards a person from your tribe. In parts of Switzerland the use of the local Swiss German dialect (as opposed to standard German) has the same effect. A choice between languages in one community can have the same function (expressing solidarity) as a choice between dialects or address terms in others.

Different groups use different linguistic strategies for the same purpose. Women and men are no exceptions. It seems possible that women and men have different preferred ways of expressing solidarity, in particular. The dimension of social distance or solidarity is a crucial one in accounting for differences in women's and men's linguistic politeness behaviour, as we shall see in the chapters which follow.

Power

Relative power or hierarchical status is another important consideration in determining the appropriate degree of linguistic politeness. It is an intrinsic component of Brown and Levinson's and Leech's theories of politeness, and Wolfson (1984) also regards power as an important factor explaining some patterns of linguistic politeness.

Power refers to the ability of participants to influence one another's circumstances. It has been defined as 'the possibility of imposing one's will upon other persons' (Galbraith 1983: 2), or the ability to control the behaviour of others (Brown and Gilman 1960). Brown and Levinson (1987: 77) define relative power in a relationship as the degree to which one person can impose their plans and evaluations at the expense of other people's. Similarly, Leech (1983: 126) discusses the power or 'AUTHORITY of one participant over another'.

The distribution of power in a particular context may derive from a variety of sources – money, knowledge, social prestige, role and so on. The power of an older child over a younger child, or of a male over a female, are further culturally constructed sources of power in many communities. Whatever the source, high power tends to attract deferential behaviour, including linguistic deference or negative politeness. We generally avoid offending more powerful people, and the way we talk to them often expresses respect (see Figure 1.3).

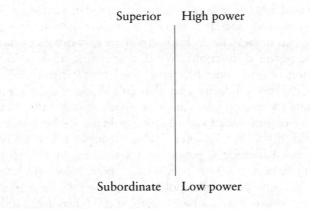

Superior   High power

Subordinate   Low power

Figure 1.3 Power dimension

Again, the terms we use to address people can illustrate this point. More formal address terms are frequently appropriate to superiors and to those who have more power or authority in a particular context. Secondary school pupils often use *sir*, for instance, as a polite form of address to their male teachers, and title plus last name to their female teachers. The managing director is likely to be addressed as *Ms Wilton* rather than *Cath* by the factory floor workers (though, as we will see in later chapters, high status does not always guarantee that women will be treated with respect). By contrast, school pupils and subordinates will often be addressed by first name by their teachers and superiors. In languages which provide a T/V choice (i.e. a choice between alternative second person pronouns, as in French *tu/vous*), politeness is a relevant factor in this choice. When power is the overriding dimension, politeness is likely to require subordinates to use the V pronoun to superiors, while the subordinates may appropriately be addressed with the T pronoun. This non-reciprocal pattern reflects the distribution of power in the relationship: the superior attracts linguistic defer- ence while the subordinate does not. The precise weighting to be given to power or status in relation to gender in any society is a matter for investigation. If one accepts the view that women are generally a subordinate group relative to men, then the inter- action of gender and other factors which contribute to the assessment of relative power is clearly a complex matter.

Obviously, too, social distance and power interact. Negative politeness strategies tend both to express distance and to emphasise power distinctions. Western societies, at least, tend to treat strangers and superiors very similarly. Positive politeness strategies express solidarity and also emphasise equality between participants. Where people want to emphasise social distance, the norms may require reciprocal negative politeness – both sides will use formal titles, for instance. Where people want to reduce social distance (despite a power or status difference), reciprocal positive politeness tends to prevail: e.g. both sides will use first names. And between equals, politeness usage will be determined by factors other than power (e.g. social distance, and the formality of the context). So the way you talk to your closest friend will depend on where you are talking.

In most western societies today, what Brown and Gilman (1960: 260) call the solidarity semantic has increasingly displaced the power semantic in many contexts: 'solidarity has largely won out over power'. In other words, solidarity is generally given more weight than power in determining appropriate linguistic behaviour. Despite power differences, people who know each other well will use first names reciprocally, for instance.

Women are regarded as a subordinate or less powerful group than men in many communities, and this is, not surprisingly, often reflected in the different politeness devices used by and addressed to women. Wolfson (1984) goes so far as to suggest that the fact that women are complimented more often than men is an indication of their subordinate status, since compliments can be regarded as patronising and prescriptive socialisation strategies (see Chapter 4). Moreover, subordinates can be treated impolitely with impunity – interrupted, talked over, ignored and even subtly insulted. The power dimension is thus an important tool for analysing the politeness patterns which characterise different groups, as will be demonstrated in Chapter 2.

Formality

Context is a fundamental influence on the expression of politeness. In a formal setting, such as a law court or ceremonial occasion, speakers tend to focus on transactional roles rather than personal relationships, and negative politeness is the prevalent pattern. Brothers who are barristers will refer to each other in court as *my learned colleague*. A Minister's secretary will generally address her as *Minister* in a formal meeting, but reciprocal first names are more likely between them in private. School pupils may use a teacher's first names in out-of-school activities, but back in the classroom the asymmetrical pattern of title plus last name for the teacher and first name for the pupil will reassert itself. Similarly, in languages with a T/V distinction, the V form may be considered the appropriately polite form for very formal contexts, regardless of the personal relationships involved.

The formality dimension is not explicitly treated as a separate factor in the politeness models of Leech (1983) or Brown and Levinson (1987).[3] They assume that, in the analysis of any parti-cular interaction, situational factors are satisfactorily accounted for as components of other dimensions, such as power and social distance (1987: 79). This emphasises the fact that assessments of relative power and social distance are always context-dependent. The relative power, for example, between you and your boss will be assessed differently at a meeting in the workplace compared to a meeting at the swimming pool. Nevertheless, in my view, it has proved more useful to take account explicitly of the relative formality of the context, especially in the analysis of certain features of interaction (such as amount of talk and verbal feedback).

In general, negative politeness strategies will occur more often in formal settings and interactions, while positive politeness tends to characterise more intimate and less formal situations (see Figure 1.4).

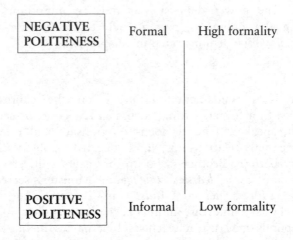

Figure 1.4 Formality dimension

In example 14, a very formal context, the addressee is referred to in the third person and the language is formal and distant – using typical negative politeness devices such as the word *please*. In the functionally equivalent utterance 15, the address form *love* is a positive politeness device, and the form of the request is a very direct question, reflecting the intimacy of the relationship, and the informality of the context.

Examples 14 and 15
(14) *Judge to witness in law court.*
The witness will please repeat his response to the last question for
the benefit of the jury.

(15) *Husband to wife at home.*
mm? what was that love?

Note that in different circumstances, such as a question from a
prosecutor in court to an accused person, the question *what was
that?* might be experienced as very threatening. Clearly, linguistic
behaviour is powerfully affected by context, and by people's
perceptions of the appropriate usage for a particular context.
When differences occur in the way politeness devices are used by
women and men, the formality of the context will be an
important factor to take into consideration as we shall see in the
following chapters. It seems possible that women and men may
have different perceptions of appropriate linguistic behaviour in
different contexts. The interaction patterns of women and men
for instance are very different in formal, public contexts and
informal, private contexts, as we shall see in Chapter 2. To some
extent this may reflect the different emphasis that women and
men appear to put on the functions of interaction in different
contexts.

Politeness is always context dependent. Judgements about the
social significance of linguistic choices must always take account
of group (including female and male) and community norms, and
can only be made in context. So using someone's first name may
be intended and interpreted as positive politeness behaviour
within a group of work colleagues. But if a new worker uses the
boss's first name on first introduction, this may be experienced
not as positively polite behaviour, but as a face-threatening
impertinent act – as impolite or rude. A lawyer who addressed
the judge by first name in court, referring inappropriately to their
personal relationship in a professional context, would be
regarded as presumptuous. While manipulation of the norms is
possible for special effects such as humour, insult, or reprimand,
misjudgements are likely to be perceived negatively. Getting it
wrong is not just failing to be appropriately polite, it generally
results in being judged as rude or insensitive, on the one hand, or

effusive and insincere on the other. If women and men have different norms, as Tannen (1990a) suggests, the potential for miscommunication is clear. But less powerful groups have more to lose. Sociolinguistic incompetence is not easily disregarded, and, when norms conflict, women's definitions of politeness are unlikely to prevail.

Cross-cultural contrasts

Though the dimensions of analysis proposed above are universal, the relative emphasis on different factors differs from one culture and social group to another. The importance of status vs solidarity, or the weight accorded to the formality of the context, is not fixed and absolute but relative and variable (see Sifianou 1992 for an excellent review of this issue). In many cultures, power or status is given more weight than solidarity, even in personal interactions. You speak respectfully to a superior no matter how well you know them. Negative politeness strategies tend to predominate in the associated languages. Javanese women, for example, are expected to speak with deference to their husbands (Smith-Hefner 1988). Japanese speakers pay a great deal of attention to the relative roles and positions of participants in a variety of hierarchies, and select the appropriate linguistic level accordingly (Ide 1982, 1990). Generally, however, Japanese women are required to express themselves with more deference than men (Smith 1992). They use a wider and more complex range of honorifics than men. and they are particularly sensitive to the complex contextual factors which determine polite usage (Ide et al. 1986). Context is a crucial determinant of appropriate ways of speaking in Tzeltal, the language of the Mayan community studied by Brown (1990). Women's Tzeltal speech is normally a paradigm of negative politeness, character-ised by restraint and circumspection. In the context of litigation, however, confrontational displays are permitted and 'women are given license to excel in public demonstrations of anger and outrage' (Brown 1990: 138). The weighting assigned to solidarity, status and context may vary quite dramatically between one culture and another.

Correctly identifying what is perceived as polite behaviour in a culture involves understanding the society's values. Japanese people, for instance, value empathy and sensitivity to the needs of others. Confrontation and directness are regarded as childish and immature in Japanese culture. Mature speakers have developed communicative skills which enable them to avoid confrontation (Wetzel 1988). In some cultures, solidarity-orientated positive politeness is emphasised and more highly valued than distance-orientated negative politeness, while in others the reverse is the case. Brown and Levinson (1987: 250), for instance, characterise the western United States of America, some New Guinea cultures and the Mbuti pygmies as 'friendly back-slapping' positive politeness cultures by contrast with 'lands of stand-offish creatures like the British (in the eyes of the Americans), the Japanese (in the eyes of the British) . . . and the Brahmans of India'. Such stereotyped perceptions of cultural differences will always be relative, as Brown and Levinson's parenthetical phrases suggest. It is impossible to describe politeness behaviour without presenting it from a particular viewpoint. New Zealanders, for instance, perceive Australians as belonging to the group of back-slapping positive politeness cultures, while Australians consider New Zealanders as somewhat stand-offish proponents of a negative politeness culture, but both these communities share the stereotypes of the American and the British described by Brown and Levinson.

As mentioned briefly above, the specific linguistic features of what is considered polite behaviour differ from one culture to another. Indian immigrants to Britain have been stereotyped as abrupt and impolite because their linguistic norms for offering services differ from those of the majority culture (Gumperz 1978, Roberts et al. 1992). Americans using Hindi or Marathi, on the other hand, will be perceived as overly effusive by South Asians who do not use explicit expressions of gratitude in commercial transactions or with family and friends (Apte 1974). Requests made in English by German speakers and Israeli Hebrew speakers are likely to be perceived as rude, if we accept the validity of questionnaire results indicating that these cultural groups use very much more direct strategies than British English speakers (House and Kasper 1981; Blum-Kulka, Danet and Gherson 1985: 135–6). By contrast, Byrnes (1986) suggests that German speakers perceive Americans and British English speakers as overly polite and wishy-washy. English complaints tend to sound like elaborate prevarications when assessed by German and Hebrew sociolinguistic norms.

Tannen's (1984) analysis of Jewish American norms of interaction illustrate clearly how even within English, the 'same' behaviour is interpreted differently by different cultural groups. What Tannen describes as the 'high involvement' style typical of Jewish New Yorkers is perceived by Californians as an aggressive impolite style with speakers constantly interrupting others. Swedes and Norwegians are perceived as rudely interrupting by Finns who pause between speakers for longer than do their Scandinavian compatriots (Lehtonen and Sajavaara 1985).

Linguistic politeness, then, is one expression of cultural values, and accurate analysis involves identifying the relative importance of different social dimensions in particular cultures. Moreover, any particular example of linguistic behaviour may be perceived quite differently by different cultural groups, and even by individual members of a particular group. One person's enthusiastic supportive feedback may be perceived by another as a confrontational disruption. Cultural context is as important as social context in analysing politeness. And information on differences in women's and men's linguistic behaviour in non-western cultures is a valuable check on researchers' tendencies to over-generalise and to regard patterns they identify as universal.

What's in store

In the chapters which follow, using data from New Zealand English, I will examine a range of different aspects of women's and men's linguistic politeness behaviour. As the definition of politeness outlined above suggests, when we say that someone is polite, or alternatively when we label someone as rude or impolite, there are many possible features of their use of language that we might be referring to. Linguistic politeness means recognising the autonomy of others and avoiding intrusion (negative politeness), as well as emphasising connectedness and appreciation (positive politeness). In western cultures, polite people tend to phrase their utterances considerately, respond encouragingly and positively to others' talk, pay compliments, and express appreciation generously. They avoid being too forceful or direct, interrupting, hogging the talking time, arriving late without an apology, giving peremptory orders, omitting expressions of appreciation – these are all examples of behaviour which may be considered rude in certain contexts.

Even within one culture, there is an infinite range of ways of expressing politeness. In the research I have undertaken on gender differences in the expression of linguistic politeness I have inevitably had to be selective. It would have been possible to focus on a small canvas in depth, as many linguists have done to good effect (e.g. Tannen 1984; Preisler 1986). I have chosen instead to spread my net wide and explore the way women and men use a number of contrasting features of linguistic politeness. I have examined how specific interactional strategies contribute to politeness, and looked at how particular linguistic forms operate as politeness devices; and I have investigated the way two speech functions which have been associated with positive and negative politeness are expressed by women and men.

Being linguistically polite involves being a considerate partici-pant in interaction. This generally involves different behaviour in different situations. In a discussion session, or when someone asks a question, it is polite to contribute in order to fill the silence. But when many people want a chance to talk and there is competition for the floor, it is polite not to talk for too long. Interrupting others is always rude provided an interruption is defined as an unwelcome disruption of another's speaking turn. But then there is the problem of distinguishing between turns at talk which are disruptive and those which are not. Providing feedback to encourage others to keep talking can be perceived as a positive politeness device, since it indicates interest in what the other person is saying. But the forms which people use to give such feedback are often indistinguishable from minimal responses which simply indicate understanding, and even from those which signal lack of interest. It is their placement and frequency which is crucial to their classification as politeness devices or not. Measuring linguistic politeness in interaction is a complex task. Chapter 2 examines evidence on the relative politeness of different interaction patterns of New Zealand women and men in different contexts.

Chapter 3 examines the ways in which particular linguistic

forms may be used as politeness devices, and the evidence that New Zealand women and men use them differently. The analysis focuses on linguistic devices which increase or reduce the strength or force of an utterance. Devices which reduce the force of an utterance are generally labelled 'hedges', while those which increase its force can be called 'boosters' (though there are many other labels too). Hedges and boosters may fundamentally affect the perception of an utterance as polite or not.

Another aspect of linguistic politeness is the way people express and use different functions of speech such as apologies, compliments, greetings or expressions of gratitude. Positive politeness is essentially other-orientated behaviour. Within limits, and taking account of their appropriateness in context, the frequency with which a person pays a compliment is likely to affect an evaluation of how polite and considerate they are. Similarly apologising for an offence is an essential feature of politeness behaviour. In Chapters 4 and 5 these functions of speech are investigated, and the distribution and form of compliments and apologies in the speech of New Zealand women and men is discussed in some detail.

The final chapter addresses the issue of the implications of differences in women's and men's politeness behaviour, in just two broad contexts – the educational and the professional world. What happens in classrooms if politeness norms differ? Whose norms prevail and what effect does this have on the learning opportunities of pupils? And when women and men work together, whose norms dominate the workplace and with what effects? There are equity implications of gender differences in politeness behaviour in the classroom and in peer talk between professionals. Does it help if people are aware of gender-based politeness patterns in these contexts? How could one change things if the situation seems unsatisfactory? The last chapter addresses these issues with the goal of improving communication between the sexes and increasing the effectiveness of interaction in the classroom and the workplace.

Caveats

I began this chapter by saying that a sociolinguist would answer the question 'Are women more polite than men?' by saying 'it depends'. It is important before proceeding with a discussion of the research which has led me to assert that women are generally more polite than men, to provide some of the qualifications which must be borne in mind when considering the evidence provided in this book.

First, it is important to be aware that the diverse range of features investigated in this book provides some idea of the complex reality of linguistic politeness, but it is still only a small section of the complete canvas. The full picture is even richer, both in ways of expressing politeness and in the range of social factors which interact with gender in determining their patterning.

The data in this book was collected from speakers of New Zealand English. New Zealand has been described as a 'gendered culture', a culture in which 'the structures of masculinity and femininity are central to the formation of society as a whole', a culture in which 'the intimate and structural expressions of social life are divided according to gender' (James and Saville-Smith 1989: 6–7). Gender, it has been suggested, is the motif and pre-occupation of New Zealand society, as class is in Britain. Women and men are more effectively trapped in gender roles in New Zealand than in Britain, it is claimed. The reasons can be traced back to the continuing influence of symbols of the pioneer origins of New Zealand Pakeha[4] society such as 'Man Alone' and 'Dependent Woman'. The strength of the concept of male mateship derives from those pioneering days, for example, as does the strength of the concept of woman as home-maker. It is also possible that gender appears so salient in New Zealand because social class categorisation is generally weaker than in Britain.

Even if one has reservations about the extent to which such claims can be sustained, they do suggest that New Zealand English may be a particularly productive source of data on differences in women's and men's use of language. Research on gender differences identified in the speech of American, British and Australian speakers of English tends to support the findings reported in this book (e.g. Thorne et al. 1983; Poynton 1985; Coates and Cameron 1989; Graddol and Swann 1989; Tannen 1990a; Coates 1993a). But perhaps, if gender is a particularly fundamental dimension of New Zealand society, as James and

Saville-Smith argue, the contrasts are starker or more pervasive than in other western cultures. New Zealand women and men may provide a particularly appropriate sample for investigating the relationship between language and gender.

Nevertheless, generalisations about politeness behaviour, and more specifically about women's and men's politeness behaviour, must always be subject to the qualifications imposed by the sample from which particular evidence is drawn. The specific features of this sample, including its size, differ from chapter to chapter, since this book documents research on New Zealand women's and men's speech based on data collected over a considerable period of time, and analysed in numerous distinct studies. However, overall, in this research, as in many other areas of linguistic research, the patterns that have been described at this initial stage of investigating specific features of politeness behaviour are predominantly those of the white western-educated middle class.

It is clear from the cross-cultural evidence that is available, that conceptions of politeness and ways of being polite differ markedly between cultures (e.g. Philips et al. 1987; García 1989). It seems very likely that different social groups within a community also have different politeness norms, although very little research has been undertaken to investigate this. While there is some discussion in Chapter 3 of differences in the way some Maori and Pakeha working-class groups use two particular pragmatic features of English, this book certainly does not explore ethnic or class differences in the use of New Zealand English. Rather it addresses the question 'are women more polite than men?' by looking at linguistic evidence collected predominantly from white middle-class females and males. Hopefully, it will stimulate others to collect data which will fill in some of the gaps.

In a book which focuses on women's and men's linguistic politeness behaviour, many of the statements about the way women and men use language will inevitably appear as gross generalisations from specific studies of particular men and women in particular situations who belong to specific cultures, social classes, age groups, occupational groups, and so on. It would be possible to qualify every statement with this kind of detailed information, but it would also be tedious in the extreme.

In discussing the research evidence every reference to women and men should be appropriately qualified, but for obvious reasons I have tended to refer simply to women and men. This is not intended to mislead or to over-generalise. Wherever possible I will provide the kind of detailed non-linguistic information which is necessary to assess the generalisability of a claim, but I will not repeat it every time I use the words women and men thereafter.

Having hedged my claims appropriately, it is time to turn to an examination of the evidence for my claim that, in general, women are more polite than men, and that in particular they are more positively polite or linguistically supportive in interaction.

Notes

1. Throughout this book I have used genuine examples of interaction wherever possible (though for obvious reasons I have changed names). It has occasionally been necessary to construct an example in order to illustrate a point concisely. In such cases the example is marked '[constructed]'.
2. It is now widely accepted that 'gender' is the appropriate term for the socially constructed categories which define appropriate feminine and masculine behaviour, while 'sex' refers to biologically based distinctions (see, for example, Eckert 1989 for a valuable discussion of this issue). In this book gender is therefore the appropriate term for describing differences in linguistic behaviour along the feminine-masculine dimension.
3. Brown and Levinson (1987) and Leech (1983) both include one further factor in their politeness models. This is labelled the 'ranking of the imposition' by Brown and Levinson (1987: 74) and 'the cost-benefit scale' by Leech (1983: 123). This factor is most relevant in the analysis of a rather restricted group of speech acts (such as directives). I have left the discussion of this factor, therefore, to Chapter 5 where it proves useful in the analysis of apologies.
4. The term 'Pakeha' generally refers to New Zealanders of European origin.

2 Who speaks here? Interacting politely

Example 1
Two friends talking over a coffee at Max's place.
Max: I got a phone call from Pat's mother saying you/ c-
　　you're a complete bastard Pat's told us what you did to
　　her// you're so inconsiderate/　　　　especially when
Nell:　　　　　　　　　　　　　oh dear
Max: she's been under such stress// well what was I
　　supposed to say/ what did they want
Nell: mm/ tricky/ did ⌈you ask her　　⌉
Max:　　　　　　⌊I didn't know ⌋what to say/
　　I mean I have no idea what story Pat had told them//
Nell: mm
Max: she's got a vivid imagination when she gets started who
　　knows w-/ who knows what fabrication they had been
　　treated to
Nell: well she was pretty stressed out /maybe they were just
　　over-reacting from worry ⌈about her d'you think ⌉
Max:　　　　　　　　　　⌊not them not them　　⌋
　　they just hate my guts// any excuse to abuse me/ I'm
　　not good enough for their daughter

[The words within the square brackets were uttered simultaneously.]

In Chapter 1, I suggested that women more often focus on the social or affective function of talk, while men tend to orientate to its referential function. In this chapter, I will examine a range of interactive strategies that provide some support for this suggestion.

Example 1 illustrates some of these strategies. This is intimate talk. Max is letting off steam to Nell who is listening sympathetically. It appears to be a good example of a male expressing affective meaning and using talk to establish solidarity. Note, however, that Max expresses frustration because he does not see the point of Pat's mother's call. What was her message? What did she expect him to do? What, in other words, was the referential meaning of the interaction? Note also that Max talks most, that he interrupts Nell twice, and that he baldly contradicts her suggestion (*not them not them*). Nell's encouraging responses (*oh dear, mm*) are neatly placed to be non-disruptive and her questions seem designed to encourage Max's train of thought. Though short, this interchange proves remarkably typical of patterns of interaction between women and men in a variety of contexts.

Talk has different significance in different contexts. Effective talk in a public context can enhance your status – as politicians and other public performers know. (Equally, of course, a poor performance can be damaging.) Getting and holding the floor is generally regarded as desirable, and competition for the floor in such contexts is common. In more private contexts, talk usually serves different functions. The purpose of intimate talk is not so much status enhancement as establishing or maintaining solidarity or 'connection' (Chodorow 1974: 44). What will polite behaviour entail in such different contexts? In this chapter I will discuss the different ways in which talk is distributed between New Zealand women and men in different contexts, and the politeness implications of these patterns.

Questions are another area where gender differences have been noted in different contexts. Who asks most in different contexts and why? What is the function of questions in different situations? We will see in Chapter 3 that superficially similar forms can have very different effects depending on who is using them to whom and why. A tag question, for example, may be a positive politeness device, inviting participation, or it may be a confrontational, critical or challenging strategy which is anything but polite. In this chapter I will focus on the distribution of different types of questions in public contexts.

Questions are one way of handing the floor over to another speaker. If you want to gain the floor, interrupting is generally considered an effective – though impolite – strategy. The interruption patterns typical of women and men have been well studied in Britain and the United States. The third section of this chapter provides some New Zealand data on gender differences in patterns of interruption, alongside a discussion of the complementary behaviour of providing positive feedback to encourage the speaker to continue – a much more obvious positively polite strategy.

In the final section the focus moves to the function of utterances in interaction – agreeing with someone is obviously a supportive speech act with a positive politeness function, while disagreeing is generally face threatening and poses a problem for politeness. The different ways in which these are handled by New Zealand females and males in interaction is obvious relevant to a consideration of politeness behaviour.

Once again, the importance of different types of context in interpreting the different patterns of male and female talk is particularly clear. In more formal contexts relative roles, power relationships and statuses are relevant, while informal and intimate contexts tend to be places for personal interactions where social distance and solidarity are the most relevant dimensions. The relative emphasis on status and solidarity in different contexts is particularly clearly illustrated when we consider possible explanations for who talks most in different contexts.

Who's got the floor?

One very simple way in which people are polite is by producing the appropriate amount of talk for the situation they are in. Being polite at a party usually involves interacting with others; being polite in a discussion may mean allowing or even encouraging others to contribute; being polite in an intimate context often involves being a good listener as well as a willing contributor. The appropriate amount of talk for a polite contribution varies quite markedly from one situation to another. Moreover, it seems possible that women and men have different interactional norms or rules in this area.

This possibility occurred to me as I identified a number of differences in the way New Zealand women and men interacted in different contexts. Not only did the relative amount of talk produced by each sex differ from one situation to another, but the pattern which emerged presented a picture of women as facilitative and cooperative contributors in a range of contexts.

Interviewer talk

On the whole talk is regarded as a 'good thing' in western culture. The opportunity to talk – especially in public – is generally valued. Consequently, male domination of the talking time is often perceived by women as inherently unfair, and as evidence of male control. While this is undeniably true in some contexts, such as formal meetings, like most generalisations, it is an over-simplification. Much depends on the purpose of the interaction and the different roles participants are expected to play. This is well illustrated by a study of the distribution of talk in three television interviews (Franken 1983). The interviewee in each case was a well-known male, and in each programme there were three interviewers: the front-person, who was a woman, and two invited guests – different people in each interview – one male and one female. It was reasonable to expect that the males being interviewed should dominate the talking time available, as indeed they did. In an interview the interviewee has the responsibility to do most of the talking. Anything else would have been anomalous, and it would be ludicrous to suggest this was evidence of male domination and control.

The role of the interviewers, on the other hand, was quite different. Their job was to elicit talk, to encourage the interviewee to contribute in an interesting way. There was no reason why any one of them should have talked more than any other, though perhaps the front-person, as the person responsible for the programme, might legitimately have been expected to contribute more than her two guest assistants. The distribution of talk, however, revealed a very different pattern, as can be seen in Figure 2.1. In a situation where each of the interviewers was entitled to a third at most of the talking time, the males in each of the three television programmes in fact appropriated at least half. In this context, then, the women behaved more politely than the men, and more appropriately in relation to their roles (a pattern confirmed by Troemel-Ploetz's 1992 analysis of German TV discussions). They facilitated the interviewee's contributions, while keeping their own contributions brief.

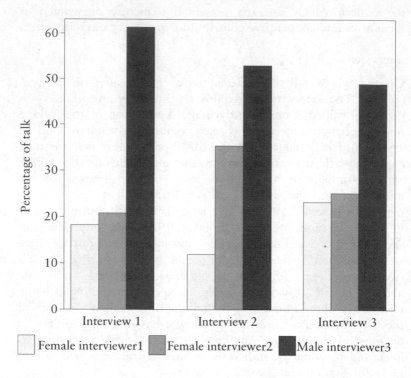

Figure 2.1 Amount of talk by TV interviewers

Interviewee talk

Another example comes from a private and less formal context and focuses on the other side of the interview, namely on the person being interviewed. Whereas one might expect interviewers to be frugal with words since their job is to elicit talk, the same is not true of interviewees. A cooperative interviewee, as mentioned above, is one who contributes plenty of talk. This was very evident during the interviews with New Zealand women and men which were collected for the Wellington Social Dialect Survey (Holmes et al. 1991). As far as we were concerned, the more talk the better. Being polite in this context meant being prepared to answer questions fully and at length. It soon became apparent that the least cooperative and polite participants were the young Pakeha males (i.e. those of European origin). They seemed determined to answer every question as briefly as possible, and in many cases monosyllabically. This despite the fact that they were being interviewed by a young man of similar age and background. (Interviewers were matched in ethnicity and gender with the people they were to interview.)

Example 2
I, the interviewer, is talking to Trevor a young Pakeha man.
I: how long you lived here
T: about a year and a half
I: what was it like/ has it changed since you've been here
T: no
I: what are the people like// are they friendly
T: oh some of them
I: um you remember the story reading about the passage in
       the boat and that um
T: yeah
I: um somebody getting into danger and that you ever exp-/
       put yourself in a position where you thought you might c- /
       not come out of it alive// kill yourself or anything//
T: nah
I: um / have you had any really bad accidents/
T: nah

By contrast most of the women were willing to talk at length. None produced anything like the kind of monosyllabic responses illustrated above, and some checked out regularly with their interviewer whether they were providing a satisfactory response.

Example 3
Female interviewee to interviewer.
Jo: is this the sort of thing you want like/ I'm just rabbiting on
       here/ are you sure this is what you want

A study which tested out more formally the hypothesis that women are particularly sensitive to the appropriate 'talk requirements' of different contexts involved a picture description task (Meyerhoff 1986). A group of ten New Zealand women and men, carefully matched for age and social class, were asked to describe a picture in sufficient detail for an interviewer to 'spot the differences' between the copy of the picture that she or he held and the interviewee's modified copy. Each interviewee performed the task with a male and a female interviewer. It was made quite clear to the interviewees that the more speech they produced the better. Overall, the women contributed more speech than the men in each context: i.e. both to the male and to the female interviewer, as illustrated in Figure 2.2. Interestingly, both women and men produced more talk to the female interviewer, while the men contributed notably less talk to the male interviewer.

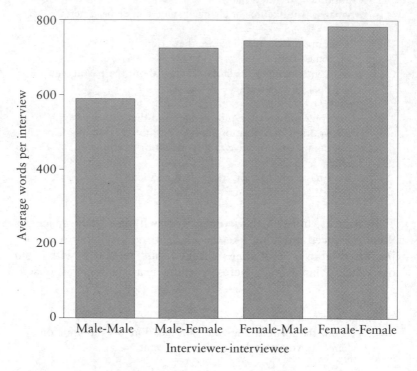

Figure 2.2 Amount of talk in picture description task

If amount of talk can reasonably be used as a measure of politeness and cooperation in this context, these New Zealand women were more polite than the men. A similar but larger study on a different topic produced the same pattern. Fifteen female and fifteen male New Zealand academics were each interviewed both by a male and a female about their physical fitness. Once again, the women interviewees were more cooperative and polite, contributing substantially more talk overall than the men (Holmes 1993).

By contrast, when talk offers the possibility of enhancing the speaker's status, men tend to talk most. There is abundant evidence from research in the United States and from Britain demonstrating that males tend to talk more than women in public contexts where talk is highly valued and attracts positive attention (see Holmes 1991 for a comprehensive review). There is also plenty of evidence that males tend to dominate the talking time in contexts such as classrooms, where talk is a valuable means of learning (a point which will be pursued further in Chapter 6). There is less evidence on differences in patterns of interaction in less formal and public contexts, but a number of American studies suggest men are much less forthcoming in intimate contexts (e.g. Soskin and John 1963; Fishman 1978, 1983; DeFrancisco 1991). When they were alone with their wives, the men in these studies contributed much less talk than the women. The women, on the other hand, worked hard to get a conversation going and keep it going.

This evidence suggests that the amount of talk contributed by women and men differs in public, formal contexts compared to private, intimate contexts. There are a number of ways of explaining this pattern. Men tend to value public, referentially orientated talk, while women value and enjoy intimate, affectively orientated talk. Each gender may be contributing more in the situation in which they are most comfortable. Correspondingly, women may experience formal public contexts as more face threatening than men do, while men, perhaps, find private and intimate contexts less comfortable. Each gender contributes least in the situation they find most uncomfortable. The New Zealand examples discussed above suggest that the amount of talk contributed by women and men differs according to what each gender perceives as appropriate in that context. In other words, politeness, or sensitivity to the needs of others, may be another contributing factor. Men appear to regard public formal contexts as opportunities for display, while they are more reticent in private interactions. Women appear to take more account of their addressee's conversational needs.

One obvious exception to this generalisation is provided by

women's and men's different perceptions of the role of talk in resolving conflict. There is evidence that women see talk as a means of resolving marital conflict, for instance, while men tend to avoid talk in such situations (Noller 1993). In these cases, women are clearly *not* responding to the conversational preferences of their spouses. One could argue, however, that their behaviour is consistent with the longer term interests of their partners, since the women see talk as a means of conflict resolution. Eder (1990) discusses a variety of ways in which adolescent girls handle conflict, and notes that some of them develop considerable skill in conflict resolution.[1] So, in a variety of contexts, one could interpret women's behaviour as evidence of a politeness rule which leads them to regulate their talk according to their perceptions of the needs of others.

This last suggestion is consistent with evidence produced by researchers exploring speech accommodation theory. In a number of studies women accommodated to their addressees' style of speech more than men did (e.g. Bilous and Krauss 1988; Mulac et al. 1988). The same point has been made about the speech of young girls and boys in interaction (Goodwin and Goodwin 1987). Females appear to focus on the needs of others and regulate their talk in a number of ways accordingly; males, by contrast, seem to assess the situation in terms of its potential for themselves. These differences of focus may well reflect each gender's assessment of what will be of most benefit to them in the long term – a point which will be explored further in Chapter 6 in a discussion of the relationship between power and politeness. In the next section, however, I will demonstrate how the distribution of questions and the different types of questions asked by males and females can throw further light on what women and men perceive as polite behaviour in different contexts.

Who's asking questions?

Women tend to regard talk as a means of maintaining and developing relationships. If women are concerned with solidarity or connection, then talk is a major strategy for connecting with others. Women's friendships and intimate relationships are sustained by talk. Women tend to assess the health of their relationships with others in terms of how much verbal interaction they engage in. For women, positive politeness involves talking to one's friends.

I want him to tell me what he's thinking, what he's feeling . . . About a month ago I said, 'Hal talk to me, just don't sit there like a bump on a log. Talk to me . . .', He'll, when we're arguing mostly, I'll say, 'just explain to me now, what are you saying, what is it?' And he won't. He takes it as an insult I guess that I don't understand what he's saying and he won't explain . . . (A 21-year-old Hispanic woman describes communication with her husband.)

(DeFrancisco 1991: 413)

Questions are an important means of generating talk. Pamela Fishman notes that 'questions are interactionally powerful devices' (1983: 94): they demand a next utterance, and so they are ways of ensuring at least a minimal interaction. In the conversations between the three heterosexual couples she studied, the women used questions to try to get their male partners to talk to them (Fishman 1978, 1983). Victoria DeFrancisco (1991: 416) reports a similar pattern in the casual interactions between the seven couples she studied: 'the women worked harder to maintain interaction than the men, but were less successful in their attempts'. Women tended to raise more topics than men in these personal conversations (Fishman 1978; Tannen 1984; West and García 1988; DeFrancisco 1991), and they used questions as a means of attempting to engage their partners in the conversation – often unsuccessfully.

The men, it seems, are not interested in talking in these intimate contexts; they are not interested in the women's topics and they appear not to value the women's contributions. Women do value this kind of talk, but their success in sustaining a conversation depends on finding topics which will interest their partners. There is little evidence of mutual cooperation in these accounts. It is male norms which prevail in these mixed-sex interactions.

Who asks the questions in formal seminars?

In public and formal contexts the pattern is quite different: in these contexts it is generally men who ask more questions. Dale Spender (1979) noted women's and men's contributions at a British conference on sexism and education in 1978. Because there was an awareness that women did not seem to be contributing as much as men in this more formal context, a decision was made to discriminate positively in favour of female speakers from the floor during the discussion session. Despite this, the men claimed almost twice as many speaking turns as the women (Spender 1979: 40). A study of nine seminars at the University of Durham produced similar results (Bashiruddin et al. 1990). At an American conference, Marjorie Swacker (1979) reported the same pattern, pointing out that although women constituted 42 per cent of the audience, they managed to claim only 27 per cent of the questions following the presentation of a paper (Swacker 1979: 157). Moreover, the men's questions were over twice as long as the women's on average. The pattern described in the previous section of male domination of the supposedly shared speaking time was once again apparent.

At a British conference in 1988, I collected similar data on the number of questions asked by women and men following each formal presentation (Holmes 1988c). The number of presentations by women and men was roughly equivalent, and the audiences were remarkably balanced, with an average of twenty-three women and twenty-six men present at any session. Despite this, and the efforts of the organisers to get a gender balance in the formal presentations, the pattern of male domination of the floor prevailed. The men averaged 7.7 contributions each, whereas the women managed only 2.6 contributions each on average. Overall, the men made well over three times as many contributions to the discussion as the women (76.7 per cent vs 23.3 per cent). (See also Bashiruddin et al. 1990).

This data supports my claim that men seem more likely than women to dominate the talking time in status-enhancing contexts where talk is valued (see Holmes 1992b). Women appear to be reluctant to contribute in such contexts. In New Zealand, I took the analysis further and examined the kinds of questions which women and men were asking.

I collected data from 100 public meetings or seminars which involved a formal presentation followed by a discussion. The presentation normally took about forty-five minutes and the discussion which followed ranged from about ten minutes to forty-five minutes. The topics were extremely varied, and so were the audiences. They included people from a wide range of government departments, diplomats, politicians, people from industry and the commercial world, bankers, trade unionists, policy makers, historians, teachers and academics.

The same pattern emerged: men dominated the discussion time asking most of the questions, or, more precisely, the elicitations. The term *elicitation* covers both questions and comments which were intended to elicit a response in the discussion. Overall, men contributed three-quarters of the elicitations, as illustrated in Figure 2.3. In such formal and public settings it is not surprising to find men made up the majority of the audience at almost every

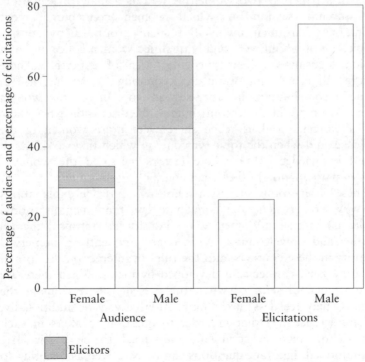

Figure 2.3 Gender of participants and number of elicitations

meeting. Figure 2.3 shows that there were approximately twice as many men as women attending these sessions. But, on average, only 17 per cent of all the women present contributed elicitations compared to 30 per cent of the men.

Even in sessions where the numbers of women and men were approximately equal, men contributed 62 per cent of all the elicitations following a presentation. Women appeared to be relatively reluctant participants in these formal and public discussions. Why?

Examining the features of the few sessions where women contributed more than men provided some clues. Men were responsible for the majority of the elicitations in all but seven of the sessions. On five of the seven occasions when women contributed more elicitations than men, women were a majority in the audience – an unusual situation overall in this sample of formal public meetings. Another occasion involved the present-ation of a paper by two women as well as a male presentation. The seventh session in which women contributed more elicitations than men involved a small group of twenty-five people, ten of whom were highly qualified women colleagues at a session focusing on their particular area of expertise. These features all proved important in accounting for an increase in women's contributions in other sessions too. In general, women were much more likely to contribute to the discussion when there was a woman speaker, when there were more women in the audience, and when the topic was one on which they could claim expert knowledge. All of these factors increased the women's level of participation in the discussion.

These observations suggest a number of possible explanations for why women generally contribute less than men in formal public interactions. Women may find formal settings uncom-fortable and unwelcoming. Women are frequently a numerical minority in these contexts, and the rules of interaction are formal and have been defined and developed by males. When there are more women present, or when the presenter is a woman, the situation may feel less threatening. Alternatively or additionally, perhaps women feel that in order to question speakers in such contexts or make a comment, they need to be particularly well-informed. Ignorant questions can be perceived as insulting to the speaker. So by avoiding elicitations women may be expressing negative politeness to the speaker. Or they may be protecting their own positive face needs by avoiding accusations that they are not adequately informed. The fact that the women who did contribute were often recognised experts on the topic supports these interpretations.

A third possible explanation is that women assess the situation in terms of the positive face needs of others. From the presenter's point of view, it is generally regarded as desirable that there be some discussion at the end of a paper; otherwise the occasion may be regarded as a failure. In most situations, there are plenty of men to fill the gap. Women may participate more when they fear no one else will. Moreover, they may feel particularly concerned to protect women presenters in this respect, and so expressing positive politeness in this context will involve women asking questions.

What kinds of questions?

It is obviously not possible to be certain which, if any, of these explanations account for women's behaviour in formal seminars. They may all contribute. However, examining the kinds of questions and comments women produce compared to men throws further light on the issue. Focusing on the function of elicitations in relation to the previous discourse (usually the formal present-ation), three broad categories can be identified: *supportive, critical,* and *antagonistic* (Holmes 1992b).

Supportive elicitations

Supportive elicitations imply a generally positive response to the content of the presentation, and invite the speaker to expand or elaborate on some aspect of it as illustrated in examples 4 and 5. (The examples are inevitably slightly edited because most are based on notes rather than tape-recordings. I have therefore used conventional punctuation. Unconscious editing of features such as hesitations is almost unavoidable, but the content of utterances is faithfully recorded.)

Examples 4 and 5
(4)   You've described the formal features of this structure very
        clearly. I wonder if you could elaborate a little on the social

implications? What do you see as the possible social
outcomes of adopting this structure?

(5)   The Thai data is really interesting. What do you think is
going on in table 2?

Supportive elicitations provide 'openings' and invite the
speaker to develop a point or expand on an area of their presentation. They have much in common with facilitative tags and were
often quite explicitly positive, as illustrated in the following
examples.

Examples 6–8
(6)   I really liked your comments on . . . could you expand a
little.

(7)   Could you comment more fully on . . . it sounds very
promising.

(8)   I liked your explanation of . . . could you tell us a little
more about . . .

Critical elicitations

Critical elicitations are less whole-heartedly or explicitly positive
and contain a hint of criticism. They often consist of a modified
agreement or a qualified disagreement, perhaps expressing a
degree of negative evaluation or scepticism, as illustrated in
examples 9 and 10:

Examples 9 and 10
(9)   It isn't always possible to collect all the information
required in order to undertake a fully comprehensive
costing, as you suggest. Are you aware, for instance, that in
a recent argument about the cost of providing a telephone
service to a particular rural consumer, no one was able to
identify the real cost?

(10) I can see what you're getting at, but it seems to me the
material in your figure 5 could be interpreted somewhat
differently.

The tone of voice in which any elicitation is expressed is

extremely important in interpreting its function in order to classify it accurately. This is particularly obvious with critical elicitations. A sceptical tone of voice can turn a superficially supportive comment into a critical one.

Antagonistic elicitations

Antagonistic elicitations generally involve challenging, aggressively critical assertions whose function is to attack the speaker's position and demonstrate it is wrong. The following examples illustrate this category of elicitations.

Examples 11–13

(11) I have to say that I disagree with your analysis. The elements you have identified as important seem relatively insignificant to me compared to the crucial influence of . . .

(12) I've listened with interest to your presentation and I found your outline of the current state of the theory fascinating. However, I simply cannot go along with your interpretation of this data. It makes no sense to me.

(13) It's not much use having a policy if it's not going to be effective is it?

Example 13 also illustrates a challenging tag question, a linguistic device which is further discussed in Chapter 3. These antagonistic elicitations are clearly very face threatening.

Who uses different elicitations?

How often are these different types of elicitation used by women and men? Figure 2.4 shows the distribution of 500 elicitations from 100 seminars according to the gender of the speaker.

Clearly, most elicitations were supportive (77.8 per cent of male and 77.5 per cent of female elicitations); most elicitations invited the speaker in a positive and non-confrontational way to elaborate on his (or more rarely her) presentation, or to develop further a point the questioner was interested in. There were no significant differences between women and men in the proportion of supportive elicitations. And both genders used much the same proportions of critical elicitations.

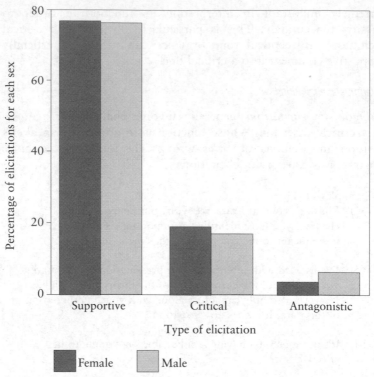

Figure 2.4 Gender of participants and types of elicitations

It was in the relative frequency of antagonistic elicitations that women and men differed. Though they constituted a small percentage of the total number of elicitations, the distribution of antagonistic elicitations differed significantly between women and men. In their contributions to the discussion, men expressed proportionately twice as many of the antagonistic elicitations as women did. In other words, the men explicitly disagreed with or challenged the presenter significantly more often than the women did. So, although during the discussion session in most seminars, facilitative elicitations were by far the most common, where antagonistic elicitations occurred, they were twice as likely to come from a man as a woman. Since antagonistic elicitations are very face threatening, this provides some support for the view that women are being more polite by taking more account of the face needs of the presenter than are men.

This is further supported by a detailed examination of the occasions when women made very critical comments. These almost always occurred in an environment where criticism and contrary views had been explicitly invited, or where it was clear that criticism was expected; for example, when a politician or policy maker had been invited to give a presentation specifically for the purpose of explaining an unpopular or controversial policy, as opposed to the more usual presentation where a guest was invited to describe their current work, or discuss an issue of general interest.

Overall, then, this detailed analysis of the types of elicitations contributed by women and men in formal seminars provides further support for the suggestion that New Zealand women tend to be more sensitive to the positive face needs of their addressees than New Zealand men. By asking more antagonistic questions men indicate at the least a concern with referential content that overrides affective or social considerations. They are more concerned with stating their disagreement or criticisms explicitly than with protecting their addressee's feelings.

Antagonistic elicitations may also act as a means of gaining status. Antagonistic elicitations are risky: if they are convincingly refuted they may lead to loss of face by the challenger. But an *effective* challenge is likely to attract admiration from others who regard interaction as a competitive activity, and so increase the social status of the challenger. Women appear to be less willing to engage in this kind of exchange; they use antagonistic elicitations rarely, and then mainly when they have some kind of official 'sanction'. Their behaviour is consistent with the claim that they are more concerned than men with the presenter's face needs.

It is also worth noting that aggressively negative questioning often leads people to take up entrenched positions – especially in a public debate – and little cognitive progress is made when this happens. Defensiveness is not an attitude which encourages creative thinking. Supportive elicitations and modified criticisms are much more likely to facilitate good quality open-ended discussion or productive exploratory talk, a point which will be developed more fully in Chapter 6 where some of the educational implications of gender differences in talk are explored.

Questions in classroom discussion

Example 14
Two adults in classroom.
May: do you have a big family
Ted: no
May: any brothers and sisters
Ted: one brother
May: how do you get on with him

There is some interesting related evidence concerning the types of questions asked by males and females in discussion groups. Analysing the questions asked by adult learners of English as a second language, I distinguished between what I called 'response-restricting' questions intended to elicit a short specific response such as May's query *any brothers and sisters?*, and 'facilitative' questions, which invite the speaker to respond more fully, such as her follow-up question *how do you get on with him?* (see Holmes 1989b). In groups of four, the learners were discussing a list of fifteen 'stresses' (such as divorce, a family death, or money problems) which they were required to rank in order of seriousness. In the context of the discussion, examples 15 and 16 were facilitative questions, and they led to extended responses, whereas, despite their apparently more open form (i.e *wh*-question rather then *yes/no* question), examples 17 and 18 were response-restricting questions as the replies demonstrate.

Examples 15–18
(15) do you have family here

(16) well for instance do you like the food here

(17) A: what have you done with 'getting fired'
      B: number five (i.e. 'I have labelled it number five').

(18) A: so what do I put here – family or spouse
      B: spouse

Among these second language learners, response-restricting questions were generally more frequent than facilitative questions. But, overall, the men used considerably more response-restricting questions (88 per cent) than the women did (66 per cent). Many of these were 'organising' questions (reflecting the fact that the men tended to take the leadership role more often than the women), asking what order others had put items in, for instance, or whether they agreed with the speaker's ordering. The effect of these questions in the contexts in which they were asked was to close off and stifle discussion. They give the impression that the questioner is concerned to elicit a short and very specific answer and proceed to the next stage of the task. And they are very clearly content-orientated rather than affective in function.

In a study which focused on fourteen year-old native speakers of English, Nancy Jenkins and Jenny Cheshire (1990) report very similar patterns. They found that girls used more questions overall than boys, and that they used them more supportively. 'The boys tended to use questions that demanded specific information, and this often interrupted the flow of conversation' (Jenkins and Cheshire 1990: 275). The girls' questions, on the other hand, either reformulated an earlier question making it easier to answer, or invited a particular individual to contribute a personal opinion or an anecdote (1990: 275). The facilitative role of females was very clear in these discussion groups.

Jenkins and Cheshire also examined 'remarks which tend to close down discussion' – in other words contributions which have the same effect as response-restricting questions: they inhibit rather than encourage others' contributions. Three kinds of contri- butions fitted this category: irrelevant and inappropriate remarks which others did not know how to respond to; very personal remarks which could not be developed; and over-hasty recourse to the written questions guiding the discussion. These were all ways in which discussion was effectively halted and exploration of the topic curtailed. Overall boys produced five times more examples of such remarks than girls.

In Chapter 1, I noted that there was some evidence that males tended to be more orientated to referential content than to affective meaning, while females were more likely than males to pay attention to the social and affective aspects of an interaction. Clearly, questions can serve a range of functions and they may be another linguistic device through which females and males express these different tendencies. Facilitative questions are addressee-orientated, since they encourage the speaker to contribute to the talk. Response-restricting questions and 'remarks which close down discussion' have just the opposite effect. Though they may keep a speaker 'on task', they tend to discourage anything other than a short contribution. So in contexts such as those examined in this section where talk is desirable for social, educational and intellectual reasons, antagonistic elicitations and response-restricting questions are often unhelpful, while facilitative questions or elicitations can be regarded as politeness devices. Once again it has been apparent that while both women and men used more supportive than antagonistic strategies in public seminars, and both used more response-restricting questions in task-orientated discussion, overall females tend to use the polite linguistic strategies more often than the males.

Who's interrupting and why?

Example 19
Woman: How's your paper coming?
Man: Alright I guess. I haven't done much in the past two
        weeks.
Woman: Yeah. Know how that ⌈can ⌉
Man: ⌊Hey ⌋ ya' got an extra
        cigarette?
Woman: Oh uh sure *(hands him the pack)*
        like MY ⌈pa– ⌉
Man: ⌊How⌋ 'bout a match
Woman: 'Ere ya go uh like MY ⌈pa – ⌉
                            ⌊Thanks ⌋
Woman: Sure. I was gonna tell you ⌈my – ⌉
Man: ⌊Hey ⌋ I'd really like
        ta' talk but I gotta run – see ya
Woman: Yeah.

[The words within the square brackets were uttered simultaneously.]
                            (West and Zimmerman 1977: 527–8)

We have seen that questions serve many functions. They can be used as positive politeness devices to encourage talk and contributions from others. Or they can be challenging and confrontational and not at all polite. Another interaction strategy which can also serve a variety of purposes in verbal interaction is the interruption. Some interruptions signal lack of interest in the other speaker's topic, as illustrated in the example above. In more public contexts, a well-timed interruption can effectively halt a speaker in their tracks. It is difficult for a speaker to ignore a loud call of 'load of rubbish', or even a more polite but well-timed 'where's the evidence?', from the floor at a public meeting. A sustained interruption may disrupt someone's talk completely and take over the floor.

Example 20
[The words within the square brackets were uttered simultaneously.]

Peter: and I must say that I think it's time we addressed this
          issue seri- seriously   and that means that means

Lisa: mm

Peter: we all have to think about it/ not just those at the top/
          all of us

Lisa: I agree/ I think that's right we need to ⌈start by –

Peter: ⌊we need to
          start by discussing some of these issues a bit more
          thoroughly// ⌈we've not done that before

Lisa: ⌊   mm right

Peter: what has your section done in this area for instance

Judith: well we have begun thinking about it/ we've been
          holding regular review   ⌊sessions on -

Peter: ⌊it'll take take a lot more
          than that I can tell you. this is a serious matter

This example from a regular meeting of colleagues in a government department illustrates some of the gender differences in patterns of interruption which have been found in a wide variety of studies. There is a substantial amount of evidence that men interrupt women more often than the reverse. Analysts differ in how they define an interruption, and some researchers have failed to reproduce Zimmerman and West's (1975) dramatic pattern of males being responsible for 96 per cent of the interruptions in conversations between male-female pairs (for example Beattie 1981; Dindia 1987; Murray and Covelli 1988; Roger 1989). Nevertheless, if we adopt a definition of an interruption as a disruptive turn, the balance of evidence from the method-ologically sounder research tends to confirm the view that, where there are gender differences, men disruptively interrupt others more often than women do, and that, more specifically, men interrupt women more than women interrupt men (McMillan et al. 1977; Eakins and Eakins 1979; Natale et al. 1979; Octigan and Niederman 1979; Leet-Pellegrini 1980; Brooks 1982; West and Zimmerman 1983; Mulac et al. 1988; Schick Case 1988).[2]

This tendency for men to interrupt women persists even where the woman has high status. In one American study, male doctors interrupted their patients twice as often as the patients inter-rupted the doctors. But the reverse was true for female doctors and their male patients; it was the doctors who were interrupted more often (West 1984). An analysis of conversations between work colleagues in Britain showed that even when women held high-status positions their male subordinates interrupted them more often than the reverse (Woods 1989). And the men suc-ceeded in gaining the floor by this means 85 per cent of the time (compared to 52 per cent for the women). This study showed that higher status at least mitigated the effect of gender differences, since the same women suffered more interruptions as subordinates than they did in high status positions. While an interruption is generally an impolite discourse strategy, refraining from interrupting is negatively polite behaviour. It avoids intruding on the speaker's verbal space. There is abundant evidence then that women are in general more polite than men. They are much less likely to interrupt others and take the floor from them.

Most of the research on interrupting behaviour has been undertaken in the United States or in Britain. The little New Zealand data available, however, confirms this general pattern for New Zealand women and men. A study which analysed the differences in interrupting behaviours between four flatmates found the men interrupting more than the women during a meal-time conversation (Stubbe 1978). The males were responsible for 60 per cent of the interruptions, despite the fact that one of them spent a good proportion of the time in the kitchen. In another study which paid particular attention to the various functions of overlapping speech, Christine Hyndman (1985) found that the interrupting behaviour of her New Zealand male student friends also confirmed the overseas patterns. She taped two separate dinner-time conversations between two male and two female students and her results demonstrated clearly that the men interrupted more than the women: 77 per cent of the interruptions were initiated by men compared to 23 per cent by the women. She distinguished in her analysis between successful and unsuccessful attempts to gain the floor and found that the men's interruptions were five times as likely as the women's to be successful in gaining the floor.

The overall pattern appears very consistent, then, in a number of English-speaking communities. But there are many possible avenues for further research. One interesting question, for instance, is when do these patterns begin? Another relates to the kinds of situations in which people interrupt each other: are there contexts in which cross-sex interruptions are more or less frequent?

A study of small group interactions between pupils in New Zealand secondary schools, suggests the pattern of male dominance in group discussion is well-established by the age of fifteen. Jane Gilbert (1990) analysed the speech of fifth formers (i.e. young people in their eleventh year of schooling) in a series of mixed-sex and single-sex small group discussions centred around the science syllabus. She found that the boys not only captured a much larger share of the talk (61 per cent vs 39 per cent) in mixed-sex groups, they also interrupted others more often than the girls. Interestingly, they were especially likely to interrupt other boys. The boys in single-sex groups interrupted each other considerably more often than students in any other group. This suggests once again that perhaps males and females are operating with different rules of interaction. What is perceived as rude, disruptive and impolite by women, may be acceptable and normal in male interaction. And when women politely (according to their norms) avoid interrupting others, they may be interpreted by males as being reluctant to get involved, or as having nothing to say.

It seems possible that these patterns of male interruption and domination of talk develop during the teenage years. They were not evident in a study of interactions between New Zealand eleven and twelve year-olds (Stubbe 1991). In this study the children worked on a discussion task in both cross-sex and single-sex pairs. The analysis focused on the difference between supportive simultaneous speech and non-supportive or disruptive interruptions. As mentioned above, interruptions to the speech of another may be negative in effect, disrupting another's turn and restricting their contribution. Stubbe called these 'non-supportive interruptions'. Alternatively, simultaneous speech, which technically 'interrupts' the other speaker, may function positively to encourage and support them. In informal contexts people often build up the discourse collaboratively, creating a 'conversational duet' (Coates 1991). Simultaneous talk, which superficially appears to be an interruption, may actually represent joint participation in the talk (see, for instance, Edelsky 1981; Coates 1989), or may be encouraging in intent, an example of what Tannen (1984) calls the 'overlap-as-enthusiasm' strategy. Stubbe called these 'supportive interruptions'. So she examined the effects of the children's interruptions in these terms – did they express support for the addressee or were they disruptive and likely to inhibit the other speaker?

With these younger children, there were no differences between the girls and the boys in the overall numbers of interruptions which occurred. Indeed, in general, the children interrupted each other relatively little. Nor were there any statistically significant differences in the number of encouraging and supportive interruptions compared to the number of negative or non-supportive interruptions. (Incidentally, Stubbe's statistics relate the number of interruptions to the amount of speech produced by the other speaker – an important variable (Stubbe 1991: 66). It is, after all, the relative number of times a speaker is interrupted that is of interest, rather than the raw number of interruptions.) And, as with the elicitations described above, she found that both girls and boys used more supportive than non-supportive interruptions. In other words, in this study of the turn-taking patterns of eleven and twelve year-olds, both genders used interruptions most often as positive politeness strategies.

It is interesting to speculate on why the usual pattern of disruptive interruptions by males was not evident in this data. It may be that at this age (pre-teens) the pattern of male dominance which is so evident later has not yet emerged. Alternatively, or additionally, the fact that the children were working in pairs rather than larger groupings may have led to a more cooperative approach to the discussion task. In fact, as we shall see below, the most interesting gender differences that emerged from this study related to the content of responses rather than to features of turn-taking.

Interestingly, this 'no difference' result was also found by Jenkins and Cheshire (1990) in their similar study of features of discussion between small groups of British fourteen year-olds. The researchers analysed a range of different functions of simultaneous speech, and concluded that most of the boys in their study 'did not use interruption to silence girls or to control the conversation' (Jenkins and Cheshire 1990: 14). They make the interesting comment that 'Interruption seemed rather to be a sign of poor listening skills' (1990: 14) – a thought-provokingly different explanation of interruptions in mixed-sex interaction.

Certainly, these studies suggest that it is very important to pay careful attention to the function of interruptions in the discourse, as well as to the kind of discourse involved. They also suggest that in this area, at least, gender differences in one aspect of positively polite behaviour – enthusiastic overlapping – are not apparent in the pre-teen and early teen years.

Back-channeling – a female speciality?

Example 21
Two women talking about a good teacher.
Tina: she provided the appropriate sayings for particular
Tina: ⌈times
Lyn: ⌊   right
Tina: ⌈and and so on   she didn't actually TEACH them
Lyn: ⌊   right
Tina: ⌈but she just//   provided a model
Lyn: ⌊   provided a model   yeah mm
Tina: ⌈you know you you must refer to this   and this
Lyn: ⌊   mm   mm mm
Tina: ⌈and she actually produced a book   that set out some
Lyn: ⌊   mm
Tina: ⌈of these ideas at the very simplest level
Lyn: ⌊   yeah

If an interruption may reflect poor listening skills, an encouraging minimal response or back-channel is generally just the opposite – it is typical of a good listener. Back-channels or supportive minimal responses are forms such as *mm*, *mhm* and *yeah* which encourage a speaker to continue talking. They indicate that the listener is paying attention and is interested in hearing more. While a supportive interruption has the same function as a back-channel, the former involves overlapping speech, while a back-channel is usually skilfully placed to avoid overlap, as illustrated in examples 20 and 21. Indeed, listeners' back-channels or minimal responses often occur totally non-intrusively between the breaths of the speaker (see Fishman 1983: 96).

Obviously here, as elsewhere, attention to variation in form and function is important. Intonation and timing are crucial in distinguishing positive feedback from discouraging, delayed, unsupportive responses (Zimmerman and West 1975; Fishman 1983). Moreover, the same forms can be used differently to achieve a contrasting effect. *Mm* may appear an obvious example of supportive minimal feedback, for instance, but repeated instance of *mm* can be used to signal that the utterer wants a turn (i.e. as bids for the floor). The relevance of this point is apparent in Jenkins and Cheshire's (1990) study of secondary school discussion goups. Girls used more minimal responses than boys in two of the three discussion groups they analysed. In the third group the distribution of forms was pretty even between the girls and boys. But the boys were using them for a different purpose.

> Although they appeared to be affirming what others were saying, they were, in fact, using these responses as a subtle form of interruption, as a way of getting their voices heard in an attempt to take the next turn . . . The boys used them to gain a foothold in the conversation rather than as a support for the current speaker. The girls on the other hand, used minimal responses in an almost wholly supportive way.
>
> (Jenkins and Cheshire 1990: 269)

As we have seen before, it is obviously very important in analysing discourse to identify accurately the range of relevant forms and their various functions.

There is overwhelming evidence from British and American research that women provide more positive minimal responses than men. This has been demonstrated in a range of contexts, including management groups (Schick Case 1988), discussion groups in very controlled laboratory or studio conditions (Hirschman 1974; Leet-Pellegrini 1980; Preisler 1986; Roger 1989), in classrooms (Munro 1987), and in casual exchanges between heterosexual couples in their homes (Fishman 1980, 1983). This evidence provides further support for the claim that women are generally more positively polite than men. Encouraging feedback is another instance of a facilitative politeness strategy which encourages others to continue talking and reflects concern for their positive face needs.

The same patterns have been found in analyses of adult and adolescent interaction in New Zealand. Casual conversations between small groups of young New Zealand women and men consistently show women using more encouraging back-channels. In two hour-long conversations, for instance, Christine Hyndman (1985) reports that the New Zealand women provided four times as many encouraging minimal responses as the men.

Analysing small-group discussions in New Zealand secondary schools, Jane Gilbert (1990) examined all the positive and negative responses used by three groups of fourteen and fifteen year-olds. She comments that, in line with previous research, the girls tended to provide more positive affective feedback overall than the boys, but there were differences in the patterns for single-sex and mixed-sex groups. In a single-sex group, the girls produced considerably more positive responses (74 per cent) to the previous speaker's contribution than did the boys in a single sex group (54.25 per cent). However, in the mixed-sex group there was no difference in the overall proportion of positive responses used by both girls and boys. At 63 per cent, the proportion of positive responses falls almost exactly between the single-sex norms, suggesting some accommodation by both parties to the norms of the other group.

Once again, Maria Stubbe's analysis of interactions between pairs of eleven and twelve year-old children revealed a different pattern. The boys in the mixed-sex pairs she recorded produced more minimal responses than the girls. Closer analysis revealed that this was related to the roles the children were taking in the discussion. As with interruptions, Stubbe points out that what is interesting is not the absolute figures, but rather the relative number of minimal responses produced by the listener in relation to the amount of speech produced by the person who holds the floor. In the mixed-sex pairs, girls tended to produce more talk than boys, which she interprets as evidence of their desire to be cooperative in relation to the task she had set. Not surprisingly, then, they produced fewer minimal responses in these inter-actions, since they were more often speakers than listeners. When they did take the role of listeners, the findings tended to follow the usual pattern: the girls' rates of producing minimal responses are overall higher than boys' rates relative to the amount of talk produced by the other person.

More detailed analysis in this area, as in others, then, reveals that supportive feedback functions differently in different contexts, as an expression of different roles and in different types of discourse. In her analysis of conversations between a group of women, Jennifer Coates (1989: 106) notes distinctions in the function and distribution of minimal responses in sections of interactive discussion as opposed to narrative sections.

> In the interaction-focussed discussion sections, they are used to support the speaker and to indicate the listener's active attention . . . In the narrative or more information-oriented sections of the conversation . . . they are used far less frequently, and . . . they signal agreement among participants that a particular stage of conversation has been reached.

Further detailed analyses of patterns of interaction reveal a more complex pattern than had initially been suspected. Generali-sations about gender differences in the use of interruptions and minimal feedback must clearly be treated with some circum-spection until we are confident that the functions of such forms have been accurately identified.

In the light of analyses which demonstrate the importance of paying attention to the function of interactional forms, it would be reassuring if we could be confident that women and men agree on the interpretations of these functions. Of direct relevance here is Maltz and Borker's suggestion (1982) that the *meaning* of minimal responses may differ for women and men, with men using them to signal agreement while women's responses mean simply 'I'm following'. Though this suggestion has been frequently · repeated, I know of no research which directly addresses it. It raises once again the possibility that women and men have different rules of interaction, and that they interpret interactive behaviour differently. Being linguistically polite may involve different behaviour for females and males.

Agreeable and disagreeable responses

Example 22
Two thirteen year-olds discussing a school-teacher.
David: he's a real dickhead he just bawls you out without
              listening at all
Oliver: yeah what an ass-hole/ I can't stand him he's always
              raving raving on

The discussion of interactive features such as interruption and minimal responses has made it very clear that the crucial aspects of these features from the point of view of politeness is their function in relation to the on-going discourse. Do they disrupt or support the talk of others? Do they threaten to take over the floor or do they encourage the current speaker to continue?

Extending the analysis further in this direction, it is obvious that the content of responses to the talk of others is another aspect of politeness behaviour. Agreeing with others, confirming their opinions and assertions, as illustrated by Oliver in example 22 and Sal and Pat in example 23, is supportive and positively polite behaviour (Brown and Levinson 1987: 112).

Example 23
Two young women watching TV together.
Sal: in that *Our House* um.......she's the mother of teenage
            kids ⌈and she
Pat: ⌊oh yeah that's an awful program isn't it
Sal: mmmm
Pat: it's got that dick who's in the Cocoon film
Sal: oh god he's insufferable!
Pat: and he's so fucking wise ⌈and so so FUCKING American
Sal: ⌊ yeah
Sal: and everybody else is always WRONG
Pat: yes and he's always right...

                                          (Pilkington 1992: 45)

This example illustrates once again the point made in the discusion of interruptions – overlapping and simultaneous talk can be supportive in effect. It also illustrates another pattern, namely, the tendency for women to agree with each other where possible. There is a great deal of evidence that in informal and casual interaction women tend to adopt the strategy of seeking agreement to a greater extent than men do, both in single-sex and mixed-sex contexts (e.g. Kalcik 1975; Leet-Pellegrini 1980; Edelsky 1981; Coates 1989). This pattern is evident from at least around age seven or eight (van Alphen 1987; Tannen 1990b), and possibly even earlier (Haas 1979; Sheldon 1990). Coates (1989: 118), for example, comments on the ways in which the women in the discussions she taped work together and collaborate with each other 'to produce shared meanings'. Participants build on each other's contributions, complete each other's utterances, and affirm each other's opinions giving an overall impression of talk as a very cooperative enterprise. Eckert (1990: 122) reports similar patterns among a group of adolescent girls, commenting that 'not one topic is allowed to conclude without an expression of consensus'. (It is interesting to note that this is also a pattern which is typical of more formal Maori interaction, suggesting that cross-cultural contrasts may mirror the gender contrasts observable in middle-class western society.)

A small but very interesting New Zealand study provides further evidence of this pattern. Jane Pilkington (1992) recorded the interactions between a group of women and a group of men working on different nights in a bakery. Her data for the women shows the same supportive and cooperative patterns in New Zealand women's speech as those described by Coates (1989) in the speech of the British women she recorded. The women developed each other's contributions, collaborating 'to produce a text by adding to what the previous speaker has just said', and they provided each other with a great deal of positive encouraging feedback. Facilitative tags were frequent as they encouraged others to comment and contribute. The women completed each other's utterances and agreed frequently. The impression is one of verbal cooperation and conversational sharing.

Example 24
Two young women working together in bakery.
Sal: perhaps next time I see Brian I'll PUMP him for
         ⌈information/ Brian tells me
May: ⌊   the goss
Sal: ⌈I know it's about six years old but
May: ⌊   [*laugh*] but
         I'd forgotten it
                                        (Pilkington 1992: 46)

The men's interactions were very different. There were very few explicitly agreeing responses. Where a woman would have been likely to agree or at least respond, there were often long pauses between speakers. Indeed, Pilkington describes the male talk as typically combative, a kind of verbal sparring, a point which will be discussed further below. This study, then, though small, provides further support for the view of New Zealand women as more positively polite than New Zealand men.

Both Gilbert and Stubbe examined the kinds of responses produced by New Zealand school pupils in the discussions they analysed. In the groups of fifteen year-olds (Gilbert 1990), the girls in the single-sex group used more agreeing positive responses than pupils in any other group (74 per cent), while the boys in the single-sex group used the fewest (54 per cent). In mixed-sex groups there were no gender differences in the overall proportion of positive responses; 63 per cent of both girls' and boys' responses were positive. Here is further evidence that the norms of interaction for each group are rather different, and again when girls and boys interact with each other, there is evidence of accommodation since these differences are reduced.

Maria Stubbe (1991) examined the relative numbers of agreeing and disagreeing responses produced by the eleven and twelve year-old children in the pairs she recorded. She found no significant differences in the proportions of agreeing responses produced by girls or boys in single-sex or mixed-sex pairs. There was an overwhelming preference for agreement in all pairs, so that agreeing responses outnumber disagreeing responses by 2:1. With these younger speakers, then, the differences between male and female pairs, in terms of the proportion of agreeing responses, disappeared.

The really interesting pattern that this analysis revealed,

however, was in the types of disagreement responses preferred by the girls and boys. Overall, the boys tended to use more 'bald' disagreements than the girls, especially in discussion with another boy.

Example 25
Two eleven year-olds discussing a problem.
Ray: I think I'd tell my friend
Rees: no that's stupid

The girls, by contrast, tended to modify or qualify their disagreeing responses, so that they were not so confrontational. Such responses allowed for, and indeed encouraged, further discussion of the point of difference between the speakers.

Example 26
Two eleven year-olds discussing a problem.
Pam: I think she should go with her mum
Hanna: but she'd really rather stay um/ with her father though wouldn't she

The pattern that Stubbe identified is summarised in Figure 2.5.

It has been suggested that in many contexts being polite means maximising areas of agreement and minimising disagreement (e.g. Brown and Levinson 1987; Leech 1983). Yet clearly people do not always agree, and it is interesting to note that when this happens, women and men tend to approach the problem posed for politeness differently. What polite options are there if one does not agree with the views expressed by a conversational partner? One can change the topic, or keep silent, but both these involve a high risk of offence if they are not skilfully managed (see West and García 1988). Softening the disagreeing response is perhaps the most obvious strategy for a twelve year-old. The girls in Stubbe's study adopted this polite disagreement strategy almost twice as often as the boys.

The boys were much more willing to contradict overtly others or 'baldly' disagree with their conversational partners – a response that is certainly regarded in many contexts as very face threatening (Brown and Levinson 1987). In fact the boys were six times more likely than the girls to respond with a bald disagreement. This again suggests that there may be different

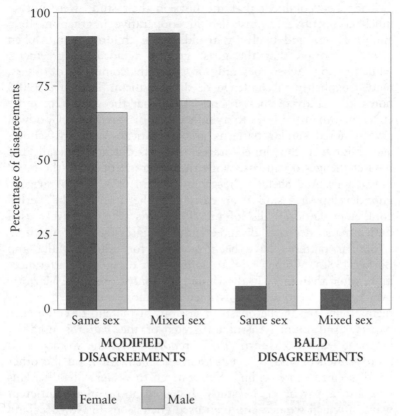

Figure 2.5 Modified and bald disagreements and gender.
(Source: Stubbe 1991: 88)

norms for females and males, or different levels of tolerance of overt disagreement.

These results are consistent with those of others. Jenkins and Cheshire (1990: 284) conclude their analysis of the interactions between young teenagers with a comment which aptly sums up the research in this area in a number of different countries. They say that

> on the whole, the girls were careful, sensitive listeners who knew when to speak and what kind of comment it is appropriate to make . . . the conversational style of the girls, overall, can be described as cooperative, generous and designed to allow the participation of everybody on equal terms.

They also comment that the boys in their study were not so much competitive as unskilled in cooperative interaction. In a study of nine and twelve year-old Dutch children, van Alphen (1987) reported that the girls' groups avoided disagreement, while the boys, when they did not ignore the comments of others, tended explicitly to challenge or dispute them. Tannen (1990b) notes in a study of 'best friends' talk' that the girls were more concerned than the boys to avoid explicit disagreement. Goodwin (1980) noted similar patterns among African-American school-age children in the United States: the girls did not generally use bald challenges or threats, while these were frequent in the boys' interactions. And Sheldon's research (1990, 1992a, 1992b) suggests girls develop such skill at an early age. She describes the 'verbal conflict mediation skills' of preschool girls who effectively used mitigating strategies to disagree without aggressive confrontation.

Similar patterns have been reported for adults (Maltz and Borker 1982). Women tend to soften their disagreeing utterances more often than men. In the United States, for example, Marjorie Swacker (1979) found that women used more modified disagreements than men in the question sessions at the end of conference papers. And in an Australian study of the patterns used by language learners, Munro (1987) reported that the women used more 'softened' disagreements than the men. Men, on the other hand, seemed more willing than women to disagree baldly. This was also apparent in the study discussed above of the different ways in which women and men used elicitations in New Zealand seminars. The men were twice as likely as the women to use antagonistic elicitations. In a detailed analysis of the interactions of a group of female and male business managers, Susan Schick Case (1988: 52) reported that 'the masculine style was an assertively aggressive one that proposed, opposed, competed'. And in her study of the interactions between New Zealand males working in a bakery, Jane Pilkington found that the men tended to challenge and disagree with each other much more explicitly and overtly than the women.

Example 27

Young men working together in bakery.
Ben: ... and ah they're very smart

Dan: well then how come they keep getting caught all the time?
Sam: maybe that's why they ⌈(......)
Ben: ⌊ they don't Dan / you've got to be
      really clever to pull one you know
                                                    (Pilkington 1992: 52)

The men provided conflicting accounts of the same event, argued about a range of topics such as whether apples were kept in cases or crates, and criticised each other constantly for apparently minor differences of approach to things. Their strategies for amusing each other were often to ridicule the previous speaker's utterance, to put them down or to insult them, as illustrated in example 28.

Example 28
Young men working in bakery discussing what apples are packed in.
Ray: crate!
Sam: case!
Ray: what
Sam: they come in cases Ray not crates
Ray: oh same thing if you must be picky over every one thing
Sam: just shut your fucking head Ray!
Ray: don't tell me to fuck off fuck(....)
Sam: I'll come over and shut yo
Jim: *(Laughingly using a thick sounding voice)* yeah I'll have a
      crate of apples thanks
Ray: no fuck off Jim
Jim: a dozen...
Dan: *(amused)* shitpicker!
                                                    (Pilkington 1992: 53)

Listening to these interactions, it is very clear that the talk of the young men contrasts quite starkly with the cooperative, agreeing, mutually supportive talk of the women (illustrated in example 24) in exactly the same context – working in the bakery – on a different night.

Women and men appear once again to be operating according to different rules of interaction. For the women, being negatively polite involves avoiding disagreement. Being positively polite is being friendly, and this involves confirming, agreeing and encouraging the contributions of others. But these politeness strategies are not typical of the interchanges described above between males. These young New Zealand men, like the young boys in the classroom discussion groups, are quite prepared to disagree baldly and to challenge the statements of others overtly. Indeed for this group, insults and abuse appear to be strategies for expressing solidarity and mateship, or ways of maintaining and reinforcing social relationships.

This kind of verbal sparring is reported by others who have examined all-male interaction (e.g. Dundes et al. 1972; Labov 1972) (but see also note 1). Labov (1972) described the ritual insults which occurred in the speech of New York adolescent gang members. In New Zealand, an analysis of the exchanges in a rugby changing room before a match demonstrated that the verbal interaction consisted almost entirely of insults – predominantly of a sexually humiliating kind (Kuiper 1991). People of both genders may use swear words to indicate their group membership (see, for example Hughes 1992), but Kuiper's study identifies insults which appear to serve as coercive devices to maintain solidarity and discipline between team members.

It appears, then, that at least in some contexts, female and male interactive norms contrast quite dramatically. The overall impression from the various studies discussed here is that male interaction is typically more competitive, aggressive and argumentative than female. For females, being negatively polite involves avoiding, minimising or mitigating disagreements; being positively polite involves agreeing with others, encouraging them to talk, expressing support verbally and ensuring they get a fair share of the talking time. For males, different norms appear to prevail. They can disagree baldly, challenge others' statements, interrupt and compete for the floor without intending to cause offence. In some contexts, aggressive and competitive verbal behaviour appears to be experienced as thoroughly enjoyable, and mutual insults may even serve as expressions of positive politeness or solidarity.

Conclusion

Example 29
I remember when I chaired the meetings I used to end up exhausted. I put so much effort into responding to each comment

and making connections between what speakers said. Eventually I noticed that my male counterparts didn't do this at all. They accepted contributions without comment and simply nominated the next speaker. So much less tiring I could see – but I was concerned people felt their contributions had been heard at least.

(Comment from a female dean.)

The evidence described in this chapter suggests that men tend to dominate interactions in public settings. They generally talk more than women, ask more questions, interrupt more often, and when they get the floor they are more likely than a woman to challenge and disagree with the speaker. In a variety of contexts, women tend to provide more supportive and encouraging feedback than men, to agree rather than disagree, to look for connections and add to and build on the contributions of others. This is positively polite behaviour, stressing shared goals and values, and expressing solidarity. Women also exhibit negatively polite behaviour in many contexts by avoiding competing for the floor or interrupting others. They appear to be more attentive listeners, concerned to ensure others get a chance to contribute.

One explanation which has been proposed for this pattern focuses on the social meaning of talk. It has been suggested that, in general, women are more concerned with solidarity or 'connection' (Chodorow 1974; Gilligan 1982), while men are more interested in status and being 'one-up' (Tannen 1990a: 38). Features of female talk, such as facilitative tags, agreeing comments, attentive listening and encouraging feedback can be seen as expressions of concern for others, and a desire to make contact and strengthen relationships. Male talk, on the other hand, appears to be more competitive, more concerned with dominating others and asserting status. Challenging utterances, bald disagreements and disruptive interruptions are examples of strategies which typify male talk in public contexts, and which seem to support this claim.

There is little doubt that talk in public contexts is potentially status enhancing; it is 'display' talk, an opportunity to display what you know. Effective contributions clearly have the potential to considerably increase a person's status or prestige. The relationships between participants in such settings are typically characterised in terms of their roles and relative statuses, rather than in personal terms. Typical examples would be public meetings, seminars, conferences and formal management meetings, though certain less formal interactions involving influential or significant 'others' may also be contexts where talk is valued as a potential source of increased status. It is in these contexts that men tend to talk most. Women, on the other hand, tend to talk more in private or informal contexts where the emphasis is on personal relationships and establishing connections with others.

The interactive patterns of interruption and back-channeling, agreement and disagreement, which characterise women's and men's talk can also be interpreted as reflecting the different social orientations of the speakers. If women are concerned with solidarity and connection, it is easy to see why they tend to talk least in formal and public contexts, and to excel in talk strategies which are appropriate for encouraging talk in smaller groups. The more private the context, the more appropriate the focus on interpersonal, affective meanings. The more public and formal the context, the more likely it is that considerations of status will be relevant. And while men appear to be comfortable contributing in contexts where demonstrating one's expertise is acceptable behaviour, women seem to be less comfortable in such status-orientated contexts. Conversely, women are more comfortable talking in less formal and more personal contexts, while men appear less likely to dominate intimate talk. (Indeed, DeFrancisco (1991: 417) notes in a study of interaction between couples that because the men contributed so little and responded so unenthusiastically to the women's talk 'these conversations were not interactive enough to necessitate interruption'!.)

This explanation is a plausible one, but I do not think it is the only reason for the different patterns of interaction that women and men display in different contexts. The studies discussed in this chapter have provided some evidence that women and men may be operating with different rules of interaction. It seems possible that they often perceive the functions of talk in specific contexts rather differently. As noted in Chapter 1, talk serves both social and referential functions. We use talk for social reasons – to make contact with others, to express how close we feel to them, as well as to establish and maintain status relationships. But we also use talk to convey information to others, for referential functions, describing, explaining and evaluating, for instance. Women tend to be more orientated to or sensitive to the social messages conveyed by talk, while men tend to be primarily orientated to the referential or informative content.

Talk in formal and public contexts such as seminars, conferences and meetings has an important referential function. Indeed, some would down-play, if not deny, the 'status-enhancing' social function discussed above, and claim that conveying information is the primary function of talk in such contexts. Much of the talk in these contexts can be described as expository – it is an exposition of facts and/or opinions. If men place a high value on this function of talk, then it is scarcely surprising that they are enthusiastic, and even aggressive, contributors in formal public contexts where it often pre-dominates.

In semi-formal contexts, such as interviews, picture description tasks and discussion tasks, the referential function of the talk is very clear: they are primarily informative, task-orientated interactions. Yet in these contexts women often contributed more talk. If men tend to be more content-orientated than women, one would expect them to dominate the talk in such interactions. The explanation for this apparent anomaly lies once again in the social function of such talk. In these private semi-formal interactions, talk does not so obviously serve a status-enhancing function, especially if the addressee is not a person with influence in the speaker's life. Any talk produced is primarily for the benefit of the interviewer or researcher, rather than the speaker. Hence by talking more in these contexts, women are acting cooperatively, since more talk is what the addressee wants. While the referential function of such talk is primary, it clearly has a social dimension – the establishment of some kind of relationship between the interviewer and interviewee. In these contexts, women's general orientation to the social functions of talk is evident in their willingness to contribute more and to contribute in a facilitative and non-competitive way. Being positively polite means cooperatively talking in an interview.

As Tannen (1990a) has illustrated well, it is in private informal contexts that women's and men's views of the primary functions of talk, and of what it means to be polite, come into most direct conflict. Many men apparently do not understand women's need for 'connection' through talk in intimate relationships. Many women cannot understand that men see talk as unnecessary and even potentially threatening in such contexts. DeFrancisco (1991) noted, for example, that the women in the couples she studied preferred to talk through problems, seeking solutions or acceptable compromises, while the men preferred to avoid conflict and keep silent. Equally, when things are going well, women tend to express this through on-going interaction and communicative exchanges, while men tend to see less need for regular talk in established intimate relationships (see also Noller 1993).

The data examined in this chapter provides further support for the suggestion that New Zealand women tend to be more polite than men. Focusing on the politeness function of linguistic devices rather than on their forms alone, I have examined evidence of different ways in which women and men behave in a variety of types of interaction. In general women are more positively polite than men in talking cooperatively in contexts where their verbal contributions are wanted by their interlocuters. Men tend to contribute more when the context is a status-enhancing one. Women contribute supportively and positively in informal contexts, by agreeing with and building on the ideas of others, and by providing encouraging feedback or back-channeling. Men tend to be less forthcoming in such contexts. In more formal contexts, women demonstrate negative politeness by avoiding interruption, and allowing others to take the floor. Men are more likely than women to interrupt and to dominate the talking time in such contexts. They are also more likely than women to make challenging and antagonistically critical contributions. By contrast, there is some evidence that when females disagree with others, the disagreement is likely to be expressed in a modified form rather than baldly – another example of negatively polite linguistic behaviour.

I have suggested that differences in women's and men's preferred ways of interacting may be attributable, at least in part, to differences in the value they attribute to the different functions of talk in different contexts. Public contexts often focus on referential talk while the social function of such talk is status-enhancing. Both these functions tend to appeal more to men than to women. Less formal contexts allow for more emphasis on solidarity, the establishing and maintaining of social relationships, and this appeals more to women. This pattern is also apparent in the different ways women and men use linguistic hedging and boosting devices. The next chapter will examine in some detail the ways in which these forms appear to serve different functions for women and men.

Notes

1. Handling conflict is another area where different cultural and social groups have clearly different norms. Eder (1990) discusses the different strategies of white American girls from different social classes, and Goodwin (1980) the norms for African-American adolescent girls and boys. Working-class and Black girls seem more likely to engage in direct confrontation than white middle-class girls.
2. Though note James and Clarke (1992) come to a different conclusion.

3 Soft and low: hedges and boosters as politeness devices

Example 1
Marie: What a great party. I really enjoyed it.
Bob: Mm not bad at all.
Marie: You seemed to get a bit plastered though didn't you?

In the last chapter we saw that being polite means being a considerate conversational partner, or a facilitative participant in more formal contexts. Being polite may also be a matter of choosing the right words. In this chapter I will discuss a number of linguistic forms which may be used as politeness devices, and look at the evidence that New Zealand women and men tend to use them differently.

As every introductory linguistics textbook asserts, there is no one-to-one relationship between a linguistic form and its function. One form may serve many functions, and particular functions are expressed by a variety of forms. You can use a form like *what?* to request information, express amazement, annoyance, or ask for a repetition. Conversely, you can express amazement with a huge variety of forms such as *you don't say, how amazing, shit* and many more. This basic fact about language means that it is not possible to study ways of being polite by simply identifying a list of relevant linguistic forms and counting them. It is crucial to look at the function of every form in context. Obviously a comparison of women's and men's use of linguistic politeness devices will also need to take account of the function of specific forms in context.

The linguistic forms discussed in this chapter are labelled 'hedges' and 'boosters' because of their effect on the utterances in which they occur. Hedges weaken or reduce the force of an utterance. The phrase *a bit*, the verb *seemed* and the tag *didn't you*, function as hedges in example 1. (Though note that with a different tone of voice *didn't you* could be heard as accusatory – a point that is discussed further below.) *Perhaps* is a hedge in example 2.

Example 2
Wife to husband concerning threatened reprimand to child.
Perhaps you should check before you get too angry.

Perhaps makes the utterance gentler. Hedges generally soften the effect of the utterance. (Other labels for 'hedges' are 'down-graders' (House and Kasper 1981), 'compromisers' (James 1983), 'downtoners' (Quirk et al. 1985), 'weakeners' (Brown and Levinson 1987) and 'softeners' (Crystal and Davy 1975).) Boosters by contrast increase the force of utterances. *Really* is a booster in examples 1 and 3.

Example 3
Mother to shop owner concerning her son's request for work.
just give him a chance/ he's really really keen/

Really makes the statement stronger. ('Boosters' have also been called 'intensifiers' (Quirk et al. 1985) 'strengtheners' (Brown and Levinson 1987) and 'up-graders' (House and Kasper 1981).) In this book, hedges and boosters include lexical items or pragmatic particles such as *you know* and *I think*, syntactic devices, such as the tag question, and features of intonation, such as the high rising terminal (usually abbreviated HRT). These will all be illustrated in this chapter.

An American linguist, Robin Lakoff, suggested in the 1970s that hedges and boosters were characteristic of 'women's language', and that they expressed a lack of confidence and reflected women's social insecurity, as well as their propensity to be more polite than men (Lakoff 1973, 1975). Other researchers have also considered these forms as politeness devices (Shimanoff 1977; Brown and Levinson 1987). This chapter will demonstrate that there is some truth in both these perceptions, since these linguistic forms are complex in function, and particularly sophisticated in the range of affective or social meanings they may express. They are most certainly important in any comparison of women's and men's expressions of linguistic politeness. They also illustrate very clearly some of the problems researchers face in comparing women's and men's linguistic politeness behaviour.

Hedges and boosters

What is a hedge?

Politeness involves taking account of other people's feelings. Linguistically this can be done in a great variety of ways (see, for example, Leech 1983, Brown and Levinson 1987). Examples 4–7 illustrate four alternative polite ways of expressing the directive to make a cup of tea.

Examples 4–7 [constructed]
/
(4) Could you make a cup of tea.
V
(5) Make a cup of tea.
/
(6) Make a cup of tea eh.
/
(7) Make a cup of tea would you.

In example 4 the speaker uses a modal verb, *could*, in example 5 a fall-rise intonation softens the directive, while a tag is used in examples 6 and 7. These linguistic devices are negative politeness strategies in that they address the hearer's 'want to have his [sic] freedom of action unhindered and his attention unimpeded' (Brown and Levinson 1987: 129). They are devices which are aimed at reducing the imposition experienced by the person that the directive is addressed to. In the everyday usage of many English speakers, 'being polite' most obviously involves this kind of non-imposing negative politeness.

As the utterances in 4–7 demonstrate, there are a variety of linguistic means by which a speaker can signal a wish not to impose. These have generally been called 'hedging' devices; they attenuate or reduce the strength of the utterance. They damp down its force or intensity or directness. The devices which may be used include fall-rise intonation, tag questions and modal

verbs, lexical items such as *perhaps* and *conceivably,* and pragmatic particles such as *sort of* and *I think*. Even paralinguistic
signals such as pauses and vocal hesitations like *um* and *er* can be
used to express a speaker's reluctance to impose. (See Holmes
1984c and Ng and Bradac 1993: 89–116 for further discussion
and more examples of hedging devices.) Consequently, all these
devices are relevant in considering whether women are more
polite than men.

Moreover, the utterance which is hedged may be a directive, as
exemplified in 4–7, or it may be an assertion as illustrated in
8–10.

Examples 8–10
(8) *Wife to husband viewing flood on kitchen floor.*
     well that wasn't the best bit of plumbing you've ever done
        \
     was it

(9) *Electrician to customer enquiring about repair.*
     I think it's not quite ready yet

(10) *One colleague to another.*
        \
     mm// unfortunately I don't see it that way

Given that example 8 was uttered with good humour, the tag
question *was it*, and the understated form of the proposition
serve to weaken the criticism. In example 9 the speaker hedges
the bare proposition 'it's not ready' by means of the pragmatic
particle *I think* and the adverbs *quite* and *yet*. In example 10 the
disagreeing utterance is attenuated with the hedge *unfortunately*.
Speakers may use a variety of forms in different contexts as
hedging devices to mitigate face-threatening acts or to avoid
imposing on their addressees.

What is a booster?

Examples 11–13
(11) *One colleague to another following a meeting.*
     you handled that just brilliantly/ I was so impressed

(12) *Two friends are chatting about A's fears about her son's performance in an exam.*
    A: but look there's absolutely no point in worrying about it/
        worrying won't change anything
    B: you're quite right of course

(13) *Teacher reassuring child that her mother will be attending their concert.*
    Child: my mum's not here yet/ she might not come
    Teacher: don't worry Liz of course she'll come/ she must
             come/she promised she'd be here.

While hedging devices reduce the strength or force of an utterance, boosting devices intensify or emphasise the force. In example 11 the intensifying devices *just* and *so* express positive politeness; they address the hearer's want to be appreciated, 'his [sic] perennial desire that his wants (or the actions/ acquisitions/values resulting from them) should be thought of as desirable' (Brown and Levinson 1987: 101). In examples 12 and 13 the speaker takes account of the positive face needs of the addressee by emphasising agreement or admiration or reassurance, implying shared values. As discussed in Chapter 1, this kind of behaviour is not generally labelled 'politeness' in English. It would normally be described as evidence of 'friendliness' or 'camaraderie', or, in the male Australasian culture, 'mateship'. But identifying this behaviour as 'positively polite', facilitates the analysis of these two complementary phenomena within a unified and potentially universal framework.

As with hedging, there are a variety of linguistic devices which may be used to boost the strength of an utterance.

Examples 14–16
(14) *Teacher to pupils*
    STOP THAT TALKING

(15) *Man responding to exhibition of the reading ability of his friend's three year-old son.*
    how amazing// he's certainly very bright indeed.

(16) *One friend to another who has just scored very highly in Scrabble.*
    shit you're incredibly good at this

Boosting devices include prosodic features such as strong stress and high volume, as illustrated in example 14, syntactic constructions such as the exclamation in utterance example 15 and modal verbs like *must* in example 13, and pragmatic particles such as *of course* as illustrated in examples 12 and 13, above, together with a wide variety of lexical items including swear words and modal adverbs, such as *incredibly, absolutely, certainly, so* and *quite* as illustrated in examples 11–16. Rhetorical devices such as repetition, and paralinguistic signals such as well-placed pauses can also be used as boosting devices to emphasise a point. (See Holmes 1984c for further discussion and more examples of boosting strategies.)

How hedges and boosters work

Boosters do not in themselves express positive politeness and solidarity. Rather they intensify the illocutionary force of any utterance in which they are used. Moreover, as example 14 (STOP THAT TALKING) illustrates, boosters may intensify or boost the effect of utterances with negative as well as positive intentions or 'affect' (see Holmes 1984c: 349). When they are used to intensify a face-threatening act, or one with negative affect, the result will usually be an increase in social distance rather than in solidarity. So a booster is not intrinsically a positive politeness device. Though a booster may contribute to the expression of positive politeness in utterances such as agreements, compliments and greetings, it may equally contribute to the degree of face threat expressed by a disagreement, a criticism or an insult. We must assess the politeness (or impoliteness) of such utterances in context.

Unlike boosters, which reinforce rather than express positive politeness, hedging devices may in themselves be the main locus of the expression of negative politeness in many different kinds of utterances. The tag in example 8, and the lexical hedge in example 10 are the main means by which negative politeness is expressed in these utterances. On the other hand, hedges resemble boosters in that they may attenuate the force both of negatively affective or face-threatening utterances such as directives, and of positively affective utterances, such as compliments (e.g. *that shirt's quite nice I suppose*). Clearly the positive versus the negative politeness effect of such an utterance can only be assessed in context.

Finally, in considering the function and meaning of particular forms which may serve as politeness devices, it is very important to recognise that these forms express other meanings too. (This point is also illustrated in the discussion of tag questions below.)

> **Examples 17 and 18 [constructed]**
> (17) He's a real actor.
>
> (18) She's certain to be selected.

In example 17, the form *real* may function referentially (or, more specifically, epistemically[1]) as a synonym for *genuine* (i.e. 'not an amateur or a fraud'); alternatively it may function affectively as a booster intensifying a criticism (i.e. 'you can't believe anything he does'). In example 18 the word *certain* may function referentially and epistemically to express the meaning 'there is no alternative – it is clear that this must be the outcome'; alternatively or additionally it may function affectively as reassurance to a doubtful addressee (i.e. 'don't worry she'll be OK'). So both example 17 and example 18 can be interpreted either as primarily referential in meaning or as primarily affective. Where it is relevant, this distinction has proved an important one in language and gender research as we will see.

Hedges and boosters and 'women's language'

In comparing the speech of women and men, many researchers have simply counted linguistic forms, regardless of their particular meaning and effect in a specific context (e.g. McMillan et al. 1977), and sometimes regardless of the relative amounts of speech contributed by women and men (e.g. Dubois and Crouch 1975). (See Holmes 1984a and Preisler 1986 for further discussion of such methodological points.) Even when account is taken of the function of a form as a hedge or booster (e.g. Crosby and Nyquist 1977; O'Barr and Atkins 1980), simple frequency counts are not enough. The researcher must also consider the illocutionary force or intention of the speech acts being modified. This is illustrated well by this quotation from a court witness recorded by O'Barr and Atkins (1980: 99).

Example 19
'Lawyer. And you saw, you observed what?
Witness. Well, after I heard – I can't really, I can't definitely state whether the brakes or the lights came first, but I rotated my head slightly to the right, and looked directly behind Mr Z, and I saw reflections of lights.'

(O'Barr and Atkins 1980:99)

It is often important in terms of *accuracy* to qualify a proposition or indicate that it cannot be asserted with complete confidence. In this example, the witness's qualifications appear to be justifiably based on his reluctance to state as an undisputed fact something about which he was genuinely uncertain. He seems to be using epistemic modal devices (i.e. devices which express degrees of certainty or confidence), not because he is powerless or socially unconfident, but in the interests of accuracy. (Note that my own use of the hedges *appear to be* and *seems* in the previous two sentences stems from a similar cause. I cannot be sure of the speaker's intention on the basis of only a decontextualised written transcript.) This demonstrates clearly that researchers must identify the specific meaning and pragmatic effect of forms in the context in which they are used before valid comparisons between speakers are possible. I will illustrate these points further in the discussion of tag questions.

Tag questions

There is a rich literature on the complex syntax and phonology of tag questions (e.g. Arbini 1969; Huddleston 1970; Armagost 1972; Cattell 1973; Hudson 1975; Oleksy 1977; Millar and Brown 1979; Cheshire 1981, 1982; Östman 1981; Holmes 1982b; Nässlin 1984). This research demonstrates that tags differ in polarity, in intonation, in syntactic derivation and in lexical form. Many language and gender researchers have ignored this variation and treated tags as invariant forms. However, an examination of my New Zealand corpus made it clear that there was no exact correlation between function and form, and that different lexical forms behaved differently. In this chapter I will focus on canonical tags, though I will also refer briefly to research on the distribution of the tag *eh*.

Functions of canonical tags

Canonical tags are tags such as *are you*, *isn't she* and *can't they* which are generally pronounced with either falling or rising intonation. They are often final in utterances, but may also be medial (Coates 1989: 116). In comparing their distribution in the speech of women and men, it is crucial to pay attention to their function in context. Though many tags express both affective and referential meaning, and it is not always easy to assign a primary function, it is generally possible to do so by paying careful attention to context (Holmes 1984b; Cameron et al. 1989). In the data I analysed, four distinct functions of tag questions could be identified: epistemic modal, challenging, facilitative and softening. Not all are equally relevant in an analysis of linguistic politeness.

Epistemic modal tags express the speaker's uncertainty. Their primary function is referential rather than affective: they focus on the accuracy of the information asserted in the proposition, rather than on the feelings of the addressee. Examples 20 and 21 provide examples of epistemic modal tags.

Examples 20 and 21
(20) *Young woman recounting school experiences to her friend.*
/
I did my exams in sixty three was it

(21) *Husband searching in newspaper for information says to wife.*
/
Fay Weldon's lecture is at eight isn't it

In both examples the tag indicates that the speaker is not totally confident about the validity of the facts. These tags express genuine speaker uncertainty rather than politeness.

Challenging tags are confrontational strategies. They may pressure a reluctant addressee to reply or aggressively boost the force of a negative speech act. Example 22 illustrates two confrontational tags in a context of unequal power.

Example 22
Superintendant to Detective Constable during interview criticising
the Constable's performance.
A: ...... you'll probably find yourself um before the Chief
              /
      Constable, okay?
B: Yes, Sir, yes, understood.

                                          \

A: Now you er fully understand that, don't you?
B: Yes, Sir, indeed, yeah.

(Thomas 1989: 152)

These tags act, as Thomas points out (1989: 27) to 'force feedback when it is not forthcoming'. Cheshire (1981: 375–6, 1982: 165) documents the use of non-standard tag forms such as *in I* with a similar challenging, aggressive function in the speech of working class adolescents (see also Cameron et al. 1989). Tags which express a coercive or challenging function are properly analysed as boosters, not hedges, and they are certainly not politeness devices. Rather they are impoliteness devices. The superintendant in example 22 shows little concern for the detective constable's face needs. He is not trying to minimise face loss; indeed, he is intent on threatening or even attacking the detective constable's face. In this context the tag question strengthens the negative force of the 'face attack act' (see Austin 1988, 1990). Courtroom cross-examination, which has the intention of destroying a witness's credibility, is another rich source of face attack acts (see Lane 1990).

Facilitative tags are quite different in function. They are examples of hedges which serve as positive politeness devices. They invite the addressee to contribute to the discourse.

Examples 23 and 24
(23) *Host, Fiona, to Tom, a guest at her dinner party.*
                                          \
      you've got a new job Tom haven't you

(24) *Primary school teacher to five year-old.*
      Mrs Short: here's a pretty one what's this one called Simon?
      Simon: mm/ erm [3 second pause]

Mrs Short: see its tail/ look at its tail// it's a fantail
\
isn't it.
Simon: mm a fantail.

The tag question in example 23 makes it easy for Tom to join in the dinner party conversation; the tag in example 24 encourages Simon to respond to the teacher's question. These tags are clearly facilitative positive politeness devices; they indicate concern for the needs of others – a feature identified as typical of women's talk strategies in Chapter 2. With their addressee-orientated affective function, these tags are obviously very relevant in comparisons of politeness between women and men. The same is true of *softening* tags which are negative politeness devices, used to attenuate the force of negatively affective utterances such as directives, as illustrated in examples 4–7, and criticisms, exemplified in examples 8 and 25.[2]

Example 25
Older brother to younger brother who has just stepped on the cat's bowl and spilled her milk all over the floor.
\
that was a really dumb thing to do wasn't it

Who uses tag questions and why?

In analysing the distribution of canonical tag questions in New Zealand women's and men's speech I used a 60,000 word corpus, carefully matched for the quantity of female and male speech produced, and for the number of women and men contributors. The corpus included approximately equal amounts of informal conversations, collected in relaxed situations in people's homes, and formal interactions from classrooms and broadcast interviews. The people contributing were predominantly middle-class, well-educated native speakers of New Zealand English ranging in age from school children to people in their sixties.

Figure 3.1 illustrates the distribution of canonical tag questions in this corpus according to the four functional categories described above. It shows that women used significantly more *facilitative* or invitational tags than men did, while men used more *epistemic* tags requesting reassurance or confirmation of the

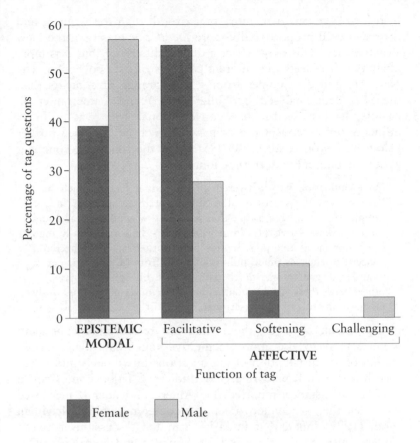

Figure 3.1 Tag questions by function and speaker's gender

validity of their propositions. Coates (1989) analysing women's speech in a relaxed setting, and Cameron et al. (1989), using mixed-sex data from the London Survey of English Usage (SEU), also identified the pattern of women using more *facilitative* than *epistemic* modal tags. And, if one interprets Hiller's (1985) category of 'expressive' tags as broadly equivalent to *facilitative* tags, her analysis, which also uses SEU data, reports the same pattern. Indeed all this evidence is consistent with the tendency for women to adopt a supportive and facilitative role in conversation which was illustrated in Chapter 2.

Unlike the men in the New Zealand corpus, the men in the

British SEU corpus used more tags overall than the women, and they also used proportionally more *facilitative* tags than the New Zealand men. This may reflect a dialect difference, but it is more likely that it reflects the different contexts of data collection. The New Zealand data comes from a wider range of contexts than the SEU data analysed by Hiller (1985) and Cameron et al. (1989). It also seems that conversational role was a likely influence on these results, a point which will be discussed further below. Cameron et al. (1989: 85) make the following comment about the unusual pattern they found:

> On examination we discovered an interesting factor which may have skewed the scores for the SEU men: three speakers in our sample texts had been aware that recording was taking place, and these speakers – two of whom were men – had abnormally high scores for facilitative tags. It may be that their speech reflected a concern to elicit as much talk as possible from other participants, in order to generate as much data as possible for the Survey. In other words these speakers had either consciously or unconsciously taken on the role of conversational 'facilitator'.

In general, however, the results are reassuringly consistent: women tend to use more facilitative tags than men. Earlier studies of the distribution of tag questions in women's and men's speech had been bewilderingly contradictory. Dubois and Crouch (1975), for instance, reported that American academic men used more tags than academic women at a conference, while McMillan et al. (1977) found that in task-orientated discussions between students just the reverse was true. Lapadat and Seesahai (1977) collected informal data which showed men used twice as many tags as women, while the informal conversations analysed by Fishman (1980) revealed that women used almost three times as many tags as men. Given the methodological naïveté of much of this research (discussed in Holmes 1984a), it is hardly surprising that the results reported were difficult to interpret and apparently contradictory. Different contexts and roles were involved, and there were also a number of uncontrolled or unconsidered factors, including the amount of data being compared from women and men, and the different functions of tag questions. More recent studies, which take account not just of the form but also of the function of tags, conclude that while the relative number of tags used by men and women may vary in different contexts and dialects, men generally use canonical tag questions more often than women do to express uncertainty and ask for confirmation, while women use tag questions more often than men in their facilitative positive politeness function.

What about the context?

Example 26
Two young students who have been reading about Lakoff's claims.
A: But it's true. Women are always using tag questions aren't they?
B: Well it depends what you mean by 'women'. Do you mean 'all women or most women' or 'some women'? And what sort of tag questions do you have in mind? Some are quite aggressive aren't they? Others are much gentler. And what about the context? In my opinion people use tags to get people talking so I bet you hear more from good teachers and facilitators than you do in board-rooms!

How far is context a relevant factor in this analysis? A number of studies have noted that tag questions occur more frequently in the speech of those who have some kind of responsibility for the success of an interaction (Johnson 1980: 72; Holmes 1984b; Cameron et al. 1989). In the professional meetings which Johnson (1980) analysed, the leader used 70 per cent of all the facilitative questions. In my New Zealand corpus, which includes formal and informal speech, two-thirds of all the tag questions used by men and three-quarters of those used by women were produced by those in such a role – teachers in the classroom, interviewers on TV or radio, or the hosts at a dinner party. I quoted above the comments of Cameron et al. (1989) on the possible influence of conversational role on the number of tags identified in the SEU data they analysed. Using broadcast data, these researchers also examined the different types of tag questions used by those in the 'powerful' as opposed to the 'powerless' roles in unequal encounters (e.g. teacher–pupil, doctor–client). The distribution of types of tag very clearly reflected the roles of the participants. Regardless of gender, 'powerful' participants used more of the facilitative tags, while 'powerless' participants used twice as many epistemic modal tags as 'powerful' contributors.[3] Preisler (1986: 165) found that in some of the small discussion groups he analysed, tags tended to be used by those who adopted a facilitative ('socio-emotional') role.

There is an obvious explanation for the correlation between the leadership or facilitator role and a high proportion of tag questions. Tag questions encourage people to talk, and that is the aim of a good interviewer or teacher or host. What is particularly interesting, however, is that in the New Zealand data, in informal interactions involving no obvious power or status differences, women used facilitative tags more often than men as positive politeness or solidarity devices, inviting the addressee's partici- pation in the discourse. In these apparently equal interactions, then, women used more positive politeness devices than men.

Tag questions nicely illustrate the complexity of analysing particular linguistic forms and comparing their use as politeness devices by women and men. I will deal more briefly with the linguistic forms considered in the rest of this chapter. It is important to remember, however, that each of the forms discussed involves similar problems in accurately identifying the relevant relationship between form and function in context.

Pragmatic particles: *you know, I think, sort of, of course*

> **Example 27**
> *Young woman describing a previous job to her friend.*
> and we started off learning/ typing I think you know sort
> of/ right from the beginning kind of thing

There are a number of linguistic forms which have been regarded as 'verbal fillers' (Brown 1977) and described in language and gender research as characteristic of 'women's language' (Lakoff 1973, 1975). The most frequently investigated of these are forms such as *you know*, *I think* and *sort of* which I have labelled pragmatic particles. These forms serve as hedging devices or boosting devices in different contexts, and their contribution to politeness also varies with context.

In the course of investigating the expression of politeness by New Zealand women and men, I have analysed a number of these particles. The patterns which have emerged are very similar. First, every particle reveals a complexity of function which emphasises the futility of simply counting unanalysed forms. Secondly, where there are differences in the distribution of such forms in women's and men's speech, women tend to use pragmatic particles to express positive politeness more often than men do. I will illustrate these points in some detail in relation to *you know*, and I will then briefly summarise additional insights provided by analyses of three further pragmatic particles, *I think*, *sort of* and *of course*.

You know

Form and function

Example 28
Young man to friends over dinner.
and I've been on this bloody speed reading course which is you know/ so one notices if one's/ you know uses two skips per line

The pragmatic particle *you know* has attracted attention from a number of researchers, especially discourse analysts who have explored in some detail both its form (e.g. Crystal and Davy 1975: 92–3; Holmes 1986a) and its functions (e.g. Edmondson 1981; Östman 1981; Schourup 1985; Schiffrin 1987).

Different instances of *you know* vary in intonation and syntactic position, and, like the tag question, *you know* conveys both referential and affective meaning. Both these aspects of meaning are captured in Östman's definition of its 'prototypical' meaning (1981: 17):

The speaker strives towards getting the addressee to cooperate and/or accept the propositional content of his utterance as mutual background knowledge.

The speaker's appeal to the addressee constitutes the affective meaning of *you know*, while the referential meaning relates to the presupposed shared knowledge. In different contexts, *you know* may focus more specifically on particular aspects of its meaning: its primary function may be to signal that the speaker attributes understanding to the listener, it may appeal to the listener's sympathy, or it may function as a booster to emphasise the mutual knowledge of the participants. These are affectively orientated functions with implications for an analysis of linguistic politeness. Alternatively, *you know* may be more referentially orientated: it may function primarily as a lexical hedge to signal linguistic imprecision or mark a qualification, or it may express uncertainty about the propositional content of an utterance.

Let us take some examples. *You know* expresses primarily referential meaning when it functions as a hedge on the validity of some aspect of the proposition. It may express uncertainty relating to the precision of the following word, for instance, or the accuracy of the way the proposition as a whole is expressed.

Examples 29 and 30
(29) *Young man requesting clarification of previous speaker, his flatmate.*

\

better/ entertainment product or better/ you know/ music
musicians

(30) *Elderly man to young neighbours.*
the house/ up above the one I was telling you / you about

/

you know the one your dad used to live in

In example 29, *you know* is a signal that the following word is causing problems for the speaker, and in example 30 it signals that there is a problem relating to referential precision.[4]

When it is used with emphasis on its affective meaning, *you know* is very clearly a positive politeness device in the New Zealand data. It refers to assumptions, values, attitudes and even earlier experiences shared by the speaker and addressee. It acts as a booster on the force of such utterances. Examples 31 and 32 illustrate instances of *you know* with this affective positive politeness orientation.[5]

Examples 31 and 32
(31) *Radio interviewee describing past experience.*
and that way we'd get rid of exploitation of man by man all

\

that stuff/ you know/ you've heard it before

(32) *Young woman in conversation with flatmates over dinner.*
                                                      \
      they obviously thought he was a bit stupid / you know

In these examples *you know* expresses the speaker's confidence
that the addressee knows or understands, on the basis of shared
experience or attitudes, the kind of thing referred to in the
proposition.

There are other instances of *you know* which, while primarily
affective are not so clearly other-orientated positive politeness
devices. Some instances, (labelled 'appealing' in Holmes 1986a: 9)
express affective meaning but are more concerned with the
positive face needs of the speaker than the addressee (see Brown
and Levinson 1987: 68). Their function seems to be to protect
the speaker's face: they express uncertainty and appeal to the
addressee for reassurance. They are hedging devices rather than
boosters of the force of the utterance. Example 33 illustrates this.

Example 33
Young woman to close friend.
and it was quite //well it was it was all very embarrassing
     /
you know

Here the speaker appeals to the listener for an indication of
understanding. *You know* is used as a positive politeness device –
but as a speaker-orientated rather than an addressee-orientated
device.

Who uses *you know* and why?

Figure 3.2 shows the results of an analysis of over 200 instances
of *you know* in New Zealand women's and men's speech in a
range of contexts along the dimensions of affective and referential
orientation, with the positive politeness instances separately
identified. When equal amounts of data for women and men are
collected in carefully matched contexts, there is little difference in
the overall distribution of *you know* between females and males
(105 females versus 102 males). However, women use *you know*
with a primarily affective meaning more often than men do, and

in particular women use *you know* significantly more often than men in its other-orientated positive politeness functions.

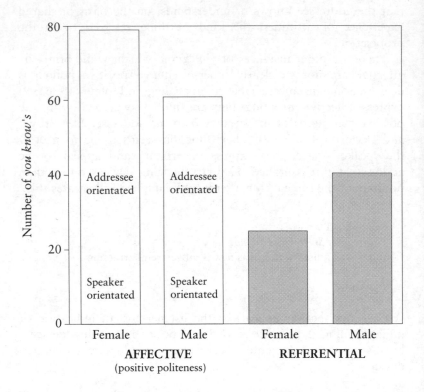

Figure 3.2 *You know* by function and speaker's gender

Clearly, there is no one-to-one correlation between the function of a form as a hedge or a booster and its role as a negative politeness or positive politeness device. It is often assumed that hedges always express negative politeness, but *you know* demonstrates that this is not the case. In the New Zealand data, *you know* sometimes served as a referentially orientated hedge, rather than as a politeness device. It sometimes served as a speaker-orientated politeness device, protecting the speaker's positive face. Thirdly, it often expressed addressee-orientated positive politeness, and this is how the women used it most often.

What about the context?

You know is a pragmatic particle which occurs considerably more often in informal interaction than in formal contexts in the New Zealand data. Of the occurrences, 92 per cent occurred in informal speech contexts. It is undoubtedly a solidarity marker, used most between people who know each other well. It reduces power and status differences and emphasises what participants share.

You know also tended to occur more often in relaxed single-sex contexts than in mixed-sex contexts (Holmes 1986a). This pragmatic particle appears to be a feature not simply of informal speech, but more specifically a reflection of relationships of friendship and camaraderie; and speakers and hearers of the same gender are more likely to share common ground. Interestingly, it appears that it may be favoured by men in single-sex contexts (Coates 1989; Holmes 1986a), though, in view of the small sample sizes, this can only be a suggestion at present.

Given that it is most frequent in informal contexts, it is not surprising to find that *you know* tends to occur most often in sections of relatively sustained narrative or accounts of the speaker's personal experiences intended to amuse, amaze, or, at least, retain the interest of the addressee. It occurs much less often in sections of discussion, argument, planning or 'phatic' talk where there is more frequent speaker-change (cf. Brown 1980). Narrations of interesting or amusing personal experiences most often occur in informal and relaxed contexts where the speaker feels some social obligation to entertain the addressee(s). All this supports the analysis of *you know* as a pragmatic particle which frequently expresses a positive politeness, solidarity-orientated function. In the New Zealand data, *you know* is used most often in this function by women, and this finding is consistent with the suggestion, which was discussed in Chapter 2, that women tend to be more comfortable talking in informal private contexts than in more public formal settings.

I *think*, *sort of* and *of course*

These three pragmatic particles contrast in a number of ways. *Sort of* is typically a hedge, *of course* is typically a booster, while *I think* may function as a hedge or a booster, though this duality has not often been recognised.

I *think*

I think is the most complex and interesting of the three. It has been identified by different researchers as an important linguistic clue to all kinds of non-linguistic facts such as the speaker's psychological state, verbal proficiency, cognitive abilities and social class (e.g. Bernstein 1962; Loban 1966; Turner and Pickvance 1972), as well as to the speaker's gender. It is amusing to note, for instance, that while Bernstein identified *I think* as a characteristic of 'elaborated code', associated with abstract reasoning, and Torrance and Olson (1984) noted such phrases in the speech of good readers and linked them to higher cognitive functioning, Lakoff labelled *I think* a hedge and described it as a feature of 'women's language' (Lakoff 1975: 54). One might reasonably conclude that women's use of *I think* reflects their cognitively sophisticated, logical, abstract reasoning processes. Before drawing such a conclusion, however, it would be necessary to take account of the fact that few researchers have considered the full range of forms and functions involved in a thorough analysis of this particle.

Like *you know*, *I think* is not a monolithic invariable linguistic form; instances vary in intonation, stress and syntactic position (Holmes 1985). Not surprisingly the function of *I think* varies with these features, and it may act as a hedge or as a booster in different utterances. Since the politeness effect of a hedge or a booster on a proposition depends on what is being asserted to whom and for what reasons, obviously the contribution of these different types of *I think* to politeness can only be determined in context.

In example 34, for instance, *I think* functions as a hedge. Since it softens a criticism, it expresses negative politeness.

Example 34
Teacher to pupil.

\
you've got that wrong I think

In example 35 by contrast the speaker signals uncertainty about the precise time with his use of *I think*.

Example 35
Elderly man recounting past experience to friends.

\
it'd be about two o'clock I think

His memory may not be perfect on this point. Here *I think* is an epistemic device expressing primarily referential meaning.

In example 34, however, the teacher is in no doubt that the pupil's answer is wrong: *I think* is a negative politeness strategy.

Both of these uses of *I think* as a hedging device contrast with a very different function where *I think* acts as a booster, strengthening rather than weakening the force of the utterance in which it occurs. The function of *I think* as a booster has rarely been discussed, yet there are instances where, from the point of view of a pragmatic analysis, it cannot be interpreted in any other way. Though, semantically, forms such as *I think* are regarded as weakening the propositions they modify, it is clear that *in context* they may function quite differently. In example 36, for instance, the statusful 'expert' speaker is in no doubt at all about the proposition she is asserting; she uses *I think* to add weight to the statement rather than to hedge its force. *I think* is (typically) in initial position and *think* gets level stress, both linguistic means of expressing emphasis and confidence.

Example 36
Statusful interviewee on TV.
I think that's absolutely right//

In such cases where *I think* boosts an agreeing proposition, it also functions affectively as a positive politeness device. The speaker is indicating that she shares the views of her addressee, the previous speaker. In other instances, as exemplified in example 37, *I think* may be strengthening a disagreement and so its affective function will be negative.

Example 37
MP in television interview.
I think that's complete rubbish

In such instances *I think* clearly does not serve as any kind of politeness device.

Once again it is apparent that lexical shape alone cannot provide sufficient information to identify the function of a linguistic form. Analyses which simply count all instances of *I think* as hedges are likely to be misleading.

An examination of the distribution of instances of *I think* showed there was no difference in the overall frequency of its use by New Zealand women and men in the corpus: women produced fifty-eight instances and men fifty-six. But there was a contrast in the predominant functions for which it was used by women and men. Women used *I think* as a booster more frequently than as a hedge (62 per cent versus 31 per cent respectively), while the reverse was true for the men (59 per cent as a hedge versus 36 per cent as a booster). And women used *I think* considerably more frequently than men as a politeness device, especially as a positive politeness device, boosting an utterance expressing agreement with the addressee.

Interestingly, while women used *I think* as a politeness device in a range of contexts, almost all of the male examples were instances of male teachers softening an alternative suggestion or a disagreeing utterance addressed to a pupil. Possibly these men were prepared to use negative politeness devices such as *I think* when they were in a powerful role, more often than in interaction with equals or with superiors. Given the small numbers involved, one can only observe trends. But it is interesting to note, first, that women used *I think* as a politeness device, and in particular as a positive politeness device, more often than men. Secondly, that the expression of negative politeness does not necessarily correlate with powerlessness, as Lakoff and others have suggested. Disagreeing with or criticising others is sometimes unavoidable, especially for those in certain roles. Negative politeness is a means by which powerful participants can mitigate negative affect towards the less powerful.

Finally, it is worth noting that there were five instances of women and five of men using *I think* to boost a disagreeing proposition, as in example 37 above and in examples 38 and 39: that is, to strengthen a negatively affective utterance.

Examples 38 and 39

(38) *Male committee convenor in radio interview.*
personally I think you can't sustain that position for long

(39) *Female member of a lobby group in radio interview.*
I think Mrs McDonald would agree with me *(where interviewer has suggested she wouldn't)*

Almost all these instances came from political interviews with women and men who presented themselves very assertively. They were high status participants interacting with interviewers in a formal context. There was certainly nothing ameliorative about these uses of *I think*, illustrating that pragmatic particles can pack a punch in the mouths of powerful participants of either gender.

Sort of and of course

The same complexity emerged in the analysis of the pragmatic particles *sort of* and *of course* (Holmes 1988a, 1989a). Like other pragmatic particles these particles express both referential meaning (degrees of certainty) and affective meaning (politeness); consequently comparing their use as politeness devices by women and men involves careful analysis. They provide an interesting contrast in that *sort of* is typically a hedge occurring in informal contexts, while *of course* generally functions as a booster and tends to occur in more formal contexts, as illustrated in examples 40 and 41

Examples 40 and 41

(40) *Female interviewee describing experiences at school to female interviewer.*
the others sort of trail along and sort of aren't considered sane

(41) *Prime Minister in a TV interview commenting on a young MP from his party who has been causing him problems.*
yes well Marilyn's got a thing about middle-aged males of course

In its affective function, *sort of* is a marker of solidarity, a positive politeness device reflecting the speaker's desire for a relaxed relationship with the addressee, as illustrated in example 40. In this meaning it tends to be used more often by women than by men (Holmes 1989a, Coates 1989). In the New Zealand corpus, women tended to emphasize the interpersonal positive politeness use of this pragmatic particle more than men did, while men tended to use *sort of* as an epistemic device expressing approximation or imprecision more often than women, especially in task-orientated interviews (Meyerhoff 1986). Examples (42) and (43) are examples from Meyerhoff's corpus (1986: 90, 100).

Examples 42 and 43
Young men describing a Dürer picture to male interviewer.
(42) it appears to be a sort of/ medieval or maybe a bit later

(43) he's wearing a sort of a um/ sort of material wrapped
    around his waist

Of course is functionally more complex and tended to occur most often in formal contexts such as TV and radio interviews, as illustrated in example 41 above. In these contexts it was used most frequently by both women and men as an impersonal, distancing device, expressing negative politeness.

As with *sort of*, however, men used *of course* in its referential epistemic function, expressing certainty, more often than women, as illustrated in example 44.

Example 44
One colleague to another in coffee-drinking area at work.
and of course Dee won't easily forgive you for that comment you made

So, although there was little or no difference in the data analysed in the total number of instances of these forms used by New Zealand women and men, in general women used them as politeness devices more often than men, and men used them more often than women as epistemic devices in their referential function. This pattern of female concern with affective meaning, and male with referential meaning was noted in the discussion of tag questions, and it illustrates once again the different orientations of women and men in interaction which was described in Chapter 2.

The pragmatic tag *eh*

Example 45
One young man to another.
\   \
it's hard yacker eh it's a bummer of a job really eh

The tag *eh* deserves special consideration in any analysis of New Zealand politeness devices. Though there are references to its occurrence in dialects of English elsewhere, such as Canada (Gibson 1976), it is regarded by New Zealanders as a distinctively New Zealand pragmatic tag. Needless to say, its functions and distribution in the speech of women and men prove very interesting.

There were only thirteen instances of *eh* in the predominantly middle-class corpus used for detailed analysis of tag questions and pragmatic particles. The Wellington Social Dialect Survey (Holmes et al. 1991), provided a much richer corpus for the analysis of vernacular forms such as *eh*. This survey involved seventy-five speakers from three age groups, two social classes and two ethnic groups, Maori and Pakeha (New Zealanders of European descent). There were 245 instances of *eh* in the casual speech of interviewees. These were analysed by Miriam Meyerhoff (1992a).

Eh is basically a hedging device, but it may soften a criticism as in example 46, or it may express varying degrees of confidence in what is being asserted, as in examples 47 and 48.

Examples 46–48
(46) *Older child to younger child* .
\
that was pretty silly eh//

(47) *Elderly male to young man.*
\
oh we've all gotta go one day eh

(48) *Young girl to friend.*
\
you're comin' tonight eh / you said you would

Its other-orientated interactive function, inviting supportive feed-back, is apparent in example 49.

Example 49
Maori man describing his relationship with his neighbours.
\
I'm afraid to walk in the house eh they might have a three-oh-three pointing at me

While recognising the range of more specific functions *eh* may serve, Meyerhoff identifies *eh* as primarily an other-orientated interactive politeness device.

Who uses *eh* and why?

In the data from the Wellington Social Dialect Survey, the tag *eh* occurred more frequently in the speech of Maori New Zealanders than in Pakeha speech. And, interestingly, working-class Maori men used *eh* most often, while working-class Pakeha men used it least, as Figure 3.3 shows.

Eh was also more frequent in young people's speech, sug-gesting a linguistic change in progress, and it was more common in working-class rather than middle-class speech (Meyerhoff 1992a). Together with the fact that it was rare in the original predominantly middle-class corpus, this suggests that *eh* is a feature of vernacular (rather than standard) New Zealand English.

The information on the social distribution of *eh* is especially interesting, because this kind of information is not available for most pragmatic particles. The New Zealand social dialect data reveals that *eh* occurs more often in the speech of the Maori ethnic minority than the Pakeha majority ethnic group. Secondly, it occurs significantly more frequently in the speech of Maori males (and especially young ones) than in the speech of any other group, a pattern consistent with its vernacular status, but initially surprising in view of the pragmatic function of this particle as an other-orientated interactive politeness device. Thirdly, young Pakeha females use this vernacular feature more often than young Pakeha males, suggesting that if there is a change in progress, it is women who are leading this vernacular change among the Pakeha group. This is a reasonably common pattern in social dialect data (see Labov 1990: 215–18; Coates 1993a), and one

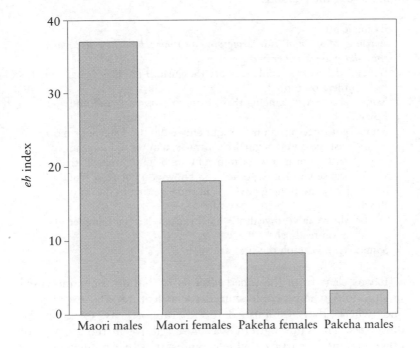

Figure 3.3 *Eh* in working class New Zealanders' speech

which is quite consistent with its function as a positive politeness device.

One explanation for these interesting patterns may lie in the coincidence of the societal and the pragmatic functions of *eh* (Meyerhoff 1992a). *Eh* is a vernacular linguistic feature which seems to be used as a marker of Maori ethnicity. Though it is used most extensively by Maori males in this function as an ethnic identity signal, the fact that Maori females also use *eh* more often than Pakeha groups supports the view that it is primarily an ethnicity rather than a gender marker. However, as a typical pragmatic particle, it also has a positive politeness function. This perhaps accounts for the fact that Pakeha women use *eh* – a vernacular form – more often than Pakeha men. For Pakeha women, it seems likely that *eh* functions primarily as a politeness device.

What about the context?

Example 50
*A young Maori man is interviewing another when they discover
they share work experience.*
Boyd: what sort of cable tray are they using? are they lying
        them on top?
Sam: ⌈no they're hanging them from the roof   yeah and you
Boyd: ⌊   yeah
Sam: got to get up oh it's alright eh we did the 14th floor me
        just me and this guy he's a tradesman we did um the
        14th floor in a week mm running behind on the 17th
        'cause you got the other you know you got your bloody
        ⌈air conditioning guys   in there getting in the way
Boyd: ⌊   yeah
        shit yeah yeah yeah it's hard yacker eh it's a bummer of
        a job really eh
Sam: yeah yeah oh the sites are yeah...

It was clear from the taped interviews that *eh* usage increased
in situations where people shared social features and experience,
and where they established good rapport, as example 50
illustrates. The same pattern was noted above in the analysis of
other pragmatic particles which express positive politeness. *You
know*, for instance, occurred with greater frequency in same-sex
conversations than it did in mixed-sex ones (Jones 1975, Holmes
1986a: 14). Similarly, Meyerhoff (1992b) found that end tags
(e.g. *and stuff, or something like that*) seemed to be more
common when both interlocutors were women. All this supports
the interpretation of these forms as verbal markers of relaxed
informal interaction.

Interestingly, as predicted by Wolfson's (1988) bulge model
which was described in Chapter 1, these forms appear to occur
more often in interactions between 'semi-intimates' than between
intimates (where 'semi-intimates' refers to friends and acquaintances, people who are neither strangers nor intimate friends).
Östman (1981: 20) points this out in comparing occurrences of
you know in conversations between friends and acquaintances
(semi-intimates) with conversations between intimates. This
suggests that a pragmatic tag such as *oh*, or a pragmatic particle
like *you know* is used as a politeness device to appeal to similar

experiences or attitudes which speakers perceive to exist between themselves and their interlocutor. Intimates do not need to make such appeals; the existence of shared experiences and attitudes can be taken for granted. The interview settings used in the Wellington Social Dialect Survey are very similar to Östman's 'semi-intimate' situations, and it seems that *eh* is functioning similarly in these interactions to identify shared experience and values..

The data on the pragmatic particle *eh* provides new insights into the possible functions of a hedging device. Unlike the other forms discussed in this chapter, *eh* was used most often by a group of young men. But they were Maori, not Pakeha, men and it is clear that for this group *eh* is primarily a signal of shared ethnic identity. In line with the distributional patterns of previous particles, *eh* is used much more often by Pakeha women than Pakeha men. For this group, it is the interactive politeness function of *eh* which is salient. Nevertheless, *eh* undoubtedly also performs an important interpersonal role in the talk of Maori people. Pragmatic devices are intrinsically multi-functional, a point which is further explored and illustrated in the discussion of the final pragmatic device examined in this chapter, the HRT.

A prosodic hedge – the high-rising terminal (HRT)

What does it mean?

Example 51
Teenage girl talking to mother's friend about an English teacher.

We had this young guy/ he was really good/ like sometimes

they bore you stiff but he was just great full of ideas and

energy// I really enjoyed his classes//

The high rising terminal (HRT) intonation pattern, like other pragmatic politeness devices, has often been described as an uncertainty signal. Talking about American women, Lakoff describes (1975: 17):

a peculiar intonation pattern, found in English so far as I know
only among women, which has the form of a declarative answer to
a yes-no question, and is used as such, but has the rising inflection
typical of a yes-no question, as well as being especially hesitant.

Is this the HRT? At present we do not have the research to
answer this question. Certainly, there are references to rising
tones in Canadian English (James et al. 1989), American English
(e.g. Ching 1982; Cruttenden 1986; McLemore 1991), and
British English (Woods 1992), but we do not know if these rising
tones are precisely the same in form, and there is relatively little
systematic evidence on their distribution. By contrast, the HRT is
a well-attested feature of Australasian speech – both female and
male (Guy and Vonwiller 1984; Horvath 1985; Guy et al. 1986;
Allan 1990; Britain 1992). However, in neither Australia nor
New Zealand do researchers suggest that the primary function of
the HRT is to express uncertainty or deference.

The functions of the HRT are similar to those of pragmatic
particles like *you know* and tags such as *eh*. Despite its super-
ficial similarity to interrogative intonation, the HRT does not
function to mark an utterance as a straightforward question.
Rather it serves interpersonal politeness functions, as illustrated in
the following examples from the social dialect data we collected.

Examples 52 and 53
(52) *Middle-aged woman to young woman interviewer.*
so there was a lot of stress in my life and I used to get
/
hidings every day

(53) *Young woman to young woman interviewer.*
as I was just sort of nodding off to sleep I could hear a
/
um like a what I thought was a moth banging on the
/
window

These utterances are not questions; nor do they express the
speaker's uncertainty about the proposition. Only the speakers
could verify the validity of the information asserted in the propositions. Rather, the HRT invites the addressee to acknowledge
the speaker's talk and indicate that they are following and

understanding the speaker (Britain 1992). In some cases the HRT, like the particle *you know* and the tag *eh*, refers to assumed shared knowledge, checking out that the addressee shares the same background information as the speaker.

Example 54
Young woman to young woman interviewer.

                            /   /

A: it reminded me of that Karla Kardno situation
B: oh yeah
A: you know she went to the shop and she hid in a shop
       /
    and that

The situation referred to here was an episode preceding a grisly murder which had been well publicised the previous year. The speaker is checking out that the listener remembers this and perceives the parallel with the incident she is describing. Clearly the HRT, like many pragmatic particles, has an interactive politeness function in discourse. This analysis is also consistent with the primary function of HRTs identified in the Sydney social dialect data (Guy and Vonwiller 1984: 12; Horvath 1985: 132). In both surveys it was found that HRTs function as positive politeness devices, seeking the addressee's participation in the discourse, emphasising the agreement and solidarity shared between speaker and listener (Britain 1992).

The data used to analyse both *eh* and HRTs came from interviews between people of the same gender and ethnicity. Similar backgrounds and good rapport appeared to increase the frequencies of both forms. Britain (1992) also reports that HRTs occurred most often in sections of narrative, rather than in sections expressing the speaker's personal opinions, for instance. This is further support for the characterisation of HRTs as other-orientated politeness devices. They invite the listener to participate vicariously and sympathetically in the narrated experience.

Who uses HRTs and why?

In general, women use HRTs more often than men, a finding consistent with others which suggest that women tend to use more positive politeness devices than men. In the New Zealand data, using a very stringent definition of what counted as an HRT, and taking account of the relative amount of talk in different interviews, Britain (1992: 90) found that women used 4.4 HRTs per 100 tone groups compared to 3.6 per cent for men. In the Sydney data, though the overall frequency of HRTs was low, women used them about twice as often as men (Horvath 1985).

As well as being more frequent in women's usage, the HRT was more frequent in lower working-class speech and in the speech of younger people in Sydney, suggesting a vernacular change in progress. As mentioned above (in relation to *eh*), there are many examples in social dialect research of vernacular changes being led by women. The reasons for this pattern may be similar to those suggested by Meyerhoff (1992a) for *eh*. A pragmatic feature which facilitates interaction, and emphasises the connection and shared background knowledge of the participants serves women's conversational aims very well. It is perhaps not so surprising, then, that such a feature has been adopted more extensively and more quickly by women.

The New Zealand data is more complicated. The distribution of HRT through all age groups, as well as its higher frequency in the speech of young New Zealanders, suggests that it may have been established longer in Wellington than in Sydney.

Figure 3.4 demonstrates that young people use HRTs more than twice as often as middle-aged people and more than five times as often as older people. And, overall, women use more HRTs than men, as mentioned above. The discrepancy between young Pakeha women (8.2 per cent) and young Pakeha men (2.7 per cent) is particularly marked. But the most interesting feature of the New Zealand HRT data is its parallelism with *eh*, namely, the high frequency with which HRTs occur in the speech of young Maori people.

David Britain's interpretation of this finding is interesting. The HRT could simply be regarded as another ethnic identity marker. But why should this particular feature serve this function? Focusing on its interactive politeness function, Britain notes (1992: 94–5) that there is growing evidence that many non western oral cultures tend to emphasise the creation of involvement in discourse. Oral cultures value shared knowledge

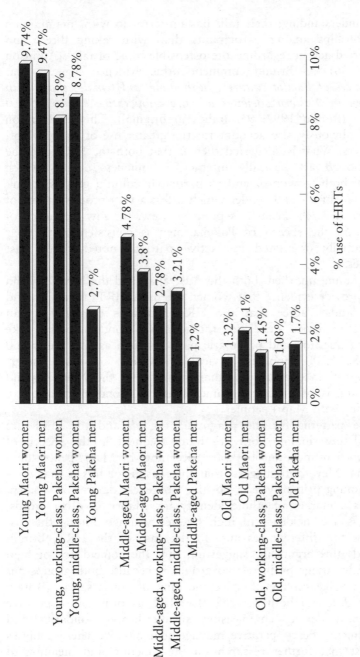

Figure 3.4 HRT use according to ethnicity, age, class and gender
(Source: Britain 1992)

and understanding; their talk has more to do with 'maintaining relationships among participants than with taking direct and concerted action regarding the ostensible topic of talk' (Atkinson 1984: 36). As Britain comments, this evidence suggests that *'members of Pacific cultures, both male and female, share with women in Western societies a more cooperative conversational style'* (Britain 1992: 95. Italics in original). This explanation could obviously also account for the greater use of *eh* by Maori speakers. What is suggested then is that both the HRT and the particle *eh* are basically interactive politeness devices which appeal both to women and to particular cultural groups, a link between culture and gender which offers a very promising line of further research. From this point of view, the low frequency of HRTs in the speech of Pakeha men is consistent with their referentially orientated interactive patterns noted in the last chapter.

Summing up, then, both the Australian and the New Zealand data provide evidence that women use more HRTs than men and both studies agree that the HRT functions primarily as an interactive device – checking the addressee's understanding. Like the tag question and pragmatic particles such as *you know* and *eh*, the HRT supports a view of women as more 'other-orientated' in conversation than men. What the New Zealand data adds is evidence that women share this concern for affective meaning with Maori people.

The patterns for the pragmatic tag *eh* and the HRT are remarkably similar. Both are more frequent in the speech of women than men, and both are used more by Maori people than Pakeha. Meyerhoff suggests that the reason for this is that *eh* is functioning primarily as a positive politeness device for women, but as a marker of ethnic identity for Maori. In other words, there is a coincidence of high frequency usage among the two groups for different reasons. In the case of the HRT, Britain extends this argument, suggesting that the coincidence of high frequency usage by these two groups is because both groups put a high value on the affective meaning of conversation (Britain 1992: 95), and both perceive the HRT as primarily a positive politeness device, emphasising speaker-hearer solidarity and assisting in the cooperative management of talk. These analyses suggest that further research on the function and meaning of pragmatic devices in the speech of different ethnic groups is likely to prove very rewarding.

How typical are these politeness patterns?

How do these conclusions about New Zealand women's and men's use of different linguistic forms compare with the results of research elsewhere?

It is difficult to provide a clear and straightforward answer to this question because of methodological differences between studies. A great deal of earlier research in this area compared the number of forms used by men with the number used by women in the same contexts during a particular period of time (Dubois and Crouch 1975; Crosby and Nyquist 1977; McMillan et al. 1977; Baumann 1979; Hartman 1979; Johnson 1980; Preisler 1986; Cameron et. al 1989; Coates 1989). In providing this information most of these researchers took account of the relative number of female and male contributors to the talk, and some controlled for the role and statuses of participants (e.g. Crosby and Nyquist 1977; Preisler 1986; Cameron et al. 1989; Coates 1989). Information on the total amount of speech contributed by women compared to men in mixed-sex contexts is not always supplied, however, and the number of instances of a particular form produced by women and men was sometimes compared, therefore, without any information on how these figures related to the total amount of speech collected from each group (e.g. Dubois and Crouch 1975; Crosby and Nyquist 1977; McMillan et al. 1977; Baumann 1979; Hartman 1979). Such information is uninterpretable.

One British study which avoids these methodological weaknesses (though it has others, such as the artificiality of the data collection context) is Bent Preisler's (1986) analysis of 'linguistic sex roles in conversation'. Preisler examined linguistic forms used by women and men to express tentativeness in conversation. Using forty-eight randomly selected workers from Lancaster manufacturing firms, he videotaped small groups in a studio discussing controversial topics such as corporal punishment and television violence. The groups were meticulously constructed to contrast on the chosen social variables of age and social status.

Preisler claims to analyse the pragmatic or politeness function of forms in the utterances they occurred in, as well as their epistemic function. He devotes some space to explaining the relationship between linguistic tentativeness and a 'socio-emotional' or interpersonal orientation in interaction. There is a clear implication in this initial theoretical discussion that tentativeness is a positive, facilitative device, especially in the context of the discussion groups he is using as his data base. His pragmatic analysis of the data then demonstrates that the women used more linguistic devices expressing tentativeness than the men. This is consistent, he notes, with the fact that they took a 'socio-emotional' or interpersonal orientation more often than the men.

The final interpretation of his findings, however, is rather different in emphasis. Despite the fact that it is the pragmatic or interpersonal function of tentativeness devices which has been the avowed focus of analysis, one is left with the distinct impression that it is their epistemic function which is the basis for the final interpretive comments. These suggest that women's greater use of tentativeness devices are not so much evidence of their interpersonal skills in discussion, as of their social insecurity. 'The female style of relative tentativeness is more likely to be the institutionalised reflection of the historical social insecurity of (lower middle-class) women' (Preisler 1986: 292). The reader feels the victim of some sleight of hand at this point.

While Preisler's results are therefore consistent with the New Zealand pattern that women tend to use hedges more often than men as politeness devices to facilitate discussion, his final interpretation is a negative one. He interprets this behaviour as evidence of women's social insecurity. Yet teachers and interviewers who use such devices to encourage discussion do not attract such charges.

In other cultures too, it has been found that women tend to use linguistic forms expressing politeness, and especially positive politeness, more often than men (e.g. Brown 1980; Ide 1982; Wetzel 1988). Examining gender differences in spontaneous conversations in Tzeltal, the language of a Mayan Indian community in Mexico, Brown focused explicitly on the function of hedges and boosters as politeness devices (Brown 1980). Taking account of factors such as relative status and social distance, as well as familiarity with the topic, she calculated the number of hedges and boosters in relation to the number of speech acts. Overall, the women used more hedges and more boosters than the men in this Mayan community. Men speaking to men used fewest particles of all. They used a relatively direct and unmodified style compared to the styles used in all other combinations. Both men and women used most hedges when talking to a woman, and most boosters in cross-sex conversations. Accepting Brown's interpretation of the function of these particles as politeness devices, the most obvious influence on the number and type of politeness devices used was the gender of the addressee. Similar results have been reported in other communities such as Japan (Ide et al. 1986) and Holland (Brouwer et al. 1979; Brouwer 1982, 1989) as well as England (Preisler 1986; Cheshire 1989).

Brown interprets her findings as indicating that women are more sensitive to the fact that what they are saying may threaten face, and so they use the extremes of negative politeness in public. In private interactions, they are sensitive to the positive face needs of intimates and friends, and so they use more positive politeness. There are obvious parallels here with the patterns of women's behaviour in public and private contexts described in Chapter 2, as well as with the patterns described in this chapter. Western women also tend to use more positive politeness strategies than men in private, while they avoid causing offence in public. Women are very clearly subordinate to men in the Mayan society, Tzeltal, and have more to lose if they offend. Men, the dominant group, generally talk to each other much more baldly and directly. There are obvious parallels here too with western societies where direct, 'straightforward' and unembellished speech is overtly valued. It would be interesting to know the Mayan community's attitudes to these different types of talk. Brown describes it as 'a society where a premium is placed on inter-actional restraint' (1990: 123), but in most contexts this seems to be more true for women than for men. There appears to be widespread recognition that women value linguistic politeness, since both women and men use more politeness particles to women in everyday public interaction.

Brown's research clearly highlights the importance of attention to context when considering norms of politeness. Women are generally expected to speak more politely than men, but she notes that in the Tzeltal courtroom they are permitted to express themselves impolitely. This is one 'institutionalised context . . . for confrontation: a dramatized outrage played against the backdrop of appropriate norms for female behavior' (1990: 137). Most of the hedges and boosters in the New Zealand data examined in this chapter occurred more frequently in less formal contexts. And this was certainly true when they were expressing positive politeness. When they occurred with other functions, and especially as epistemic devices, it was often ·in more formal contexts such as interviews or formal transactions. *Of course*, for instance, was used as a distancing device in formal interviews, by those with social status. This was also true of *I think* when it was used as a booster rather than a hedge. In more formal contexts, such as TV and radio interviews, women were as likely as men to use these forms. In less formal contexts, where hedges and boosters occurred more often as positive politeness devices, women's usage most obviously contrasted with men's. The formality of the context is clearly a crucial variable in accounting for the patterns of politeness of hedging and boosting devices, just as it was for interactive strategies in Chapter 2.

A related point which is also suggested by Brown's analysis is the relevance of the particular type of discourse to the frequency of occurrence of hedges and boosters. She notes that the particles she examined tend to occur most frequently in speech expressing feelings and attitudes, and that in her data women spent more time talking about feelings and attitudes towards events than men did (1980: 125). It seems possible that the association of particular linguistic devices with women's speech may reflect the fact that they occur more often in discourse types favoured by women. Ide et al. (1986) suggests this may be one explanation for the politeness patterns she describes for Japanese women's speech. A number of the pragmatic devices discussed in this chapter occur more frequently in particular types of discourse. The HRT for instance tends to characterise informal narratives. *You know* seems to occur most often in semi-intimate conversations about personal experiences, while *of course* was more frequent in formal interviews, especially with politicians. It is important to bear this in mind when considering the sources of popular stereotypes of women's speech. The association of hedges and boosters with women's speech may simply reflect the fact that they occur more often in discourse types which are favoured by women (see Coates 1989, for example). Boosters which occur in compliments have a very different effect from those which intensify insults. Women tend to use them more often than men in positively affective rather than negatively affective speech acts as we shall see in Chapters 4 and 5. The analysis in this chapter has suggested that once attention is paid to the functions of these forms, the picture of women's speech is much more positive than that painted by some earlier researchers.

This leads to a consideration of the crucial role of interpretation in the study of women's and men's language. There is no doubt that in a great deal of the research generated by Lakoff's claims, the use of hedging devices is regarded negatively. 'Women's language' was described by Lakoff as a handicap and as less effective than men's language, apparently regardless of context. Others have continued to interpret the use of hedging devices in the same way, as evidence of 'insecurity' (Brouwer et al. 1979: 47; Preisler 1986: 292) and 'powerlessness' (O'Barr and Atkins 1980). It is clear, however, that the interpretation of the function and effect of such devices depends largely on the subjective assessment of the interpreters. One (female) person's hedge may be another (male) person's perspicacious qualification. It is interesting to note, for instance, that the association of linguistic markers of tentativeness and a high incidence of epistemic modal devices with insecurity, lack of confidence, powerlessness, and subordinate status, is to a large extent restricted to studies of 'women's language'.[6] Epistemic devices are not interpreted in this way when used in scientific discourse (which is dominated by men). There they are regarded as evidence of judicious restraint and meticulous accuracy. Similarly, when such features are used more frequently by middle-class than by lower-class subjects, they are perceived very positively. Indeed, in different contexts, such expressions have been interpreted as evidence of higher cognitive functioning (Torrance and Olson 1984), high ability (Rubin and Nelson 1983: 286) and as reflections of cognitive sophistication (Loban 1966; Turner and Pickvance 1972). This suggests that women's subordinate societal status may account not so much for the way women talk, as for the way their talk is perceived and interpreted.

Conclusion

In this chapter I have discussed a range of different linguistic forms which may function as politeness devices in different contexts, and which are used differently by women and men. In order to reach reliable conclusions about the expression of linguistic politeness by New Zealand women and men, it is clear that much more research is necessary. The discussion has raised as many questions as it has answered.

The analysis has demonstrated that simply comparing the number of linguistic forms used by women and men, regardless of their function, will not provide useful information. Nor will simply counting hedges and boosters. Though this distinction takes account of function, it is also necessary to consider the overall effect of these pragmatic devices in different speech acts. There are also very difficult problems of scope. If one is comparing groups for linguistic politeness, then in the final analysis every conceivable linguistic expression of politeness will require thorough analysis. The level of detailed analysis required in order to correctly identify the functions of forms in context has meant that most researchers have focused on only a few of the potentially relevant forms. Preisler's (1986) study is the most ambitious attempt to identify the full range of epistemic devices relevant to a comparison of women's and men's language. But even his very thorough analysis did not consistently separate out the politeness functions from the referential effects.

And how does one weigh up the relative effect of different devices? The degree of linguistic delicacy required for satisfactory linguistic analysis has so far precluded coverage of the range of social contexts and groups that would render such analyses generalisable. Nevertheless, the parameters are now much better defined and it is true to say that some interesting trends have emerged in the many and varied analyses of the contribution of a range of different forms to linguistic politeness.

Every device examined throws interesting additional light on the ways in which hedges and boosters are used by women and men in interaction. The analysis of the tag question, for instance, demonstrated that these forms are not always used as politeness devices. The confrontational tag is anything but polite. Hedges may express a primarily referential or a mainly affective function, as illustrated by the analyses of the pragmatic particles *you know* and *I think*. In all these analyses, consideration of contextual factors was crucial in distinguishing between epistemic meanings and affective functions. The analyses of the tag *eh* and the prosodic HRT pattern demonstrated yet further the complexity of meaning of which hedges and boosters are capable. The same forms appear to be used differently by different ethnic groups. Maori people may use them as ethnic identity signals, expressing solidarity with others of the same ethnic background. It is also possible, however, that members of Maori culture may share with western women a more cooperative interactional style. Hence Maori speakers may use some hedges and boosters as Pakeha women do, that is, as facilitative interactional devices with a positive politeness, addressee-orientated function expressing solidarity.

Overall, in the data examined, New Zealand women tended to use the hedging and boosting devices analysed as politeness strategies more often than men. Where an epistemic function was identified, men tended to use tag questions and particles such as *you know*, *I think*, *sort of*, and *of course* to express epistemic meaning more often than women. It seems possible that the functions of hedges and boosters are perceived differently by women and men. Overall, women's usage tends to emphasise the interpersonal function of interaction, while men's usage tends to focus more often on the referential function. Women tend to use more facilitative devices and expressions of positive politeness. This pattern will be explored further in the next chapter which examines in some detail one particular way in which people may express solidarity with others; we will look at the use of compliments in New Zealand women's and men's speech.

Notes

1. Epistemic forms indicate the extent of the speaker's confidence in the truth of the proposition expressed in the utterance.
2. It is interesting to note that I did not find any examples of what Robin Lakoff described as 'illegitimate' tags which serve as 'an apology for making an assertion at all' (1975: 54). But then interpreting the function of tags is a subjective business and is doubtless as vulnerable to the dangers of stereotyping and pre-conceived perceptions (or in Tannen's words (1986: 146) the

'culturally conditioned epistemological system of the researcher') as other areas of women's behaviour (see Holmes 1984a: 168–71; Cameron 1985: 53–6).

3. Following Holmes (1984b), Cameron et al. (1989) categorise the tags in their data using the terms 'modal' and 'facilitative'. However, they include in their count of facilitative tags, instances which they describe as assertive and challenging in function rather than facilitative and softening. As discussed above, I believe these two functions should be kept distinct. It should also be noted that I have since adopted a suggestion from Jennifer Coates that the label 'epistemic modal' is more informative than simply 'modal'.

4. In my earlier analysis (Holmes 1986a) I suggested that instances of *you know* which signal the linguistic imprecision of what follows serve as negative politeness devices. I now think that since their focus is the validity of (components of) the proposition, categorisation as referentially orientated instances is more accurate.

5. Jennifer Coates (personal communication) notes that in her British data *you know* does not function primarily as a positive politeness device, that it occurs more often in formal contexts and, as one might predict given the different function and context, it is used more often by men than women. This underlines the importance of identifying the function of such chameleon-like forms and examining them in context. She also notes a manipulative use of *you know* (by politicians, for example) attributing shared knowledge to an addressee who might not wish to be identified with the proposition presented. *Of course* was used in a similar manipulative way by some speakers in my corpus (see Holmes 1989a).

6. Coates (1987, 1989) is a notable exception since she explicitly identifies the positive functions of epistemic modal forms in women's talk.

4 What a lovely tie! Compliments and positive politeness strategies

Example 1

Two friends meet at the swimming pool.

Liz: Hi Jill. How's things?

Jill: Hi Liz. Oh not bad. You look as if you had a good holiday!

Liz: Mm did we ever! Lots of sun and sailing – it was great. You're nice and brown too.

Jill: Thanks. We went to Taupo. Those new togs?

Liz: Mm, I needed some – the others had faded.

Jill: They're a great colour. Shows off your tan.

The last chapter illustrated some of the ways in which women more often focus on the social or affective function of talk, while men tend to orientate to its referential function. This was apparent in the different ways women and men use linguistic hedging and boosting devices. In many contexts the same forms appear to serve different functions for women and men. In this chapter we will examine the possibility that this is equally true of speech acts such as compliments.

When we describe someone as polite, or alternatively when we label them rude or impolite, there are many possible aspects of their use of language that we might be referring to. Arriving late without an apology, giving peremptory orders, failing to thank someone for a gift – these are all examples of behaviour which may be considered rude in certain contexts. Polite people tend to apologise for their offences, request assistance in an indirect way, express appreciation for gifts, and pay appropriate compliments.

Expressions of gratitude and sympathy, invitations, jokes, greetings and other phatic or social utterances, as well as the use of friendly address forms, are all ways of expressing positive politeness in appropriate contexts, as example 1 illustrates.

Do women and men differ in the way they use particular speech acts to express politeness? How would one measure any differences? Should the relative frequency with which women and men use compliments, greetings, or expressions of gratitude be considered, for instance? The form of a directive (e.g. *Shut up!* versus *Let's have a bit of hush now*) is very obviously relevant in assessing how polite it is in any particular situation (Leech 1983; Brown and Levinson 1987). What can we deduce about female and male patterns of politeness by examining who uses particular speech acts to whom? In this chapter and the next I will focus on two speech acts – compliments and apologies – to show how analysing particular speech acts can provide interesting suggestions about gender differences in politeness behaviour.

Paying compliments

Example 2
Two colleagues meeting in Pat's office to discuss a report.
Chris: Hi Pat. Sorry I'm late. The boss wanted to set up a time for a meeting just as I was leaving.
Pat: That's OK Chris. You're looking good. Is that a new suit?
Chris: Mm. It's nice isn't it. I got it in Auckland last month. Have you had a break since I last saw you?
Pat: No, work work work I'm afraid. Never mind. Have you got a copy of the report with you?

Positive politeness can be expressed in many ways but paying a compliment is one of the most obvious. A favourable comment on the addressee's appearance, as illustrated in example 2 is a very common way of paying a compliment as we shall see. Compliments are prime examples of speech acts which notice and attend to the hearer's 'interests, wants, needs, goods', the first positive politeness strategy identified and discussed by Brown and Levinson (1987: 102).

What is a compliment?

But what is a compliment? There are a number of positively polite speech acts in the exchange between Pat and Chris – greetings, friendly address terms, expressions of concern and compliments. I would want to count *you're looking good* and *is that a new suit* as examples of compliments. The first is a direct compliment, while the fact that the second counts as a compliment is inferable from the discourse context and the fact that things which are new are generally highly valued in western society (see Manes 1983). When collecting and analysing examples of a particular speech act, it is important to have a clear definition in order to decide what counts and what does not. This is how I have defined a compliment:

> A compliment is a speech act which explicitly or implicitly attributes credit to someone other than the speaker, usually the person addressed, for some 'good' (possession, characteristic, skill, etc.) which is positively valued by the speaker and the hearer.
>
> (Holmes 1986b: 485)

As the utterance *is that a new suit* illustrates, a compliment may be indirect, requiring some inferencing based on a knowledge of the cultural values of the community. There are other ways in which a compliment may be indirect too. Compliments usually focus on something directly attributable to the person addressed (e.g. an article of clothing), but examples 3 and 4 demonstrate that this is not always the case.

Examples 3 and 4
(3) *Rhonda is visiting an old schoolfriend, Carol, and comments on one of Carol's children.*
Rhonda: What a polite child!
Carol: Thank you. We do our best.

(4) *Ray is the conductor of the choir.*
Matt: The choir was wonderful. You must be really pleased.
Ray: Yes, they were good weren't they.

The complimenters' utterances in these examples may look superficially like rather general positive evaluations, but their function as compliments which indirectly attribute credit to the addressee for good parenting in (3), and good conducting in (4), is unambiguous in context.

Why give a compliment?

Compliments are usually intended to make others feel good (see Wierzbicka 1987: 201). The primary function of a compliment is most obviously affective and social, rather than referential or informative. They are generally described as positively affective speech acts serving to increase or consolidate the solidarity between the speaker and addressee (see Wolfson 1981a, 1983; Holmes 1986b; Herbert 1989; Lewandowska-Tomaszczyk 1989). Compliments are social lubricants which 'create or maintain rapport' (Wolfson 1983: 86), as illustrated in all the examples above, as well as in example 5.

Example 5
Two women, good friends, meeting in the lift at their workplace.
Sal: Hi how are you? You're looking just terrific.
Meg: Thanks. I'm pretty good. How are things with you? That's a snazzy scarf you're wearing.

Compliments are clearly positive politeness devices which express goodwill and solidarity between the speaker and the addressee. But they may serve other functions too. Do compliments have any element of referential meaning, for instance? While the primary function of compliments is most obviously affective, they also convey some information in the form of the particular 'good' the speaker selects for comment. They provide a positive critical evaluation of a selected aspect of the addressee's behaviour or appearance, or whatever, which in some contexts may carry some communicative weight. Johnson and Roen (1992), for instance, argue that the compliments they analysed in written peer reviews, simultaneously conveyed both affective (or interpersonal) meaning and referential (or ideational) meaning in that a particular aspect of the review was chosen for positive attention. It is possible that some compliments are intended and perceived as conveying a stronger referential message than others. Very clearly, the relationship between the complimenter and recipient is crucial in accurately interpreting the potential functions of a compliment.

In some contexts, compliments may function as praise and encouragement. In an analysis of over a thousand American compliments, Herbert (1990: 221) suggests some compliments serve as expressions of praise and admiration rather than offers of solidarity. This seems likely to reflect the relationship between the participants. Praise is often directed downwards from superordinate to subordinate. So the teacher's compliment about a student's work in example 6 would generally be regarded as praise.

Example 6
Teacher: This is excellent Jeannie. You've really done a nice job.

Tannen seems to be referring to this function of compliments when she identifies compliments as potentially patronising.

> Giving praise . . . is . . . inherently assymetrical. It . . . frames the speaker as one-up, in a position to judge someone else's performance.
> (Tannen 1990a: 69)

It is possible, then, that in some relationships compliments will be unwelcome because they are experienced as ways in which the speaker is asserting superiority. Compliments directed upwards from subordinate to superordinates, on the other hand, are often labelled 'flattery'. In analysing differences in the way women and men use and interpret compliments, it will clearly be important to consider compliments between status unequals, exploring the possible alternative interpretations which they may be given.

Compliments may have a darker side then. For some recipients, in some contexts, an apparent compliment may be experienced negatively, or as face-threatening. They may be patronising or offensively flattering. They may also, of course, be sarcastic. When the content of a compliment is perceived as too distant from reality, it will be heard as a sarcastic or ironic put-down. I was in no doubt of the sarcastic intent of my brother's comment 'You play so well' as I was plonking away at the piano, hitting far more wrong than right notes. Focusing on a different perspective, Brown and Levinson suggest (1987: 66) that a compliment can be regarded as a face-threatening act to the extent that it implies the complimenter envies the addressee in some way, or would like something belonging to the addressee. This is perhaps clearest in cultures where an expression of admiration for an object imposes an obligation on the addressee to offer it to the complimenter, as in example 7.

Example 7
Pakeha woman to Samoan friend whom she is visiting.
Sue: What an unusual necklace. It's beautiful.
Eti: Please take it.

In this particular instance, Sue was very embarrassed at being offered as a gift the object she had admired. But Eti's response was perfectly predictable by anyone familiar with Samoan cultural norms with respect to complimenting behaviour. In other cultures and social groups too, compliments may be considered somewhat face-threatening in that they imply at least an element of envy and desire to have what the addressee possesses, whether an object or a desirable trait or skill (see Brown and Levinson 1987: 247). And in 'debt-sensitive cultures' (1987: 247), the recipient of a compliment may be regarded as incurring a heavy debt. In such cultures, then, the function of a compliment cannot be regarded as simply and unarguably positively polite.

Even if intended as an expression of solidarity, a compliment might be experienced as face threatening if it is interpreted as assuming unwarranted intimacy. Lewandowska-Tomaszczyk (1989: 75) comments that in her Polish and British compliment data, compliments between people who did not know each other well caused embarrassment. Compliments presuppose a certain familiarity with the addressee, she suggests. This is likely to be true of certain types of compliments in many cultures. Compliments on very personal topics, for instance, are appropriate only from intimates, as in example 8.

Example 8
Young woman to her mother who is in hospital after a bad car accident.
Oh mum you've got your false teeth – they look great

The mother had been waiting for some time to be fitted with false teeth to replace those knocked out or broken in the car accident. There are not many situations in which such a compliment could be paid without causing embarrassment.

At the darkest end of the spectrum are utterances which have been called 'stranger compliments' or 'street remarks' (Kissling and Kramarae 1991, Kissling 1991).

Example 9
Man on building site to young woman passing by.
Wow what legs. What are you doing with them tonight sweetie?

These serve a very different interpersonal function from compliments between friends and acquaintances. Though some women interpret them positively as expressions of appreciation, others regard them as examples of verbal harrassment. It seems likely that both the speaker's intentions and the hearer's interpretations of these speech acts are extremely variable, and require detailed analysis in context. Though I have mentioned them here for completeness, the discussion below is not based on data which included 'stranger compliments'.

Different analysts have thus identified a number of different functions of compliments in different contexts:

1. to express solidarity;
2. to express positive evaluation, admiration, appreciation or praise;
3. to express envy or desire for hearer's possessions;
4. as verbal harrassment.

These functions are not necessarily mutually exclusive, but the relationship between the participants is crucial in interpreting the primary function of a particular compliment: analysis in context is essential. Distributional data can also be suggestive, however, as we shall see in the next section which describes the way compliments are used between New Zealand women and men, and discusses what this suggests about their function as politeness devices.

Who pays most compliments?

Shall I compare thee to a summer's day?

The following analysis of the distribution of compliments between New Zealand women and men is based on a corpus of 484 naturally occurring compliments and compliment responses. The data was collected using an ethnographic approach (Holmes 1986b), a method which derives from anthropology, and which has been advocated by Hymes over many years (1962, 1972, 1974), and very successfully adopted by researchers such as Nessa Wolfson (e.g. 1983, 1988). This approach combines some of the advantages of qualitative research with the generalisability gained from quantitative analysis. Compliments and their responses are noted down, together with relevant features of the participants, their relationship, and the context in which the compliment occurred. Using a number of people as data collectors, it was possible to gather a large number of compliments from a wide variety of contexts. Most, however, were produced by adult Pakeha New Zealanders, and it is therefore the compliment norms of this group which are being described.

The New Zealand compliments collected in this way revealed a very clear pattern. Women gave and received significantly more compliments than men did, as Figure 4.1 illustrates.

Women gave 68 per cent of all the compliments recorded and received 74 per cent of them. By contrast, compliments between males were relatively rare (only 9 per cent), and, even taking account of females' compliments to males, men received overall considerably fewer compliments than women (only 26 per cent). On this evidence, complimenting appears to be a speech behaviour occurring much more frequently in interactions involving women than men.[1]

Other researchers report similar patterns. Compliments are used more frequently by women than by men, and women are complimented more often than men in two different American studies (Wolfson 1983; Herbert 1990), and in research on compliments between Polish speakers (Lewandowska-Tomaszczyk 1989). This same pattern also turned up in a rather different context – that of written peer reviews (Johnson and Roen 1992). In this more information-orientated context which involved

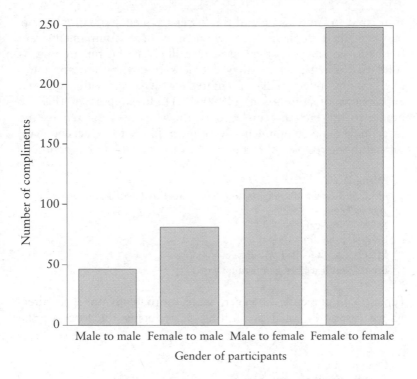

Figure 4.1 Compliments and gender of participants

writing rather than speech, one would not have predicted gender contrasts. But even in writing women tended to use more compliments (or 'positive evaluative terms' to quote Johnson and Roen's precise measure) than men, though the differences were not quite statistically significant (Johnson and Roen 1992: 38).

These differences in the distribution of compliments between women and men have led to the suggestion that women and men may perceive the function of compliments differently. Women may regard compliments as primarily positively affective speech acts, for instance, expressing solidarity and positive politeness, while men may give greater weight to their referential meaning, as evaluative judgements, or to the potentially negative face-threatening features discussed above.

Herbert (1990), for instance, draws a parallel between the lower frequency of compliments given by South Africans compared to Americans, and the lower frequency of compliments between men compared to women. Where compliments are frequent, he suggests, they are more likely to be functioning as solidarity tokens; where they are less frequent they are more likely to be referentially orientated or what he calls 'genuine expressions of admiration' (1990: 221). In support of this, he points to the fact that in his data the responses elicited by the rarer male-male compliments were more likely to be acceptances, reflecting the recipients' recognition of their evaluative function.

Example 10
Mick and Brent are neighbours. They meet at Brent's gate as he arrives home.
Mick: New car?
Brent: Yeah.
Mick: Looks as if it will move.
Brent: Yeah it goes well I must say.

Female compliments, however, were more likely to elicit alternative responses, such as shifting or reducing the force of the compliment.

Example 11
Friends arriving at youth club.
Helen: What a neat outfit!
Gerry: It's actually quite old.

Responses which shift or reduce the compliment's force reflect the function of such compliments as tokens of solidarity, he suggests, since they indicate the recipient's desire to restore the social balance between speakers. There were no such gender differences in compliment responses in the New Zealand corpus, so this explanation cannot account for the less frequent use of compliments by New Zealand men.

It is possible, however, that men may more readily perceive compliments as face-threatening acts than women do. They may feel embarrassed or obligated by these unsolicited tokens of solidarity. The male threshold for what counts as an appropriate relationship to warrant mutual complimenting may differ from the female. Wolfson's 'bulge' theory, which was outlined in Chapter 1, suggested that certain linguistic behaviours, such as compliments, occurred more frequently between friends than between strangers or intimates. The bulge represented the higher frequency of such polite speech acts to friends and acquaintances. But the 'bulge' or the range of relationships within which compliments are acceptable politeness tokens may be much narrower for men than women. Female and male norms may differ. (This point is discussed further in the next chapter.) While one cannot be sure of the reasons for the imbalance in the distribution of compliments in women's and men's speech, it is widely agreed that women appear to use compliments mainly as a means of expressing rapport, while they do not appear to function so unambiguously for men.

This interpretation would be consistent with the research discussed in previous chapters which suggested that women's linguistic behaviour can often be broadly characterised as facilitative, affiliative, and cooperative, rather than competitive or control-orientated. In much of the research comparing patterns of male and female interaction, women's contributions have been described as 'other-orientated'. If women regard compliments as a means of expressing rapport and solidarity, the finding that they give more compliments than men is consistent with this orientation. Conversely, if men regard compliments as face-threatening or controlling devices, at least in some contexts, this could account for the male patterns observed.

In studies of compliments elsewhere, women also received more compliments than men (Wolfson 1984; Holmes 1988b; Herbert 1990; Johnson and Roen 1992). Compliments between women are most frequent in all the studies, but it is noteworthy that men compliment women more often than they compliment other men. One explanation for this might be that women's positive attitude to compliments is recognised by both women and men in these speech communities. Perhaps people pay more compliments to women because they know women value them.

Alternatively, one might focus on why people do not compliment men as often as they do women. It appears to be much more acceptable and socially appropriate to compliment a woman than a man. One possible explanation based on an analysis of the power relations in society points to women's subordinate social position. Because compliments express social approval one might expect more of them to be addressed 'downwards' as socialising devices, or directed to the socially insecure to build their confidence. Nessa Wolfson (1984: 243) takes this view:

> women because of their role in the social order, are seen as appropriate recipients of all manner of social judgements in the form of compliments . . . the way a woman is spoken to is, no matter what her status, a subtle and powerful way of perpetuating her subordinate role in society.

In other words, she suggests, compliments addressed to women have the same function as praise given to children, that is they serve as encouragement to continue with the approved behaviour. They could be regarded as patronising, socialisation devices. Interestingly, even in classrooms it seems that females receive more praise or positive evaluations than males (e.g. de Bie 1987). It is possible that one of the reasons people do not compliment males so often as females is an awareness of men's ambivalence about compliments and of the possibility that men may regard some compliments as face-threatening acts, as embarrassing and discomfiting, or experience them as patronising strategies which put the speaker 'one-up'. If this is the case, then it is not surprising that the fewest compliments occur between men.

The way compliments are distributed suggests then, that women and men may use and interpret them differently. While women appear to use them as positive politeness devices, and generally perceive them as ways of establishing and maintaining relationships, men may view them much more ambiguously as potentially face-threatening acts, or as having a more referential evaluative message which can serve a socialising function. In the next section an examination of the syntactic patterns of compliments will throw a little further light on these speculations.

How do women and men pay compliments?

Examples 12–16
(12) You're looking nice today.

(13) What great kids!

(14) That's a beautiful skirt.

(15) I really love those curtains.

(16) Good goal.

Compliments are remarkably formulaic speech acts. Most draw on a very small number of lexical items and a very narrow range of syntactic patterns. Five or six adjectives, such as *good, nice, great, beautiful,* and *pretty* occurred in about two-thirds of the New Zealand compliments analysed. Wolfson noted the same pattern in her American corpus of nearly 700 compliments (1984: 236). And syntactic patterns prove similarly unoriginal. One of just four different syntactic patterns occurred in 78 per cent of all the compliments in the New Zealand corpus (Holmes 1986b). Similarly, three alternative syntactic patterns accounted for 85 per cent of the compliments in the American corpus (Manes and Wolfson, 1981). Compliments may be polite but they are rarely creative speech acts.

Nor are there many gender differences in this aspect of politeness behaviour. Most of the syntactic patterns and lexical items occurring in compliments seem to be fairly equally used by women and men, as Table 4.1 demonstrates. There are, however, two patterns which differ between women and men in an interesting way in the New Zealand corpus. Women used the rhetorical pattern *What (a) (ADJ) NP!* (e.g. *What lovely children!*) significantly more often than men. Men, by contrast, used the minimal pattern *(INT) ADJ (NP)* (e.g. *Great shoes*) significantly more often than women. The former is a syntactically marked formula, involving exclamatory word order and intonation; the latter, by contrast, reduces the syntactic pattern to its minimum elements. In other words, a rhetorical pattern such as *What a splendid hat!* can be regarded as emphatic and as increasing the force of the speech act. (D'Amico-Reisner (1983: 111–12) makes the same point about rhetorical questions as expressions of disapproval.) Using a rhetorical pattern for a compliment stresses its addressee- or interaction-orientated characteristics.

But the minimal pattern represented by *nice bike*, which was used more by men, tends to reduce the force of the compliment; it could be regarded as attenuating or hedging the compliment's impact. Interestingly, too, there were no examples of the more rhetorical pattern (*what lovely children!*) in the male-male interactions observed. So there seems good reason to associate this pattern with female complimenting behaviour.

Table 4.1 Syntactic patterns of compliments and speaker gender

Syntactic formula*	Female %	Male %
1. NP BE (LOOKING) (INT) ADJ	42.1	40.0
e.g. *That coat is really great*		
2. I (INT) LIKE NP	17.8	13.1
e.g. I *simply love that skirt*		
3. PRO BE (a) (INT) ADJ NP	11.4	15.6
e.g. *That's a very nice coat*		
4. What (a) (ADJ) NP!	7.8	1.3
e.g. *What lovely children!*		
5. (INT)ADJ (NP	5.1	11.8
e.g. *Really cool ear-rings*		
6. Isnt NP ADJ!	1.5	0.6
e.g. *Isn't this food wonderful!*		
Subtotals	85.7	82.4
7. All other syntactic formulae	14.3	17.6
Totals	100.0	100.0

Notes: *Following Manes and Wolfson (1981) copula BE represents any copula verb; LIKE represents any verb of liking: e.g. *love, enjoy, admire*; ADJ represents any semantically positive adjective; and INT represents any boosting intensifier: e.g. *really, very.*

Examples 17–19

(17) I love those socks. Where did you get them?

(18) I like those glasses.

(19) *Referring to a paper written by the addressee.*
    I really liked the ending. It was very convincing.

Studies of compliments by other researchers provide support for this suggestion that women's compliments tend to be expressed with linguistically stronger forms than men's. Having analysed over one thousand American compliments, Herbert (1990: 206) reported that only women used the stronger form *I love X* (compared to *I like X*), and they used it most often to other women. In written peer reviews, Johnson and Roen (1992) noted that women used significantly more intensifiers (such as *really, very, particularly*) than men did, and, as in Herbert's data, they intensified their compliments most when writing to other women.

These observations provide further support for the point that was discussed in Chapter 3, that it is important in analysing hedging and boosting behaviour to examine the particular types of speech acts which are being boosted, and, in particular, to note whether the speech act is intended and perceived as affectively positive or negative. It is possible to strengthen or alternatively to reduce the force of a positively affective speech act such as a compliment in a variety of ways. By their selections among a narrow range of syntactic formulas and lexical items, men more often choose to attenuate the force of their compliments, while women tend to increase their compliments' force. This supports the suggestion that women expect addressees to interpret compliments as expressions of solidarity rather than as face-threatening speech acts. By contrast, men's tendency to attenuate compliments supports the proposal that men perhaps perceive compliments as less unambiguously positive in effect. In other words, the differences which have been noted in the distribution of syntactic and lexical patterns between women and men is consistent with the view that women tend to regard compliments as primarily positively affective acts while men may feel more ambivalent about using them.

Examples 20 and 21
(20) You're looking stunning.

(21) I especially liked the way you used lots of examples.

In general, it is also true that women use more personalised compliment forms than men, while men prefer impersonal forms. There is some evidence for this in the New Zealand data, as Table 4.1 illustrates, but it is even more apparent in Herbert's (1990) American corpus, and Johnson and Roen's (1992) written peer reviews. Well over half (60 per cent) of the compliments offered by men in Herbert's corpus were impersonal forms, for example, compared to only a fifth of those used by women. By contrast women used many more forms with a personal focus (Herbert includes both *you* and *I* as personalised forms). Almost 83 per cent of female-female interactions used personalised forms compared to only 32 per cent of male-male compliments (Herbert 1990: 205). The peer reviews analysed by Johnson and Roen revealed a similar pattern. The women used more personal involvement strategies, especially to other women (1992: 44).

This evidence echoes the patterns noted in Chapter 2, and more generally in research on verbal interaction, which suggested that women tend to prefer personalised and expressive forms as opposed to impersonalised forms (see Kalcik 1975; Swacker 1979; Aries 1982), and supports a view of women's style as more interpersonal, affective and interaction-orientated compared to the impersonal, instrumental and content-orientated style more typical of male interaction (e.g. Piliavin and Martin 1978; Baird and Bradley 1979; Preisler 1986; Aries 1976, 1987; Schick Case 1988; Tannen 1990a). So, where the linguistic features of women's compliments differ from men's, the differences tend to support the proposition that women regard compliments as other-orientated positive politeness strategies which they assume will be welcome to addressees, whereas for men, and especially between men, their function may not be so clear-cut.

What do women and men compliment each other about?

Examples 22–25
(22) *Appearance compliment.*
I like your outfit Beth. I think I could wear that.

(23) *Ability/performance compliment.*
Wow you played well today Davy.

(24) *Possessions compliment.*
Is that your flash red sports car?

(25) *Personality/friendliness.*
I'm very lucky to have such a good friend.

Women and men tend to give compliments about different things. To be heard as a compliment an utterance must refer to something which is positively valued by the participants and attributed to the addressee. This would seem to permit an infinite range of possible topics for compliments, but in fact the vast majority of compliments refer to just a few broad topics: appearance, ability or performance, possessions, and some aspect of personality or friendliness (Manes 1983; Holmes 1986b). In fact, compliments on some aspect of the addressee's appearance or ability accounted for 81 per cent of the New Zealand data.

Within these general patterns, there is a clearly observable tendency for women to be complimented on their appearance more often than men. Over half (57 per cent) of all the compliments women received in the New Zealand data related to aspects of their appearance. And women give compliments on appearance more than men do, so that 61 per cent of all the compliments between women related to appearance compared to only 36 per cent of the compliments between males, as Figure 4.2 demonstrates. Men, by contrast, appear to prefer to compliment other men, but not women, on possessions.

Provided it is not sarcastic, a compliment on someone's appearance such as *you're looking wonderful* is difficult to interpret as anything other than a positively polite utterance. An appearance compliment is clearly an expression of solidarity, a positively affective speech act. The predominance of this type of compliment in women's interactions is consistent with the view that women use compliments primarily for their positively polite function. Compliments on possessions, on the other hand, are much more vulnerable to interpretation as face-threatening acts since, as illustrated in example 7 above, there is the possibility that the complimenter will be heard as expressing desire for or envy of the object referred to. To this extent, men's greater use of these compliments reinforces the suggestion that they are more likely to perceive and experience compliments as potential FTAs. In other words, if possession-orientated compliments are experienced as more face-threatening than others – which seems feasible since they focus on things which are in theory transferable from complimenter to recipient – then men certainly use more potentially face-threatening compliments than women.

Compliments on appearance seem to cause some men embarrassment.

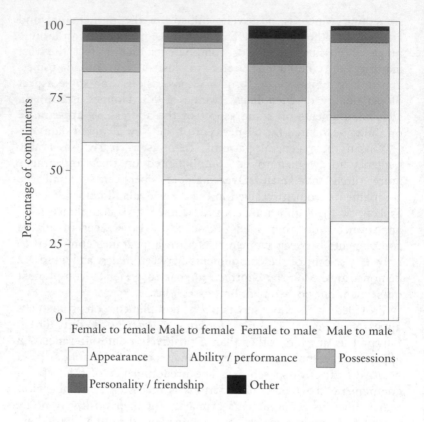

Figure 4.2 Compliment topic and gender of participants

Example 26
Middle-aged male to elderly male at a concert.
Male 1: I haven't seen you since the Festival.
Male 2: We haven't been here much since the Festival.
Male 1: You've got a new tie in the meantime.
Male 2: It's a very old one actually.
Male 1: It's quite splendid anyway.
Male 2: (*Looks extremely embarrassed.*) No no. What have you been up to anyway?

The recipient's response to the first somewhat indirect compliment is a disclaimer, while his response to the second overt compliment is acute embarrassment followed by a rejection.

Wolfson comments (1983: 93) that appearance compliments are remarkably rare between American males. It seems that in America compliments on appearance may be experienced by males as very big face-threatening acts. And while New Zealand men do give and receive compliments on their appearance, there are a number of examples where compliments on their appearance clearly caused surprise.

Example 27
Two colleagues meet at coffee machine at work.
Bill: You're looking very smart today.
Tom: (*Looking very embarrassed.*) I'm meeting Mary and her mother for lunch.

Appearance compliments are clearly not the common currency of politeness between men that they are between women.

A number of men have commented that at least one of the reasons for the scarcity of appearance compliments between men is fear of the possible imputation of homosexuality.

To compliment another man on his hair, his clothes, or his body is an *extremely* face threatening thing to do, both for speaker and hearer. It has to be very carefully done in order not to send the wrong signals.

(Britain, personal communication)

In support of this David Britain provided the following example.

Example 28
Male flatmate, Alex, to Dave, referring to the latter's new haircut.
Jesus Christ tell me who did that and I'll go and beat him up for you!
Laughter. Then
No it's OK.
Finally, a week later.
That's a good haircut.

In this case, it took a week for Alex to get round to saying he liked Dave's haircut, that is to pay a clearly identifiable compliment on his appearance to another male.

Figure 4.2 also shows that nearly half (44 per cent of all) the compliments given by males to females were compliments on abilities, skills or performance. Women do not compliment men or other women so often on this topic. This raises the question of whether a compliment can act as a power play. As mentioned above, praise is often directed downwards. A compliment could be experienced as patronising if the recipient felt it was given as encouragement rather than as a token of solidarity. Compliments on skills and abilities are particularly vulnerable to being interpreted in this way.

Example 29
Husband to wife about her painting of a wall.
You've made a pretty good job of that.

One has the feeling that the husband is a little surprised his wife has done so well and is patting her on the head approvingly. The tendency for men to compliment women on their skills and abilities may reflect women's subordinate social status in the society as a whole, as well as, perhaps, a male tendency to perceive compliments as means of conveying referential or evaluative, as well as affective, messages. The next section will illustrate that the way compliments are used to those of different status provides further support for such an interpretation.

Can a compliment be a power play?

People pay most compliments to their equals. As Wolfson puts it, 'the overwhelming majority of all compliments are given to people of the same age and status as the speaker' (1983: 91). New Zealanders' compliments followed this pattern (see also Knapp et al. 1984, Herbert 1990). Almost 80 per cent of the corpus consisted of compliments between status equals. Compliments typically occur in informal interactions between friends.

The distribution of the small proportion of compliments that occurred between people of different status is interesting, however, because it throws further light on the question of the functions of compliments for women and men.

If it is true, as Wolfson suggests, that the fact that women receive more compliments than men reflects their subordinate status in the society as a whole, then one would also expect more compliments to subordinates than to superiors, regardless of gender. Wolfson's American data evidently confirmed this expectation. She comments that 'the great majority of compliments which occur in interaction between status unequals are given by the person in the higher position' (1983: 91).

Example 30
Manager to her secretary.
You are such a treasure Carol. What would I do without you!

Another American study which was based on self-report data rather than observation, reports the same pattern (Knapp et al. 1984). Most compliments occurred between status equals, but when there was a status imbalance, higher status participants complimented more often than lower status ones. In other words, people seem generally less willing to compliment someone of higher rather than lower status. Neither of these studies examined the interaction of gender and status, however.

In the New Zealand data, as mentioned, the great majority of compliments occurred between status equals. There were no significant differences in the numbers addressed to those of higher rather than lower status. But, interestingly, it was found that higher status females were twice as likely to receive compliments as higher status men.

Example 31
Secretary to boss.
That's a lovely dress.

If high status generally reduces the likelihood that one will receive compliments, then this data indicates it reduces it less with women than with men. This is true whether the complimenter is male or female, as can be seen in Figure 4.3. In fact, despite the general pattern that women pay more compliments than men, males are even more likely to compliment women of higher status than women are.

Example 32
Male caretaker to woman executive as she leaves work.
You're a hard working woman Mrs Thomas. I hope they pay you well.

This is further support for the view that it is more acceptable to compliment high status women than high status men.

Perhaps higher status women are perceived as more receptive to compliments (especially from men) than their male counterparts, because in the society as a whole women are generally regarded as socially subordinate, and less powerful and influential than men. This may legitimate behaviour that might otherwise be considered presumptuous. Tannen's (1990a: 69) suggestion that giving praise 'frames the speaker as one-up' is again relevant here. Higher status males may be perceived as high risk addressees by both genders. But female gender apparently overrides high status in determining how risky a compliment is perceived as being. Alternatively, perhaps women are seen as more approachable because they value solidarity more highly than status, and tend to reduce rather than emphasise status differences (Troemel-Ploetz 1992).

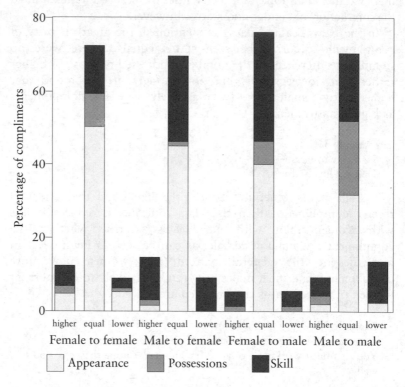

Figure 4.3 Compliments by relative status and gender of participants and topic

This interpretation of the patterns is consistent with the suggestion that men are more likely to experience a compliment as a face-threatening act whereas women are more likely to perceive compliments as positively affective speech acts, regardless of relative status. If true, this would be likely to encourage complimenters to address compliments upwards to women, and discourage compliments to higher status men where the risk of offence would be too great. Note the male's discouraging reaction in the following example.

Example 33
Young woman to Minister's personal secretary at a reception.
Woman: What an interesting job you have. You must be very
    bright.
Man: I just do my job.

The young woman was lively and friendly. The tone of the man's reply made it clear he thought her presumptuous. Complimenting a higher status male is obviously a risky business. There is further support for this interpretation when we look at differences in the way women and men use compliments on appearance, in particular. As Figures 4.2 and 4.3 illustrate, appearance was the most common topic of compliments in this corpus, as in others. Figure 4.3 shows that appearance was also by far the most frequent topic of compliments between equals (30–50 per cent of all compliments). But status differences reduced the likelihood of appearance compliments quite dramatically, especially in cross-sex relationships. Fewer than 2 per cent of the compliments analysed were appearance compliments between cross-sex pairs of different status – a clear indication of the link between appearance compliments and solidarity-based relationships.

On the other hand, appearance compliments are the most obvious examples of compliments which are likely to be interpreted or experienced differently by women and men, as discussed above, and illustrated in the following example.

Example 34
Office receptionist to high status male whom she knew only slightly.
Receptionist: That's a nice suit.
Male: Mr Avery's expecting me I think.

The man ignores the compliment completely. The receptionist was almost certainly being positively polite and intended her compliment as a solidarity signal. But an appearance compliment is vulnerable to being interpreted as presumptuous when addressed by a subordinate to a superior of either gender. If men also tend to regard compliments as potential face-threatening acts and find compliments on their appearance particularly discomfiting, the negative effect will be even greater.

The patterns revealed by the distribution of compliments in this corpus suggest, then, that women and men may use and interpret compliments differently. While women seem to use compliments to establish, maintain and strengthen relationships, they are much less clearly positive politeness devices for men, where they need to be used with care – especially to other men – since they can be face-threatening. The fact that men pay more compliments to women than they do to men may indicate that men are aware of the value of compliments in women's eyes – a solidarity-based explanation. Alternatively, this pattern may reflect the fact that men perceive compliments as appropriate encouragement or evaluative feedback to subordinates. In other words, male compliments to women may reflect the different social power positions of women and men.

Compliment responses

The way people respond to compliments is another aspect of linguistic politeness. In general, and especially in social exchanges, there is a preference for agreement in interaction (Leech 1983: 138). So the recipient of a compliment is under some pressure to agree with the complimenter and accept the compliment, as in the following example.

> **Example 35**
> *At a party. Joan has had her hair cut very short.*
> Margie:Your hair looks so nice.
> Joan: Thanks. It feels really good like this.

Indeed, Herbert (1990: 207) says, 'There is virtual unanimity among speakers of English that the prescriptively "correct" response to a compliment is *thank you*'.

Pomerantz (1978: 80), too, points out that the professed ideal in American culture is to accept a compliment graciously, but she notes that there is also strong pressure on speakers to avoid or minimise self-praise, a pressure towards being modest (Leech 1983: 136). These opposing pressures present an interactional dilemma when a person is paid a compliment. Consequently people will sometimes deflect a compliment with a response like the following.

Example 36
Harry is admiring Ken's new mountain bike wheels.
Harry: Neat set of wheels.
Ken: I got them at *Sam's*. They weren't expensive.

Social pressure to act modestly or minimise self-praise may even lead people to reject compliments, and disagree with the complimenter, though this is not common in the New Zealand data.

Example 37
After a meal at Fiona's flat.
Alice: You're such a good cook.
Fiona: No no not at all. Just ordinary, nothing special.

Compliment responses can usefully be divided into three broad categories, then: *accept, reject/deflect,* and *evade.* (See Holmes 1986b for a more detailed discussion, and compare also Pomerantz 1978; Herbert 1989.) Do women respond to compliments differently from men?

Figure 4.4 and Table 4.2 show that the women and men in the New Zealand corpus responded to compliments in very similar ways. It is clear that the most common response to a compliment by both women and men is to accept it, albeit with qualification in some cases. It was relatively rare for a person to overtly reject a compliment: less than 5 per cent of responses consisted of direct disagreements. Disagreeing responses were also relatively uncommon in Herbert's American data (10 per cent), while there were none in his South African corpus where acceptance was decidedly the preferred response (Herbert 1989).

Table 4.2 also shows that both genders were most likely to accept with an agreeing comment as in example 35, and least

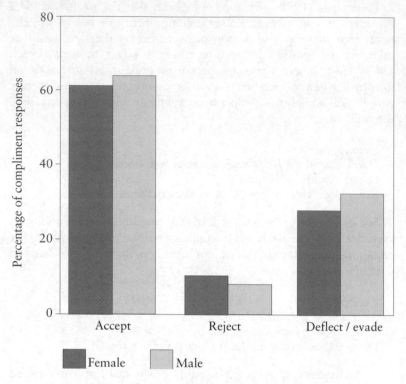

Figure 4.4 Compliment responses amd responder's gender

likely to reject a compliment by challenging the complimenter's sincerity, as in example 38.

> **Example 38**
> *Tom and Linda are colleagues who have met by chance at the swimming pool.*
> Tom: You swim like a professional.
> Linda: You don't really mean that. You're just being nice.

Nor were there any differences in the likelihood that male compliments or female compliments would be accepted in the New Zealand data. In Herbert's American data, by contrast, women were more likely than men to agree with the semantic content of a compliment (1990: 214), and male compliments

Table 4.2 Compliment responses and speaker gender

Response type	Female No.	%	Male No.	%
A. ACCEPT				
1. Appreciation/agreement token e.g. *thanks, yes*	52	15.8	18	15.8
2. Agreeing utterance e.g. *I think it's lovely too*	110	33	40	35
3. Downgrading utterance e.g. *it's not too bad is it*	29	8.8	11	9.6
4. Return compliment e.g. *you're looking good too*	14	4.2	4	3.5
Subtotal	205	62	73	64
B. REJECT				
1. Disagreeing utterance e.g. *I'm afraid I don't like it much*	23	7	5	4.4
2. Question accuracy e.g. *is beautiful the right word?*	7	2.1	3	2.6
3. Challenge sincerity e.g. *you don't really mean that*	3	0.9	1	0.9
Subtotal	33	10	9	7.9
C. DEFLECT/EVADE				
1. Shift credit e.g. *my mother knitted it*	5	1.5	–	–
2. Informative comment e.g. *I bought it at that Vibrant Knits place*	33	10	9	7.9
3. Ignore e.g. *it's time we were leaving isn't it?*	8	2.4	6	5.3
4. Legitimate evasion Context needed to illustrate	29	8.8	16	14
5. Request reassurance e.g. *do you really think so?*	17	5.2	5	4.4
Subtotal	92	27.8	36	31.6
TOTAL*	330	100	114	100

Note: *There were forty compliments followed immediately by a second compliment (e.g. *What a lovely jacket. It really suits you.*). While formally these can be analysed as two syntactically different compliment patterns, they generally elicited just one response. Hence the total number of responses (444) is smaller than the total number of compliments analysed (484).

were much more likely to be accepted, especially by women (1990: 212). This suggests the possibility of interesting cross-cultural differences which may reflect differences in the relative status of women in different communities.

Overall, gender differences in the New Zealand compliment responses were relatively minor, and involved only small numbers of exchanges (see Holmes 1988b). Women tended to disagree with a compliment more often than men (a pattern also noted in the American data (Herbert 1990: 213)). This may well reflect the influence of the social pressure to be modest, which, as noted above, permits disagreement to be regarded as a polite response to a compliment.

Example 39
Helen: You've made a lovely job of the garden.
Mary: Oh no it's a mess really.

Perhaps women feel more pressure to acknowledge a compliment, even if they cannot accept it, as in example 39. Men, on the other hand, tended to prefer different strategies for resolving the interactional conflict presented by a compliment: they were more likely to ignore the compliment or evade it than to disagree with it. They changed the topic, for instance or responded to some other aspect of the previous speaker's utterance than the positive evaluation, as in example 36. In Herbert's (1990) data, too, males were most likely to ignore or question compliments, especially from other males.

Example 40
After a soccer match.
Liam: You played well today Davy.
Davy: You must be joking. I missed a couple of sitters.

These avoidance responses are consistent with a perception of compliments as embarrassing, or patronising, and provide support for the suggestion that compliments are more often experienced as face-threatening acts by men than by women.

In the New Zealand data there were no differences in types of compliment response according to the gender of the complimenter. Americans, however, were more likely to reject or disagree with a compliment from a woman, than with one from a man, supporting Wolfson's argument that compliment patterns reflect and reinforce women's subordinate status. People tend to avoid disagreeing with a superior; they are generally much more willing to disagree with an equal and an intimate. Compliments may be more frequently perceived as potential socialising devices in the American community sampled by Herbert. These contrasts in the New Zealand and American patterns once again suggest the possibility of cross-cultural differences.

This is certainly an area where cultural differences exist (Wolfson 1981a; Ngan-Woo 1985). In Malaysian society, compliments are more often rejected than accepted, especially by women (Azman 1986). The pressure to be modest and avoid self-praise prevails over the preference for agreement. In Mexican society, which is relatively highly stratified, only intimates rejected a compliment with a disagreeing response (Valdés and Pino 1981: 59). The norms for different social and cultural groups clearly differ, and interpretation of gender differences in different speech communities thus requires some care.

This analysis of a corpus of New Zealand compliments and compliment responses suggests that women and men may operate with different socio-pragmatic rules. It seems possible that women use and perceive compliments more often as solidarity signals, while men may more often experience them as patronising or embarrassing face-threatening speech acts, or in some contexts as more referentially orientated evaluative utterances. Women use compliments to each other much more often than they do to men or than men do to each other. Women use linguistic forms which strengthen the positive force of the compliment more often than men do, while men more often than women use a form which attenuates or hedges on the compliment's strength. Women compliment each other on appearance more often than on any other topic, and this is a topic which is generally regarded as most appropriate between equals, friends and intimates, least threatening, and most other-orientated. Compliments on possessions, on the other hand, which are perhaps most obviously perceived as face-threatening acts are used significantly more often between males. Women of higher status are more likely to receive compliments than higher status men, suggesting that complimenters may be more sensitive to the risk of discomfiting higher status men with a face-threatening act. Finally, men's evasive compliment responses more often take the form of a marked avoidance strategy than women's do, suggesting they are more anxious to avoid recognising and responding to a compliment than women. The cumulative effect of these patterns supports the notion that women and men may have very different rules for using and interpreting compliments.

More detailed analyses of gender differences in compliment exchanges are now needed to provide further clues concerning the ways women and men use amd interpret compliments. In what kinds of situations do women and men reject or respond evasively to compliments, for instance? Are some types of compliment accepted more readily than others from particular complimenters? Is there support for the suggestion that some compliments are perceived more readily as solidarity tokens, while others are regarded as potential face-threatening acts? There is obviously considerable scope for more detailed analysis of the content of specific compliments and compliment responses in context in order to explore these issues more thoroughly.

What about other speech acts?

The compliment is generally regarded as the paradigm of a positive politeness strategy, but there are many other speech acts which may express positive politeness. At present, however, we have little information about the ways they are used by women and men. Greetings, invitations, expressions of gratitude or appreciation, commiserations, friendly address forms, and leave-takings are obvious examples of positively polite speech acts. Given the patterns of gender differentiation in compliment use described in this chapter, one would expect them to be used more frequently by women than by men. What little evidence there is, supports this prediction. One study (Greif and Gleason 1980) found that mothers expressed gratitude more often than fathers, for instance. In an analysis of peer reviews, Johnson and Roen (1992: 48) found that 62 per cent of women used a positive evaluation as a closing remark, especially to other women, while only 28 per cent of men did so. The research available on address forms, however, is more complex and deserves fuller comment.

What shall I call you? Forms of address

Example 41
Male police officer at enquiry desk finishes what he is doing
before paying attention to the woman who is standing waiting.
Male: Mornin' love.
Woman: Good morning officer. And it's not 'love' it's 'sergeant'.

While research on compliments has tended to focus on their positive politeness function, and has paid little attention to the possibility that compliments might be used patronisingly to emphasise status differences, just the opposite is true of research on address terms. Comparisons of the address terms used to women and men have consistently noted the asymmetrical nature of the English address system, reflecting the power differences between women and men (Kramer 1975; Wolfson and Manes 1980; Poynton 1985, 1989; Braun 1988). The use of address terms as positive politeness devices has received far less attention (but see Troemel-Ploetz 1992).

Analysing Australian data, Cate Poynton (1985: 80–4) argues that the address system is fundamentally skewed or asymmetrical, especially in relation to gender. The address terms used to females and males are by no means parallel. So, as illustrated in example 42, a male boss may address junior staff or his female secretary by first name (regardless of her age), while she will often be expected to reciprocate with Mr X (regardless of his age).

Example 42
Male boss: I need this for 10 o'clock, Sharon.
Female secretary: OK Mr Freed. No problem.

Alternatively, where she uses his first name, he may use an endearment (Poynton, 1985: 80).

Example 43
Female secretary: There's a message on your desk about that policy
                     meeting Tom.
Male boss: Thanks love.

Poynton (1985) also notes the practice of men (often complete strangers) addressing women in public by a variety of endearments, approbatory or derogatory terms. (The parallels with 'stranger compliments' or street harassment are clear.) The reverse is much less common – at least in Australia and New Zealand. Endearments such as *dear, love*, and *sweetheart* express intimacy when used reciprocally between equals, but used non-reciprocally they suggest one is talking to an inferior or subordinate. Example 41 illustrates this, as well as the woman's effective challenge based on her superior occupational status which the police officer was unaware of. Non-reciprocal usage is generally a clear indication of a power or status differential. Teachers use first names to pupils, for example, but generally receive a respect term, such as *sir*, or title and last name. Parents, older relatives, neighbours and even shopkeepers, address children with terms such as *sweetie, darling, lovie, sugarplum*, and so on. But they would be shocked if the child were to reply in kind.

In the United States, Cheris Kramer (1975) noted that, in public, women receive more endearment terms, and a much wider range of them, from people such as salespersons than men do. In her study, women were addressed by terms such as *dear, little lady, sweetie, lovey* and *baby*. Men, however, were generally called *sir*, though young men might receive *dear* from an older saleswoman. In another analysis of over 600 service encounters in American shops and garages, Wolfson and Manes (1980) also found extensive evidence of a non-reciprocal pattern reflecting women's subordinate power position in society. When addressing women, they found that people tended to use either *ma'am*, or an endearment term, such as *dear, honey*, or *sweetheart*, treating these rather different forms as if they were equivalent choices. The same is true in New Zealand where terms such as *dear* are commonly used to women in shops.

Example 44
Butcher's shop in New Zealand.
Butcher: What can I do for you today dear?
Customer: Half a kilo of mince please.
Butcher: There you are dear. That'll be $2.50. Can I get you
           anything else dear?
Customer: No thank you. That's fine.

This pattern of address usage is clearly non-reciprocal. In the north east of the United States, such endearment terms were used in 75 per cent of service encounters, while *ma'am* was used in only 25 per cent of the interactions observed. *Ma'am* indicates respect for a customer, but the use of non-reciprocal endearments is certainly not respectful. Using endearment terms to women in service encounters is generally interpreted by these analysts as patronising; they reflect society's perception of women as subordinate and dependent.

Cheris Kramer (1975) also found that men used a wider variety of address forms for women and men than women did. Poynton (1985) makes the same point about the options for Australian women and men. In particular, she suggests there are fewer positive, solidarity terms available to women, as well as fewer derogatory terms. There is no female equivalent, for instance, for the widespread term *mate*, or the (very Australian) male address form *sport*.

Forms of address clearly reflect social relationships. In all the communities studied, it seems that strangers or salespeople address women with terms which are appropriate for children, subordinates or close friends, while women appear to be much more restricted in the choice of address forms they can use, at least in public contexts. Studies of gender differences in this area of usage have focused to date on the use of address forms to express status and power difference, that is on the use of address forms to women which function as patronising and possibly face-threatening strategies.

But what of the use of such terms as positive politeness devices between friends and equals? One might expect very different patterns. Reciprocity is generally identified as one feature of interactions between friends and status equals. If the pattern identified for compliments is typical, we would expect women to use more address terms which express positive politeness than men. This is an area where social and cultural norms are likely to differ, so that women's and men's usages in different English-speaking communities may be very different. It is one obvious and fascinating area for further research.

What's the significance of a genuine invitation?

Another positively polite speech act which seems likely to be particularly interesting in terms of gender differences is the invitation. Wolfson (1981b) points out that invitations can be broadly divided into two types – ambiguous and unambiguous. Invitations tend to be unambiguous and specific between those who know each other well, and also between those who differ in status. Examples 45 and 46 are specific invitations between good friends.

Examples 45 and 46
(45)   *Friend knocks on office door at noon.*
       Lunch?

(46)   *Close friends on the phone.*
A: I'm having the most awful day.
B: Poor you. Have you got time for a drink after work?
A: That would be great.
B: OK. Let's meet at the wine bar at six. You can tell me all
    about it then.

Inequality of status also favours unambiguous invitations (Wolfson 1981b: 17). People are specific when issuing invitations to superiors or subordinates, as in example 47.

Example 47
Boss to employee.
Boss: We're having some people round on Saturday for
            drinks before the match. Would you and Carol like to
            join us?
Employee: That would be great.
Boss: About two o'clock then.

As this example illustrates, specific invitations generally specify time, date, place and so on. With non-intimate equals, on the other hand, invitations often remain ambiguous and non-specific, as illustrated in the following examples.

Examples 48 and 49
(48) *Friends on the telephone.*
A: We haven't been in touch for ages.
B: Mm true. We're both so busy.

A: Well let's have lunch together some time soon?
B: Yes that's a great idea. I'd love to. Give me a ring next week.

(49) *Example from Wolfson (1981b: 14)*
A: OK, good talking to you. Let's get together some time.
B: I'd love to.
A: Good, I'll call you soon and we'll have lunch together.
B: Great.

Wolfson suggests that the reason for this ambiguity is the desire to avoid the possibility of refusal. The invitation is deliberately left vague so that the person invited is not put in the position of refusing outright. It is also clear that a non-specific invitation allows a general indication of good will without any great social commitment. In other cases, the invitation may end up being specific, but it gets there as the result of a process of negotiation.

Example 50
A: OK, thanks for the information. Let's get together soon.
B: I'd love to.
A: Good, I'll give you a call and we'll make a date for lunch.
B: If you want, we can make a date now. When are you free?
A: Uh, OK, let's. I'm available almost any day next week. What about you?
B: Well, Wednesday is my best day.
A: OK, let's make it Wednesday.
B: Noon OK for you?
A: Noon is fine. Shall I pick you up at your place?
B: That would be great.
A: I'll be there at noon Wednesday.
B: Great. See you then.

(Wolfson 1981b: 14)

Extended and careful negotiation of this kind usually occurs between non-intimates of approximately equal status (Wolfson et al. 1983: 126).

So do women offer more invitations than men? Which gender offers most ambiguous invitations and which most unambiguous and specific invitations? One would predict that women would issue invitations more often, since they are positively polite speech acts, but it would be interesting to examine the form such invitations take. Given the tendency for men to focus on referentially orientated speech or 'report talk', as Tannen (1990a) calls it, one might predict that men would tend to give fewer, but more specific, invitations than women. Correspondingly, women's concern for 'rapport talk' would lead one to expect them to issue more invitations overall, but most might be ambiguous and non-specific. Wolfson's research would predict that men's more specific invitations would be directed to subordinates and intimates, while women's invitations would include more negotiated invitations with a wider range of addressees. In other words, it seems possible that, like compliments, non-specific invitations may operate as tokens of solidarity, and it would therefore be interesting to examine their distribution between women and men.

Hello–goodbye: Greetings and partings

Example 51
Woman: Hi
Man: Gidday
Woman: It's windy up top.
Man: Mm.

It seems likely that greetings, partings and expressions of gratitude might display similar patterns. These are all very obvious positive politeness speech acts, and their functions as tokens of solidarity is self-evident. Laver (1981: 301–2) suggests that the form of British greetings differs between those who know each other well and those who do not, as well as on the basis of status differences. While neutral or impersonal phrases such as 'Nice day' or 'Frosty night' are available to all, regardless of their relationship, there are status constraints, he suggests, on more personalised greeting forms. In particular, he proposes that status is very relevant between non-acquainted speakers so that only a superior may, with politeness, use other-orientated phrases such as 'How's the family?' or 'That looks like hard work' to someone they do not know well. A person of lower status will more appropriately use self-orientated phrases such as 'Hot work, this' or 'I do like a breath of fresh air' when greeting a stranger. People who know each other well may choose from any category, Laver claims.

Laver's observations are not based on empirical research, and they may not be generalisable beyond Britain (if they hold there). They do present, however, an interesting area for further research. In general, women tend to use more personalised compliment forms than men, who markedly prefer impersonal forms. Herbert's (1990) data suggested that where there were differences between women and men in the use of self-orientated versus other-orientated compliments, women used more self-orientated ones while men used more other-orientated ones. Projecting from Laver's interpretation of this pattern in greeting behaviour, this might suggest that men more often felt themselves to be of superior status in such interactions, while women's preferred pattern could be seen as reflecting lower social status. There is clearly considerable scope for further research here too.

Leave-takings are another area of positive politeness where one would expect gender differences. Kipers (1984, cited in Wolfson 1988: 34) notes that, as with invitations and compli- ments, partings between non-intimates differ from those between intimates.

> Where there is no framework of social contact in place to assure casual friends and acquaintances that a future meeting will take place, partings reflect concern over the survival of the relationship . . . lengthy negotiations over future meeting time reassure both participants that even though they may not designate a definite time when they will see one another again, they both value the relationship enough to want it to continue.

Partings between non intimates are thus considerably more extensive and elaborated than between intimates. Kipers makes no comment on gender differences in her data, but, given the compliment patterns described above, one would predict that women's partings will be more elaborated than men's. Women tend to pay more attention than men to the face needs of others, especially their positive face needs. Partings are occasions which provide opportunities for attention to positive face needs, for example, reassurances that the participants regret the need to part and that they wish to meet again soon. It seems likely, then, that women will provide more extensive and elaborate reassurances than men on parting with friends.

The interaction of status and social difference in politeness behaviour is another area which needs further attention. The evidence discussed in this chapter suggests that there will be differences in the frequency, function and interpretation of the same speech acts by equals compared to non-equals. Although most compliments occurred between equals, for instance, men in particular used more downwards. Similarly, we might expect more invitations to be issued downwards than upwards. The fact that status and social distance or solidarity interact is also likely to be relevant. Solidarity may override status differences, for instance, and this may be more apparent in the patterns of use for one gender than the other. When a boss and her female secretary are close friends, for example, either may issue an equally specific invitation. With less close relationships, or between males the form of the invitations may differ – the boss's may be more specific. There is clearly a great deal of potential for further research in this area.

Conclusion

In concluding this chapter it is worth emphasising the range of functions any utterance may perform. The detailed analysis of compliments illustrated well that the 'same' utterance may simultaneously convey a range of meanings. The 'same' utterance may also be used and interpreted differently by different social groups, including women and men. Just as a gift expresses solidarity and appreciation in some cultures, but is a form of one-upping a rival in others (Tannen 1990a: 295–6), so at least some compliments may be accepted as tokens of solidarity by women but experienced as an embarrassment by men. The same is likely to be true of other potential positive politeness devices. They are likely to be used and interpreted very differently in different contexts and cultures.

On the basis of a number of different aspects of the distribution of compliments in the New Zealand corpus, I have suggested that women tend to perceive and use compliments as positively affective speech acts and expressions of solidarity, whereas the responses of men may be more ambivalent. It seems possible that in some situations, at least, and with some types of compliment in particular, men may be more likely to interpret compliments as face-threatening acts. The pattern I have suggested provides an intriguing mirror-image of Kuiper's (1991) analysis of the way insults which would certainly be experienced as face-threatening acts by women, appear to perform a solidarity-maintaining function for at least some men. Kuiper describes the verbal interaction of members of a rugby team in the locker room before a match. The team members insult and abuse each other, using terms of address such as 'wanker', 'fuck-face' and the more overtly sexist 'fucking old woman', and 'girl's blouse'. For this group 'sexual humiliation is used as a means of creating group solidarity through the loss of face the individuals who belong to the group suffer' (1991: 200). (See also Labov 1972 on ritual insults among Black gang members and Dundes et al. 1972 on Turkish boys' verbal duelling.) Insults function for these men as expressions of solidarity, whereas the data in this chapter has suggested women prefer compliments for this function.

It also seems possible that the way men use compliments to women, in particular, may reflect the subordinate status of women in the society generally. Like endearments, compliments gain their force from the context of the relationship in which they are used. When used non-reciprocally by superiors to subordinates, these may underline patterns of societal power which place women in a clearly subordinate position to men.

In this chapter I have been concerned with speech acts which typically express positive politeness, especially when used between status equals and friends. The content of speech acts such as compliments and invitations is positive, as well as their intended effect on the addressee. In the next chapter I will discuss a speech act which is generally considered a negative politeness strategy – the apology.

Notes

1. As noted in Holmes (1988b), the predominance of females among the data collectors was a potential source of bias. The figures nevertheless suggest that even with equal numbers of female and male data collectors, compliments between females will be more frequent than compliments between males, though the imbalance would not be so dramatic.

5 Sorry! Apologies and negative politeness strategies

Example 1

Woman surveying damage to neighbour's car which her son has just backed into.

Oh god we've done something awful to your paintwork. I'm terribly sorry. We'll get it fixed up don't worry. I'll ring the insurance.

Speech acts such as compliments, invitations and greetings are generally regarded as positive politeness devices, expressing solidarity and friendliness. Apologies, by contrast, are usually perceived as negative politeness devices, expressing respect rather than friendliness. An apology is a polite speech act used to restore social relations following an offence. Apologies therefore focus on redressing face-threatening behaviour, and they acknowledge the need of the addressee not to be imposed upon or offended.

Negative politeness is 'the heart of respect behaviour' (Brown and Levinson 1987: 129). In fact, there are few speech acts which are intrinsically negative politeness speech acts. Linguistically expressed negative politeness generally takes the form of expressions or strategies which reduce the effect of face-threatening speech acts such as directives, threats, insults, complaints, disagreements or criticisms. The hedging devices which were discussed in Chapter 3 are obvious examples of linguistic forms which can have such a mitigating effect. Tag questions, and pragmatic particles such as *you know, I think*, and *sort of*, can serve very effectively to attenuate the force of a face-threatening act. Indirect requests, deferential address forms, and linguistic devices such as the passive, which tend to distance the speaker from the hearer, are further ways of expressing negative politeness. The apology, however, is the most obvious example of a speech act whose primary purpose is redressive action.

Why apologise?

Example 2

Jenny walks into Helen's office to find her talking to a client.
Oh sorry sorry I didn't mean to interrupt. I didn't realise you were busy.

Apologies, like compliments, are speech acts which pay attention to the face needs of the addressee. They are primarily aimed at maintaining, or enhancing the addressee's face (Goffman, 1967). Compliments generally express solidarity while apologies express respect, but both are intended to have a positive rather than negative effect on the person they are addressed to. They could be described as 'face-supportive acts'. (In other words, they contrast with speech acts such as threats and insults which Austin (1990) has called face attack acts.) The term 'apology' has generally been used to describe what Goffman refers to as a 'remedy' (1971: 140), one element in a 'remedial interchange'. This term nicely highlights the central function of apologies – to provide a remedy for an offence and restore social equilibrium or harmony (see also Edmondson 1981: 280; Leech 1983: 125). The following broad definition of an apology takes function as the crucial criterion:

> An apology is a speech act addressed to B's face needs and intended to remedy an offence for which A takes responsibility, and thus to restore equilibrium between A and B (where A is the apologiser, and B is the person offended).

It is difficult to further define an apology in any helpful manner since the remedial function may be achieved linguistically in an infinite number of ways depending on the offence addressed. It is possible, however, to categorise the range of strategies used to apologise, as I will illustrate below.

An apology will typically address an offence performed by the speaker.

Example 3
Hannah bumps into Chris, who is standing still.
Hannah: Sorry.
Chris: That's OK.

It is sometimes the case, however, that an apology will be made on behalf of someone for whom the apologiser feels responsible, such as a child, a spouse, a friend, or a member of the same group as the person apologising.

Example 4
Ann's child spills her drink on Pam's carpet.
Ann: Oh look I'm terribly sorry. I'll clean it up. Have you got a cloth?
Pam: Don't worry. I'll do it. It wasn't very much.

For this reason, the definition above refers to the person who takes responsibility for the offence rather than the offender herself.

As with many linguistic forms, utterances which serve as apologies may express other functions too (see Thomas 1985). So, for instance, utterances which express regret for an offence may also serve as an admission of guilt or responsibility, with the addressee learning of the offence through the utterance which acts as an apology. Example 5 is a case in point.

Example 5
In trying to undo a bottle for B, A breaks the cap.
Alice: Oh dear, I'm afraid I've broken it.
Bronwen: Never mind, at least it's open now!

While Alice's utterance clearly serves as an apology, it simultaneously performs the function of conveying bad news (see Coulmas 1981; Brown and Levinson 1987: 68).

Who apologises most?

The following analysis of the distribution of apologies between New Zealand women and men is based on a corpus of 183 naturally occurring remedial interchanges, that is apologies and apology responses, collected over a wide range of contexts.[1] In an article called 'A plea for excuses' Austin comments whimsically on his method of collecting examples of apologies and excuses: 'I do not know how many of you keep a list of the kinds of fool you make of yourselves' (1961: 186). The method used to collect apologies given by New Zealand women and men was a refinement of Austin's – an ethnographic approach identical to that used in collecting compliments. As with compliments, the instances collected were predominantly produced by adult Pakeha New Zealanders, and it is therefore the apology norms of this group which are described.

There has been little systematic comparison of male and female norms for apologising. Bruce Fraser comments on the basis of examples noted ethnographically that there was 'no apparent systematic or predictable frequency' in the occurrrence or non-occurrence of apologies from women and men in a range of contexts, and that '[c]ontrary to popular stereotype, we did not find women offering more apologies than men' (1981: 269). But he does not provide precise figures to support his observations, nor any idea of how many apologies he noted in total. (Note, too, a real problem with analysing data of this kind is the absence of information on when an apology could, or even should, have occurred but did not.)

In the New Zealand corpus there were significant differences in the distribution of the apologies used by women and men. In fact, the distributional pattern for apologies was remarkably similar to that for compliments discussed in Chapter 4. Figure 5.1 summarises the apology patterns.

Women gave 75 per cent of all the apologies recorded and received 73 per cent of them. It is always possible with ethnographic data that the environments in which the data was collected provided a higher proportion of female than male speech acts of the kind under investigation. The sampling method, which involved researchers collecting twenty consecutive apologies without interruption or editing, was an attempt to protect against such bias. So at least in this corpus, over a range of contexts, New Zealand women apologised more than New Zealand men did, and they were apologised to more frequently than the men. Figure 5.1 also illustrates the fact that apologies were most frequent between women, while apologies between males were relatively rare (only 8.5 per cent). As illustrated in the

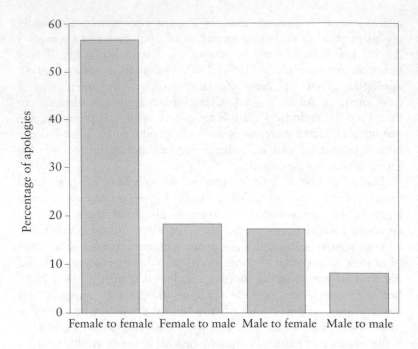

Figure 5.1   Apologies and gender of participants

last chapter, these patterns closely parallel the distribution of New Zealand compliments.

One might have expected that compliments and apologies would have rather different distributional patterns of use between women and men. It is superficially surprising, for instance, that apologies to males are so much less frequent than apologies to females (27 per cent versus 73 per cent). One might expect negative politeness strategies to be used more frequently to the powerful and to those with status. This is the pattern in a number of studies of directives, for instance. Young American children involved in role play indicated that they perceived mothers as appropriately addressed more often with direct imperatives, while fathers received more mitigated directives (Andersen 1989).

Examples 6 and 7
(6) *Julia to her mother.*
Mum read me a story

(7) *Julia to her father.*
I'm thirsty Dad. Can I have a drink of juice?

Similarly, a study of directives in middle-class American families found that children used less polite imperatives to their mothers, and more mitigated directives to fathers (Ervin-Tripp et al. 1984). The researchers suggest that these studies reflect the fact that mothers are perceived as less powerful than fathers, and as less deserving of respect or negative politeness. (Though it is worth noting that unmitigated directives are normal between intimates. The children may feel closer to their mothers.)

So, as signals of concern for offending or interfering with another person's freedom of action, apologies could be expected to occur most often 'upwards'. As noted in previous chapters, it is generally accepted that males are perceived as the dominant and powerful group in communities such as New Zealand, the United States and Britain, among others. So, one might expect, in particular, more apologies to men from women. But, in fact, as Figure 5.1 demonstrates, the number of apologies between women and men is remarkably evenly distributed. The resolution of this puzzle will involve exploring other social features of apology behaviour between women and men.

As with compliments, part of the answer may lie in differential perceptions by women and men of verbal politeness devices. The contexts, types of relationship, and kinds of offence which elicit apologies may differ between women and men, for instance. Norms for appropriate use may differ between women and men. Women may regard explicit apologies for offences as more important in maintaining relationships, for example, than men do. The very low frequency of apologies between men supports this suggestion. In other words, it seems possible that apologies function differently for women and men.

To explore this suggestion further, it will be useful to consider a number of features of the apologies in more detail. First I will describe the apology strategies used by women and men in the data. Then a number of features of the social interactions in which apologies occurred will be considered.

How do women and men apologise?

There are a number of linguistic strategies which can be used to apologise and a number of researchers have developed systems for classifying different apology strategies (Fraser 1981; Cohen and Olshtain 1981; Olshtain and Cohen 1983; Owen 1983; Blum-Kulka and Olshtain 1984; Trosborg 1987). In classifying the New Zealand data, I have built on the work of these earlier researchers, and I have followed Olshtain and Cohen's framework, in particular, very closely. Four broad basic categories have been used, with a number of sub-categories where required (Holmes 1990b.)

The simplest and most frequent apology form is an explicit expression of apology, *sorry*. But there are other forms which explicitly apologise too, some of which are rather formal: *I must apologise, I do apologise*. Less formal expressions, such as *please forgive me* and *excuse me*, though technically less direct are conventionally identified as relatively explicit apologies. Sometimes an explanation can serve as an apology, as in the following example.

Example 8
Jane is apologising for breaking an arrangement to meet Molly for lunch.
Oh help I've double booked. I was just about to write you a note. I've got a meeting. Let's make another time.

There is no explicit apology here, and yet this sequence of utterances explaining the problem functions as a remedy for the offence. In other cases, an acknowledgement of blame acts as an apology, as in example 9.

Example 9
David bumps into his wife Rose in the basement.
Oh that was silly of me. Didn't mean to hurt you. It's so dark down here.

Sometimes an apology will involve an explicit promise that the offence will not be repeated as in example 10.

Example 10
Computer trainer to person who has lost some files due to
computer crash.
How awful. Look I promise that won't happen again.

Table 5.1 Apology strategies and apologiser gender

| Apology strategy | Apologiser gender | | | |
| | Female | | Male | |
	No.	%	No.	%
A. Explicit expression of apology				
1. An offer of apology	8	3.7	7	8.6
e.g. *I apologise*				
2. An expression of regret	114	53.3	34	42
e.g. *I'm sorry*				
3. A request for forgiveness	10	4.7	7	8.6
e.g. *Excuse me*				
Subtotal (As)	132	61.7	48	59.2
B. Explanation or account				
e.g. *I wasn't expecting it to be you*	50	23.4	17	21
C. Acknowledgement of responsibility				
1. Accepting the blame	4	1.9	5	6.2
e.g. *It is my fault*				
2. Expressing self-deficiency	5	2.3	4	4.9
e.g. *I was confused*				
3. Recognise B entitled to apology	2	0.9	–	–
e.g. *You're right*				
4. Expressing lack of intent	7	3.3	–	–
e.g. *I didn't mean to*				
5. An offer of repair/redress	11	5.1	5	6.2
e.g. *We'll replace it for you*				
Subtotal (Cs)	29	13.5	14	17.3
D. A promise of forbearance				
e.g. *I promise it won't happen again*	3	1.4	2	2.5
TOTAL	214	100	81	100

Table 5.1 provides information on female and male
preferences in strategy selection. It includes all the apology
strategies used by women and men in the 183 remedial exchanges
in the corpus. In many cases an apologiser used more than one

strategy as part of the complete apology; hence the total number of apology strategies is 295. (See Holmes 1990b for further discussion of combinations of apology strategies. There are no significant differences in the combinations used by women compared to men (Holmes 1989d).)

Table 5.1 demonstrates that overall both women and men make use of the same range of apology strategies, and they use them in similar proportions. There are, however, a few small but suggestive differences. Though the numbers of apologies involved are small, men tend to use formal sub-strategies (e.g. *I do apologise, I must apologise*) more often than women. The following examples illustrate these patterns.

Examples 11 and 12
(11) *Ken has taken a colleague out for lunch.*
I must apologise for the lousy service here. They're not usually this bad. But the food's pretty good you see.

(12) *John apologises to a client who has been given the wrong form to fill in.*
There seems to have been some mistake. I do apologise.

If these tendencies hold over a large number of interactions and other corpuses, this might indicate that men regard apologies as signals of social distance, appropriate mainly in relationships with people they do not know well, since formal linguistic strategies are generally not considered appropriate between people who are close friends.

Alternatively, or additionally, since formal strategies may also be used to attempt to remedy great offences, men may regard apologies as devices to be used only in cases of relatively serious offences.

Example 13
John has borrowed his flatmate's car without asking and has scratched the door slightly.
Look I am most terribly sorry. I apologise most abjectly (*laughs in an embarrassed way*) . . .

There is some support for this suggestion in the analysis below.
Table 5.1 also shows that though there is little overall

difference in the likelihood that women rather than men will acknowledge responsibility for the offence, within this category there are subtle differences of emphasis. Women tend to use strategies which focus on the harmony of their relationship with the other person; only women used the strategies of expressing lack of negative intent and recognising the other's right to an apology.

Examples 14 and 15
(14) *Elizabeth interrupted her friend.*
Sorry I didn't mean to interrupt you.

(15) *Jill acknowledges she has made an error in marking Fiona's test.*
Sorry. You're quite right. You've got that right. You deserve an apology.

Men, on the other hand, tend to use more strategies which focus on the relative status relationship with the other, accepting blame and expressing self-deficiency.

Examples 16 and 17
(16) *Len has overfilled Ron's glass.*
Hell that was a daft thing to do.

(17) *Gordon puts milk in Fay's coffee though she asked for it black.*
Oh sorry I wasn't thinking.

These strategies emphasise the fact that an offence puts the apologiser at a social disadvantage – the apology acknowledges a 'one-down' position relative to the offended person. With such a small number of apologies involved, such differences may be due to pure chance, but they are suggestive. If the pattern were sustained, it supports an argument that women's motivation for apologies may be related to their perception of what is necessary to maintain the relationship with the person offended. Their strategies could be described as 'other-orientated'. They make explicit the apologiser's concern that the offence should not damage the relationship. Where men's strategies differ from women's on the other hand, they appear to reflect a concern with status relationships and an awareness that an apology damages the apologiser's face and puts him one down (compare Tannen 1990a: 231–4).

These differences in preferred sub-strategies are small, but where they occur they suggest that perhaps women and men regard apologies as doing different jobs. They provide some support for the suggestion that the lower numbers of apologies used overall by men reflect a different assessment by women and men concerning the circumstances in which politeness requires an apology. If that is the case, even though women and men largely use the same range of strategies, they presumably carry different weight for each group.

What deserves an apology?

Example 18
Karen, a postgraduate student, in a note to her supervisor with material due.
Sorry the writing's so awful but I strained my wrist giving birth to the first of the season's lambs (i.e. I assisted the ewe!) back home so this is all rather painful.

When is it polite to apologise and when is it unnecessary? What are the contexts in which we consider it essential to apologise? In Chapter 1, I pointed out that relative social distance or solidarity, and relative power or status were factors that had been identified by a number of researchers in the area of politeness. More specifically, Brown and Levinson's model of politeness suggests that the weighting of any face-threatening act will reflect a third additional factor, namely, the degree of imposition involved in the relevant speech act. In other words, the degree of face threat represented by any utterance will be determined by the power differences between those involved, how well they know each other, and how much of an imposition the content of the speech act represents. As the degree of face threat, or the weighting of the face-threatening act, increases, so will the appropriate degree of politeness as illustrated in Figure 5.2.

These factors are obviously among those relevant in determining appropriate apology behaviour too. A detailed examination of the relationship between the frequency of apologies and the

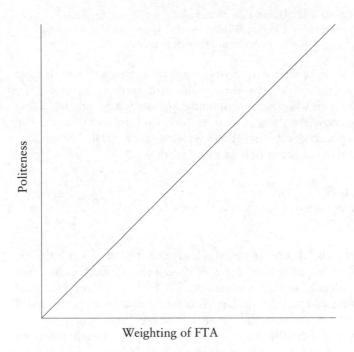

Figure 5.2 Weighting of face-threatening act in relation to degree of politeness.
(Based on: Brown and Levinson 1987.)

types of apology strategies used showed a clear relationship between power, social distance, and the seriousness of the offence on the one hand, and the frequency of apologies and their elaborateness on the other. So, for instance, the greatest number of apologies were for slight offences such as bumping into a friend or acquaintance, and involved a simple strategy such as *sorry*. A small number of exchanges involved much more elaborate apologies. These generally involved a more serious offence between people who did not know each other well, or a situation where the person offended was more powerful or influential in the apologiser's life, as in example 19.

Example 19
Jon has forgotten a lunch date with his uncle who has been a source of advice and financial support in the past. He telephones.

Look I'm so sorry Uncle Tim. What can I say? I just forgot – I
should get a diary I know. What a nerd. My memory's collapsing.
Please forgive me. Let's make another date please.

It is not surprising that people tend to apologise more readily
and more extensively to those who are more powerful. The
potential repercussions for offending are obviously greater. How
well you know someone is also an obviously relevant factor. We
tend to apologise most to those we know less well. We assume
intimates will tolerate offences more readily.

Example 20
Ned steps back and bumps into his wife Tina.
Oops.

Said with an appropriately apologetic tone of voice, this is
assumed to be enough of a remedy between intimates. And the
type of offence and its seriousness is also a relevant factor in
determining whether an apology is offered, and how elaborated it
is in form. A serious offence merits more 'face work' than a
minor one. Forgetting to turn up to an appointment with the
managing director could require weeks of remedial work.
Damaging someone's prized possession may take considerable
skill in remedial exchange. Repeated failure to meet expectations
may require an extended apology.

Example 21
Anne has failed yet again to meet a work deadline.
I'm afraid I've got nothing to report yet again (*apology*). I haven't
managed to do any analysis this week at all (*acknowledges
offence*). I've been plagued with nasty headaches every day
(*explanation*). Anyway the important thing is to make more effort
next week. I'll do my best I promise (*promise of forbearance*).

But, accepting these overall patterns, are there differences
between women and men in their use of apologies in different
contexts? I will first examine the effect of the offence type and its
seriousness in discussing whether women and men differ in this
aspect of politeness behaviour.

How have I offended?

Example 22
Female shop assistant has brought woman customer a skirt to try on.
Customer: I'm sorry but this is the wrong size.
Shop assistant: So sorry dear. My fault. I'll get you another. Just wait here a moment.

What kinds of things do people perceive as needing an explicit verbal apology? What types of offence are serious enough to require remedial work? There are obviously many ways in which different types of offence could be classified. A careful examination of the data suggested the following six broad categories:

1. *Space* offences: e.g. bumping into someone, queue jumping.
2. *Talk* offences: e.g. interrupting, talking too much.
3. *Time* offences: e.g. keeping people waiting, taking too long.
4. *Possession* offences: e.g. damaging or losing someone's property.
5. *Social gaffes*: e.g. burping, coughing, laughing inappropriately.
6. *Inconvenience* offences/inadequate service: e.g. giving someone wrong item.

Do women and men differ in the types of offence for which they apologise? Do some offences seem more offensive to women than to men and vice versa? Distributional data can only be suggestive but it is clear from Figure 5.3 that there are some differences in the types of offence for which New Zealand women and men apologised.

There are two areas where significant gender differences appear. First, men apologised more for time offences, that is for being late, or for keeping someone waiting.

Example 23
Max arrives late at weekly staff meeting.
Sorry I'm late. Phone call just as I was leaving.

Wolfson (1988: 27) comments that

The notion that [middle-class Americans] consider themselves under obligation to be prompt and/or to avoid keeping another

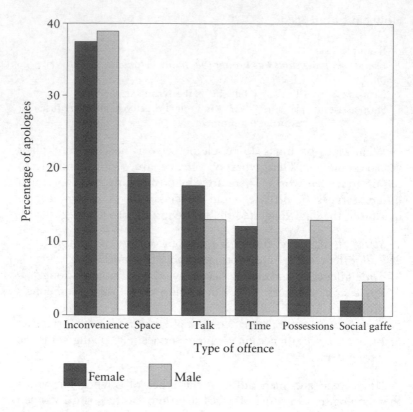

Figure 5.3 Apologiser gender and offence type

person waiting is, in fact, evidenced by the large number of apologies that refer to just this situation.

Wolfson does not provide figures so it is difficult to know how time apologies compare with other types of offence in her American data. In the New Zealand data it is clear that time offences are more frequent reasons for apologies among men than women. It is possible that men are late more often than women and so have more reason to give apologies for lateness. Keeping someone waiting is impolite behaviour and women tend to avoid being impolite more than men do. It may also be the case that when we think of time as a very valuable commodity, we are reflecting 'male as norm' values (Spender 1980a). It would be interesting to compare female and male behaviour in this area in different contexts, private and public, formal and informal.

A second area of significant difference between women and men in the type of offence which elicited an apology was space offences, that is when the apologiser intruded on another person's space in some way.

Example 24
Woman has taken someone's library space.
Oh I'm sorry. I didn't realise you were coming back.

In general, women apologised more than men for intrusions on the space of another person. They were more likely than men to apologise for bumping into another person, for instance. In fact when women bumped into each other, both generally said *sorry*. It is perhaps not suprising to find a predominance of apologies for accidental body contact in a group who are the main victims of sexual harassment. It is very plausible that women are more sensitive to space impositions, and as a result they more readily apologise for intrusions on another's space. An apology can serve to make it clear that the contact had been unintentional. Men, on the other hand, may not regard space impositions as so offensive. In this respect it is worth noting that there are no examples in the corpus of space apologies between men.

There are two further differences between the types of offence for which women and men tend to apologise which are worth comment in the light of the suggestion that women and men may see apologies as appropriate in different contexts, or as serving different interactional purposes. First, men tended to apologise more often than women did for offences which involved other people's property or possessions.

Example 25
John: Where's my Parker [pen]? Didn't you borrow it Ken?
Ken: Look I think I've lost it – sorry. I'll have to get you a new one.

Possession apologies related to damage or loss to a range of things including the other person's pen, car, books, clothes and washing machine. Offences which cost the other person money (e.g. failing to pay a bill on time) were also included in this category. The fact that men apologised more often than women for offences involving another person's possessions is consistent with the finding noted in Chapter 4 that men pay compliments relating to possessions more often than women do. It is also consistent with a widely held belief that men value 'things' more than women do, while women tend to give greater weight to social relationships than men do.

Further support for this line of argument is provided by another difference apparent in the data illustrated in Figure 5.3. Women apologise for talk offences more than men.

Example 26
Ann has been talking to a small group of colleagues for about four minutes without interruption.
I am sorry to go on so about this but I think it's really important.

Talk offences involved things such as interrupting others, or taking up what the speaker perceived as an unfair share of the available talking time, or not hearing what the other person said. The fact that women apologised more than men for such offences, if generalisable, is somewhat ironic, since women are in fact more often the victims of such talk offences than men, as was apparent in Chapter 2. As with space offences, however, it may be that women are, for this very reason, particularly sensitive to such offences.

If the offences we consider worth an apology reflect our concerns and pre-occupations, this data suggests that women are particularly concerned about intrusions relating to a person's personal space and infringements of the talking rights of others. Men are more concerned by inconvenience which costs another person time or money, and offences which result in damage to another's possessions. All this provides some support for the suggestion that the reason for differences in women's and men's apology behaviour may relate to differences in their perceptions of the kind of situations where being impolite requires an apology. Women and men may use apologies differently because they differ in their perceptions of when they are appropriate.

How serious was my offence?

Example 27
Avery is a house guest in Rhonda's house.
Avery: I'm sorry I've made a hell of a mess. I dropped the
          sugar jar and spilt the sugar. I've cleaned the bench
          but I'll need the vacuum cleaner to get down the side
          of the stove.
Rhonda: (*With a smile*) Oh that's terrible. You can't come
          again.

Another factor which is worth considering in an analysis of
gender differences in the use of apologies is the relative seriousness of the offence in context. How serious are the offences
which elicit apologies from women compared to those for which
men consider it appropriate to apologise? This analysis required a
careful consideration of a range of contextual factors. The degree
of offence caused by losing someone's book, for instance,
depends on factors such as how urgently they need it, as well as
its rarity or monetary value. I identified three different degrees of
seriousness in the offences noted in the apology corpus.

1. *Light offences*: e.g. bumped into someone accidentally, forgot
   to return a library book on time.
2. *Medium offences*: e.g. broke someone's stapler, kept someone
   waiting so they were late for a film.
3. *Heavy offences*: e.g. knocked someone over so they were hurt,
   inflicted serious damage on someone's car, insulted someone in
   public.

Figure 5.4 illustrates the differences found in the number of
offences of different degrees of seriousness which elicited apologies from women compared to men.

The pattern illustrated in Figure 5.4 provides some support for
the suggestion that women and men weigh offences differently. It
suggests that perhaps women apologise more readily than men.
Men's apologies take up a greater proportion of the more heavily
weighted offences than women's do, while a greater proportion
of women's apologies relate to the lightest weighted offences. It is
possible, of course, that women may interpret situations
differently from men. The 'same' behaviour may elicit an apology

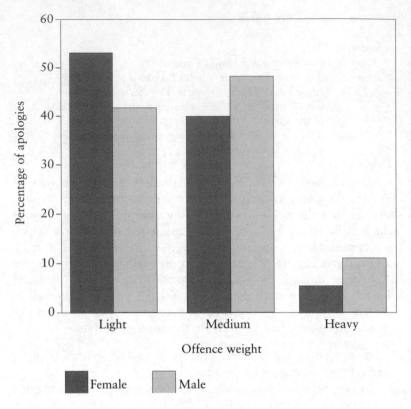

Figure 5.4 Apologiser gender and offence weight

from a woman but not from a man. The contexts in which women consider an explicit verbal apology is needed for the sake of politeness appear to involve less serious offences than those in which men provide apologies. This may be another factor, then, accounting for the fact that women apologise more frequently than men do.

Offending the boss is a serious matter

Example 28
Secretary spills coffee on boss's desk.
Oh excuse me. I'll get a cloth.

Offending the boss is likely to elicit a pretty quick apology whereas bumping into a child or borrowing the secretary's pen without asking may not warrant an apology at all. We are more likely to apologise to those who are more powerful. And we are likely to apologise more profusely and extensively if the offence is serious.

Example 29
Daphne and her husband forgot an invitation to dinner at
Daphne's head of department's home and had to be rung up on
the evening concerned to remind them. They arrived very late.
Look we're so sorry. I'm afraid we've both been so busy and the kids, you know. But I should have written it in my diary. There's really no excuse. What a terrible thing to do. Please forgive us.

This apology went on for days. Every time the two people met for several days afterwards Daphne apologised. The relative status or power of the apologiser and the person offended is an obvious factor to consider when examining apologies from the point of view of politeness.

Three categories were used to classify apologies according to the relative status of the people involved.

1. *Upwards*: i.e. apology to a superior or person of greater power.
2. *Equal*: i.e. apology to an equal.
3. *Downwards*: i.e. apology to a subordinate or person of lesser power.

Most of the apologies in the corpus occurred between status or power equals (63 per cent). The distribution of the remaining apologies among those of different status throws some interesting light on the issue of how apologies are perceived as tokens of politeness by women and men. In general, one would expect that where participants differ in power or status, apologies upwards to those of higher status or greater power would be more frequent than apologies downwards to those of lower status or less power. Figure 5.5 shows that this pattern describes the New Zealand women's behaviour better than the men's. Twice as many of the women's apologies were directed upwards to those of greater power than were directed downwards.

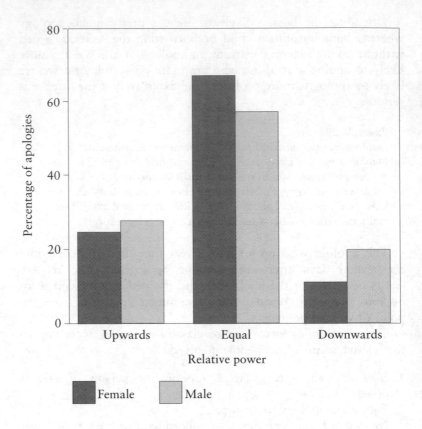

Figure 5.5   Apologiser gender and power of recipient

Example 30
Student to tutor as she bumps into her desk.
Sorry. I'm so clumsy today.

Women are sensitive it seems to the need to ensure that possible offences are remedied, especially when those involved have greater power.

Figure 5.5 suggests that men, by contrast, do not distinguish to the same extent between those of higher and lower status; they give roughly similar proportions of apologies to both (24% vs 20%). It is interesting to note, however, that men apologise proportionately more than women do to those with unequal

power compared to their status equals. Correspondingly, men use
relatively fewer apologies to equals than women do. This suggests
that men may regard apologies as more often superfluous or
dispensable between equals than do women. Such a belief would
mesh with the men's tendency to use apologies more often than
women for more heavily weighted offences. Apologies are
perhaps not the common everyday currency of politeness for men
that they are for women. The pattern that is emerging supports
the suggestion that men's norms for using apologies may be
rather different from women's.

It may be that apologies are regarded by men not so much as
'other-orientated' politeness devices, but rather as admissions of
weakness, inadequacy or failure to measure up in some way. In
other words, men may focus more on the effect of an apology on
the apologiser's face, rather than on the attention and respect it
pays the person addressed. In discussion of these issues male
friends confirm that this explanation is plausible. One
commented: 'You don't apologise if it isn't necessary. Good
mates don't get offended about little things.' Another said:
'Apologising is such a formal thing. Reminds me of school when
the teacher insisted you had to apologise for ridiculous things.
Yea I suppose I do feel it's belittling. You don't apologise if you
don't have to. No need to put yourself down unnecessarily.'
Women, on the other hand, with their tendency to look for ways
of attending to the face needs of others, seem to regard apologies as
tokens of concern, and even solidarity (see Tannen 1990a: 232).

Further examination of the apology data provides some
support for these suggestions. Men apologised twice as often to
women as they did to men, regardless of the women's position in
relation to the apologiser. Interpretation must be speculative, but
for men perhaps it is easier to apologise even to a woman boss or
social superior than to a man. If apologies are regarded as
admissions of inadequacy, then it may be easier for men to use
them to subordinates and to women (a socially less powerful
group in the society). Using them upwards to a male may be
uncomfortable, since the apology emphasises the existing power
difference.

In fact, both genders apologise much more often to women
than to men, regardless of relative power or status. It is clear that
women place a very high priority on apologies to female equals:

these are by far the most frequent apologies in the whole corpus. It seems likely that while apologies may be experienced as admissions of inadequacy by men, that is they emphasise power differences, they are regarded by women primarily as ways of restoring social harmony and expressing concern for the other person. Additionally, it may be the case that the society as a whole, both women and men, recognise the high priority that women place on politeness strategies as interactive tokens.

Friends and forgiveness

Example 31
Avril is a guest at Jenny's place.
Avril: I'm terribly sorry I've done a terrible thing. I've broken that little knob on the dryer. It's fallen inside the filter and I can't get it out.
Jenny: (*Looks in dryer*) Oh that's easily fixed. And it'll run OK without the filter.

Men's patterns for using apologies appear to give more weight to status differences and the seriousness of the offence involved than do women's patterns. Women's patterns, on the other hand, seem to reflect the fact that social distance or solidarity counts for more with women. Are there any differences, then, in the frequency with which men and women apologised to other people on the basis of how well they knew them?

One incident I observed illustrated nicely the fact that the same offence might elicit different types of apology between friends and strangers. Both exchanges took place in the library as a person returned an overdue book.

Examples 32 and 33
(32) *Person returning book does not know library assistant.*
I'm sorry this is overdue. I must owe you something.

(33) *Person returning book is a friend of the library assistant.*
Overdue as usual. What's new! What's the damage this time?

In example 33 there is no explicit apology. Yet the utterances serve as a remedial exchange. How well you know someone can affect the form the apology takes. There are also differences in the frequency with which women and men apologise to friends compared to strangers.

Three categories were used to classify the data in terms of the relative social distance between the participants:

I: intimates or very close friends: e.g. spouses, partners, family members;
F: friends or colleagues;
S: strangers or distant acquaintances.

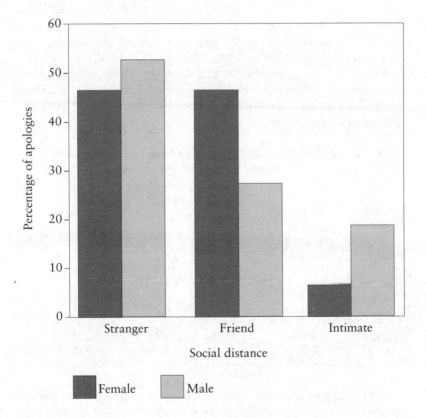

Figure 5.6 Apologiser gender and social distance of recipient

Figure 5.6 shows the distribution of the apologies according to how well the participants knew each other. Brown and

Levinson's (1987) model of politeness suggests that the greater the social distance between those involved, the more politeness is required towards the other person. So one might expect to find people apologising more often to strangers than to friends and intimates. Figure 5.6 shows men do this, but not women. There are twice as many examples of men apologising to those who are strangers or acquaintances as to friends. Women, however, apologise as often to their friends as to strangers. Again this supports the view that men regard apologies to friends as less crucial and as more dispensable than those to strangers. Men may reflect or signal friendship by *not* apologising for what they regard as 'trivial' offences. To apologise to a mate for a minor offence may be regarded as an insult or a distancing device. One young man commented: 'Mates don't expect apologies for piddly things. It's insulting.' Paying attention to face needs by apologising may be interpreted as indicating lack of confidence in the strength of the bond between male mates. If you need to apologise, it suggests you are not close mates.

Table 5.2: Apologies by social distance and gender of participants

| | | Apologiser gender | |
| | | Female | Male |
Relative distance	Recipient gender	%	%
Stranger	Female	29.2	38.6
	Male	16.9	13.6
Friend	Female	40.8	11.4
	Male	6.2	15.9
Intimate	Female	5.4	15.9
	Male	1.5	4.5

Table 5.2 throws more light on this issue. As suggested above, apologies may be regarded by males as admissions of inadequacy. The apologiser puts himself in a one-down position as Tannen (1990a) points out. Men's awareness of status differences and of asymmetries in relationships may mean they are unwilling to apologise to other men unless they judge it really necessary.

Apologies to women may be more acceptable since women's subordinate social status means the apologiser will not be so reduced in status relative to his addressee in these cases.

The data in Table 5.2 is consistent with both of these interpretations. Women apologise most to their women friends (41 per cent), while by far the largest proportion (39 per cent) of male apologies are directed to female strangers or acquaintances. These figures suggest that both women and men are aware of the importance that women attach to face needs, and both groups recognise that it is important to apologise to women one has offended. It appears that women rate women friends as requiring most attention, while men appear to consider female strangers as needing most attention. It is interesting to speculate on the reasons for this. The potentially dangerous social interpretations when a male offends a female stranger may be one relevant consideration. When a man accidentally bumps into a woman, for example, he will want to make sure his action is not interpreted as deliberate. Addressing a stranger familiarly, mistaking her for a friend, will require some redress. An apology is one way of making sure unintended offences are properly perceived.

The pattern of apologies to people classified as intimates is also consistent with this interpretation. Men apologise more to women they know really well than to very close male friends. Both women and men appear to apologise more to females than to males with whom they have a close relationship, though the numbers here are very small. So men are least likely to apologise to a close male mate, and they differentiate between females and males with whom they are close, using apologies to the women more often than the men. Once men have developed close relationships with women, it may be that they use the face-supportive strategies which women value in an effort to maintain the relationship. Men may not regard apologies as necessary in close relationships with other males. It is also possible that they find it less face-threatening to apologise to a woman than a man, because of the general social asymmetry between women and men. The following example occurred between a man and a woman. Apologies of this sort were not observed between men.

Example 34
Man bumps into woman coming out of shop.
Oh I'm terribly sorry. Are you alright?

It seems, then, that the distribution of apologies according to the social distance between the apologiser and the person offended supports the suggestion that women evaluate the need for an apology differently from men. Women seem to regard an offence against a female friend as weighing more heavily than one against a stranger, while the reverse may be true for men. Women appear to treat apologies as tokens of concern and friendship, while men may regard them as debt-incurring hostages to fortune.

How do people respond to an apology?

If apologies are aimed at restoring social harmony, or even if they are regarded as admissions of inadequacy, responses to apologies can provide an indication to the apologiser of whether the offended person is satisfied or not. Has the goal of re-establishing social harmony or equilibrium been achieved? Does the offended person feel satisfied that the offence has been adequately acknowledged?

Example 35
Male student to male professor in tutorial.
Michael: Sorry we're late. We got stuck in the lift.
Professor: Michael you're always late.
Michael: Sorry Prof. I promise I'll be early next time.
Professor: I'll believe it when I see it.

This good-humoured exchange indicates clearly to the student that the professor does not regard the offence as a very serious one and that good relations prevail.

In the data as a whole, six categories of response strategies were identified. The most likely response from both women and men was to accept the apology, with a remark such as 'That's OK' or 'No problem'. A lateral comment, sometimes responding to some other aspect of the apology, was the next most frequent response, as in example 36.

Example 36
Joe is phoning Sam to cancel a lunch date.
Joe: I'm sorry. I can't make it after all. I've got an unexpected
        meeting. It's a real pain.
Sam: Let's make another time.

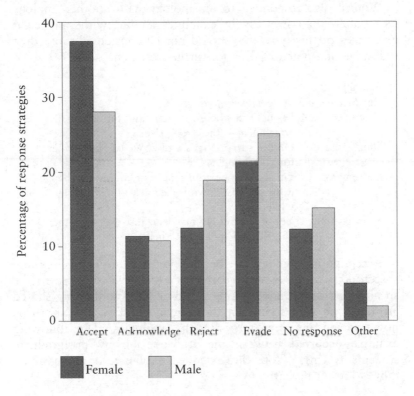

Figure 5.7 Apology response strategies and gender

As Figure 5.7 indicates, there were few gender differences in
apology responses. In general, women appeared to be more likely
to explicitly accept an apology than men, while men were more
likely than women to reject an apology, or say nothing in
response.

Example 37
In restaurant kitchen with male waiter and male chef.
Chef: Don't take that.
Waiter: Sorry I thought it was ready to go.
Chef: Don't take anything till I say.
Waiter: Sorry.
Chef: *says nothing.*

Women also responded to an apology with another apology more often than men, as in example 38; but with only eight exchanges of this type, this should not be considered more than indicative of a potential area for further research.

Example 38
Female customer to female shop assistant.
Customer: I bought this here yesterday and I'm afraid the attachment is the wrong size.
Shop assistant: Oh I'm sorry. That's a pity. We can get it altered for you though.
Customer: I'm sorry to be a nuisance but could you change it for me now. I won't be back in town for a while.
Shop assistant: Yes of course. No problem. Just wait a moment and I'll find someone to help.

Accepting an apology can be interpreted as a positively polite speech act. An acceptance represents a positive response to the speaker, indicating understanding and perhaps confirming shared attitudes and values between those involved. This appears to be how women interpret responses to apologies. The following example occurred between me and one of my postgraduate students recently. Note the extended explanation and gradual move to restoring harmony.

Example 39
Mary telephones me to change an appointment.
Mary: Did you get the note I left for you yesterday afternoon?
Janet: No.
Mary: Oh I thought you mightn't have. Look I'm sorry I've double booked myself for this afternoon.
Janet: Oh that's a pity. We'd better make another time then.
Mary: Yes I am sorry I'd forgotten about this other thing and basically you're easier to change.

Janet: Oh! (*a bit surprised at this comment*)
Mary: Sorry well no that wasn't meant to be rude – it's just that you are more reliable.
Janet: Oh well that's a good way of putting it.

On the other hand, an acceptance could be regarded as a threat to the accepter's face, since the acceptance implicitly confirms that the offender has imposed on the speaker. This may be how men interpret acceptance, since they seem to be less willing to explicitly accept an apology than women are, and they are more likely than women to reject or fail to acknowledge an apology.

Example 40
Male doctor to his female receptionist who has accidentally put a call through to him which should have gone to his nurse.
Doctor: Who put that call through to my room?
Receptionist: Sorry Doctor Keith. It certainly wasn't intentional.
Doctor: It's just not good enough Diane.
Receptionist: Sorry doctor.

An acceptance restores the social balance and preserves the offender's face. It is an other-orientated response. Silence or rejection threatens the offender's face and preserves the face of the person offended, and is thus more self-orientated. An evasion allows the speaker an 'out' in these circumstances, and avoids admitting the loss of face resulting from the offence. Example 36 above illustrates this. Sam does not explicitly accept Joe's apology, releasing him from any obligation and restoring social harmony. Rather his response is a means of avoiding the loss of face involved in having an appointment with him cancelled for something which Joe obviously considers more important. Men seem less 'other-orientated' than women in this data, in that a higher proportion of male than female responses could be categorised as avoidances or evasions.

Tannen (1990a: 234) provides an alternative interpretation. She says

> accepting an apology is arguably quite rude. From the point of view of connection, an apology should be matched. And from the perspective of status, an apology should be deflected. In this view,

a person who apologises takes a one-down position, and accepting the apology preserves that asymmetry, whereas deflecting the apology restores the balance.

Though her evidence appears to be anecdotal, the point she makes is an interesting one. Acceptances can be regarded as preserving rather than reducing the asymmetry introduced by the offence, she suggests. Nevertheless in my view, after examining the exchanges in the New Zealand corpus, responses involving acceptances or a responding apology appear to have the goal of restoring harmony and balance to the relationship. They are appeasing in tone. Silences and rejections, on the other hand, are not responses which appear to be aimed at achieving balance. Rather they preserve the asymmetry introduced by the apology. Men clearly use a higher proportion of these than women, while women accept apologies more often than men.

Why apologise? Some answers

Apologies, like compliments, are hearer-orientated face-supportive acts. While compliments are generally regarded as positive politeness strategies, apologies have been seen as negative politeness strategies aimed at remedying the effects of an offence or a face-threatening act and restoring social harmony and equilibrium. It is also true, however, that apologies inevitably damage the apologiser's face to some extent, as pointed out by Brown and Levinson (1987: 68). This provides one possible explanation for why men and women perceive apologies differently. Men may give more weight to their function as self-orientated face-threatening acts, damaging the speaker's face – and therefore to be avoided where possible. Women by contrast may perceive them primarily as 'other-orientated' speech acts aimed at facilitating social harmony.

It is clear from the distribution of apologies in the corpus that, as with compliments, women use these polite speech acts more often than men. Moreover, just as with compliments, there are obviously grounds for suggesting that the reasons for the frequency difference between women and men may be related to different interpretations of the social significance of these speech acts. Detailed contextual analysis will be necessary to make further progress with many of the questions raised by the distributional evidence, but that evidence does provide some basis for exploring further the hypothesis that men and women attach different weight to the 'same' offences, and so assess the need for an apology differently, and that men and women interpret the interpersonal effects of apologies differently.

The evidence can be summarised as follows:

- Women use significantly more apologies than men; they use more to each other than to men, and they use many more to each other than men do to each other.
- Women tend more than men to use apology strategies which recognise the claims of the person offended and focus on the harmony of the relationship. Men tend more than women to use strategies which focus on the apologiser's loss of face and the resulting status imbalance.
- Women's apologies more often than men's serve as remedies for space and talk offences – areas of interaction where women are particularly vulnerable and where they may have developed a greater sensitivity. Men, on the other hand, pay particular attention to time offences, suggesting that they may have different priorities from women.
- Women's apologies are predominantly directed to light offences, whereas men use more apologies than women for more serious offences.
- Whereas both women and men use most apologies to power equals, men use proportionately more than women to women of different status, that is, 'upwards' and 'downwards'.
- Women use most apologies to female friends whereas men use most to socially distant women.
- Though the most frequent response for both women and men is to accept apologies, men reject more apologies than women do, and women accept them proportionately more than men do.

These patterns suggest that women and men may regard apologies differently. Being polite seems more likely to involve an apology for a woman than a man. Women and men seem to evaluate the need for apologies differently. Men seem to avoid apologies where possible, using them only in cases where they judge they are likely to cause greater offence by the omission of an apology. They are regarded perhaps as acknowledgements of inadequacy. Between female friends, by contrast, apologies appear to play an important part in the normal face-attention required of such a relationship. They are an intrinsic part of the politeness behaviour between friends and could even be regarded as tokens of concern and friendship. Between men apologies may be much more dispensable. In fact, a signal of the strength of male friendship may be that the offender feels able to omit an apology. Face-saving appears to be more important and is perhaps recognised as such between men.

One way of interpreting the data described in this chapter is to suggest that men's apology behaviour broadly conforms to Brown and Levinson's model of politeness: the frequency of men's apologies is sensitive to increased social distance and the seriousness of the offence. Women's apology behaviour, on the other hand, appears to conform more closely to Nessa Wolfson's 'bulge' model, which was outlined in Chapter 1 (Wolfson 1988). Wolfson's model suggests that, in general, speech behaviour tends to be most frequent and most elaborated between those who are acquaintances and casual friends, rather than between intimates or strangers. Strangers know where they stand with one another, as do intimates. Relationships with casual friends are often much less certain and more ambiguous; they are more 'dynamic and open to negotiation' (Wolfson 1988: 33) and in need of regular redefinition and reassurance, and this is one of the functions of positively polite speech acts. This accounts for the observation, which was supported by the data in Chapter 4, that speech acts such as compliments, greetings and invitations occur more frequently in interactions between friends than with intimates, or strangers. The pattern described both female and male behaviour in the use of the speech acts discussed in Chapter 4. Though it was more pronounced for women, both women's and men's compliments followed the bulge model. But apologies follow different patterns for men and women. Women's apologies conform much more closely to the bulge model than men's do. The bulge model illustrates very neatly the women's pattern of apologising to friends more than to strangers or intimates.

The bulge model is essentially a model which focuses on solidarity/social distance. It seems possible that women apologise more to those to whom they feel a need to signal positive attitudes in order to resolve possibly threatening alternative inter-pretations, and less to those with whom their relationships are clear-cut and unambiguous, because intimate or transactional. In other words, the distribution of women's apologies follows the pattern of their compliments, suggesting that apologies perhaps function similarly for women as tokens of friendship or solidarity. The distribution of men's apologies, on the other hand, is better described by Brown and Levinson's model which focuses on the degree of face threat involved in different speech acts.

These interpretations can be no more than suggestive at this stage. Closer analysis of the type of apologies which occur in different contexts will doubtless shed interesting illumination on the reasons for the differences identified in women's and men's apologising behaviour.

Speech acts and politeness – what next?

In fact, there is abundant scope for further research in terms of the way different speech acts express politeness, as well as into differences in the way they are used by women and men. There is some research on gender differences in the use of directives, but little on other potentially interesting speech acts. There is evidence that mitigated directives, reflecting concern for the addressee's feelings, are more likely to occur in female than male speech. A study of white American children found that the boys produced more explicit directive forms, while the girls produced more utterances expressing positive politeness (Haas 1979). Among African-American adolescents, the girls used more mitigated directives than the boys (Goodwin 1980). In these cases, a variety of strategies were used to reduce the face-threatening effect of the directive, and so express negative politeness. But few other speech acts have been examined for possible gender differences.

The mitigation of complaints by females and males, for instance, would be an interesting area to explore. Complaints are potentially a rich source of information on politeness, since at least two contrasting types can be distinguished. First, there are complaints which directly or indirectly attribute blame to the addressee for a particular offence.

Examples 41 and 42
(41) *One flatmate to another.*
You've fucked up the vacuum cleaner again Rob.

(42) *Customer to shop assistant.*
This material is complete rubbish.

These are clearly face-threatening speech acts and so one would expect to find them used more by men than by women. It is also likely, given the gender differences identified in the use of directives mentioned above, that women would mitigate or hedge their complaints more than men. A second type of complaint involves a much less face-threatening speech act, however. General complaints about life, the weather, the state of the economy, and so on, invite agreement or commiseration rather than acting as face-threatening acts.

Examples 43–46
(43) This wind is driving me mad.

(44) This is the worst summer I can remember.

(45) More job losses. It's so depressing.

(46) This weather is just appalling.

These are essentially phatic in function and could be regarded as positively polite speech acts: they seek common ground and areas of agreement; they are attempts to establish rapport and solidarity. So, one might expect these more general phatic complaints to be used more often by women than men.

Criticisms or expressions of disapproval are another area where gender differences are likely to be apparent. D'Amico-Reisner (1983: 111–12) noted that imperative forms and rhetorical forms increased the force of expressions of disapproval, and that both tended to occur more often in intimate exchanges.

Examples 47–49
From D'Amico-Reisner (1983: 110–11).
(47) What do you mean 'that's not true'?

(48) How can you say that?

(49) It's too loud. Turn it down huh?

She also noted that longer exchanges were more likely to develop into altercations. She does not, however, explore differences in women's and men's use of disapproval expressions. As with directives and complaints, one would expect men to use more explicit and strongly expressed expressions of disapproval, while women would be likely to use fewer, and would be more likely to mitigate them. An American study based on criticisms in role plays provides some support for this view (Tracy and Eisenberg 1991), though there are methodological problems which mean the results cannot be confidently generalised.

Direct expressions of disapproval tend to occur almost exclusively with intimates or with strangers in service encounters, a pattern which, it is interesting to note, inverts Wolfson's bulge model. Refusals follow the same pattern. It is interesting to note that refusals are most elaborated and negotiated with friends and acquaintances, most brief and direct with intimates and strangers (Beebe and Cummings 1985). This suggests that positive politeness speech acts tend to be used most to friends and acquaintances, in ambiguous or uncertain relationships which need nurturing, while negatively affective speech acts, such as criticisms and refusals, will be used least in such relationships; and when they do occur they will be most mitigated and hedged. In other words, friends are the group that people make most interactional effort with.

But does this pattern hold for both women and men? It would be very interesting, given the different patterns of female and male apologies, to explore these patterns further with speech acts such as complaints, criticisms and refusals, speech acts which are quite clearly 'impolite' face-threatening acts. I suspect that with appropriate modifications, Wolfson's bulge model may account better for women's speech behaviour than for men's in this area too.

The gender of addressees – the people to whom speech acts are addressed – is also an important consideration in studying the distribution and form of different speech acts, as the patterns for compliments and apologies have suggested (see also Brouwer et al. 1979; Zimin 1981; Brouwer 1982). Johnson and Roen's study of compliments in peer review underlines this. They noted that about equal numbers of women and men writing peer reviews tended to pair a directive or a criticism with a positive evaluation or compliment (1992: 46). But this pairing, which mitigates the negative effect of the criticism or directive, was used much more often to women than men. And, in fact, men never used this softening, or hedging strategy to other men. In this context it was clearly possible to interpret the compliment as a patronising pat on the back, rather than as a negative politeness device mitigating the face-threatening act. Possibly male writers of the reviews saw this interpretation as most likely when male recipients were involved, and so men avoided using this strategy to other men. Women perhaps were judged more likely to accept the compliment as a positive politeness token. So the gender of the recipient of a speech act is another factor which needs to be considered when investigating differences in the politeness norms of women and men.

The discussion in this chapter has made it clear that the classification of speech acts as face-threatening acts, or as negative or positive politeness devices, is not a straightforward matter. The way a speech act is interpreted will depend on its use in context. The analysis has also suggested that women and men may interpret what appear to be the 'same' speech acts differently. It seems reasonable to interpret the agreeing responses discussed in Chapter 2 as welcome and positively polite speech acts, and the bald disagreements as less positive speech acts. But the analysis in Chapter 4 suggested that compliments, which would appear to be clearly positively polite speech acts, may in fact be interpreted as face-threatening or patronising by some. And the discussion of apologies in this chapter has suggested that apologies, which appear to be clearly mitigating negatively polite acts, may in fact serve as positively polite tokens of solidarity between women. In the final chapter, then, when we examine the implications of the politeness patterns discussed in this book, it will be important to bear in mind that the interpretation of patterns, and especially the explanation of patterns, may be complex. Attempts to generalise force one towards simplification, and this is useful when exploring the implications of the data. But it is important to remember that the richness of the data itself constantly reasserts the complexity of human interaction whenever one returns to examine any particular exchange in depth.

Note '

1. A more detailed analysis of all the material in this chapter is provided in Holmes 1989d and 1990b.

6 Why politeness matters

Patterns of politeness

Example 1

Last week my colleague Chris brought a young woman to see me for some academic advice. Chris brought her into the room and she immediately sat down, even before he had finished explaining why she was there. Some years ago my instinctive reaction would have been:

> That feels rather rude – she should wait to be invited to sit. Sitting down implies I am willing to see her now and that I will devote some time to her problem.

This reaction would have reflected a misunderstanding of the politeness norms that Tufaina was using. As a Samoan, she sat down out of respect not rudeness. I was sitting down so she could not politely stand, since she would then have been higher than me. Samoan politeness required that she reduce her height to be lower than me.

What is considered polite behaviour varies from one culture to another. As example 1 illustrates, what is polite for one group may seem rude to another (see also Wierzbicka 1985; García 1989; Kasper 1990). What is polite for one group may seem unbearably tedious to another cultural group, and may appear embarrassing or jaw-breakingly formal to yet another. Politeness is culturally determined. In this book I have suggested that what is considered polite linguistic behaviour may differ even within one cultural and social group – middle-class Pakeha New Zealanders – if they belong to different genders.

We have seen a range of evidence that New Zealand women tend to be more verbally polite than New Zealand men. In general, women are more orientated to affective, interpersonal meanings than men. Women give more encouraging verbal feedback to their conversational partners than men do, and they disruptively interrupt others less often. Women ask questions and introduce topics aimed at maintaining talk that is of interest to others in informal and private interactions. In public where the floor is more highly valued, they participate much less, and more often leave the floor to men. Women use pragmatic particles in ways that are 'other-orientated' more often than men. Women agree with others, compliment others, and apologise more often than men, demonstrating sensitivity to the feelings of other people, and using these speech acts as tokens of solidarity.

New Zealand men's norms of interaction are clearly different from New Zealand women's. Men seem to be more concerned with the referential functions of talk than with its affective functions. In private interactions with female partners, they tend to make less effort than the women to maintain or sustain conversation. But their verbal patterns are different in public. The social meaning of language to which they are most responsive is the public, status-orientated aspect of interaction. Getting and keeping the floor in public is one means of asserting a claim to status. Men agree with others less often than women, and they are more likely than women to disagree without softening their assertions. Pragmatic particles are used more often by men to indicate the validity of a proposition, for example, than to signal the relationship between the speaker and addressee. The focus is often on information rather than feelings. They give fewer compliments and apologies than women, and seem to experience compliments with mixed feelings. Accepting a compliment can be seen as incurring a social debt. Similarly, giving an apology is an admission of inadequacy; apologisers put themselves one down in the status hierarchy. This may explain why men use these speech acts less frequently than women, especially to other men.

What are the implications of these gender differences in norms of interaction? How do these different preferred patterns of interaction affect women's and men's potential contributions in different contexts?

Women as social models of politeness?

Example 2
· Mrs Godley, an early New Zealand settler, believed in the
civilising influence of women.
> 'When two young men she knew were about to take up a
> sheep station in Canterbury in 1852, she warned them that
> they would become "semi-barbarous". She begged them to
> have a "lay figure of a lady, carefully draped, set up in their
> usual sitting-room, and always behave before it as if it were
> their mother".'
>
> (Bassett et al. 1985: 67)

One obvious implication of the patterns identified in previous
chapters is that what society calls polite linguistic behaviour is
largely based on women's norms of interaction. Being linguistically polite involves using language in a way that reflects
consideration for others. Positively polite behaviour expresses
friendliness; negatively polite behaviour expresses respect.
Consideration for the feelings of others has been the hallmark of
every aspect of women's verbal behaviour which has been
examined. It would appear, then, that despite their lack of social
power, women have considerable social influence: their linguistic
behaviour determines the overt and publicly recognised norms of
polite verbal interaction in the community.

Unfortunately, though this is true, to assess its real significance
it needs to be considered in context. Women's norms are
accepted as defining polite behaviour – but in a relatively limited
sphere. Since men are the power brokers in society, it is men who
determine what this sphere will be. Men consider explicitly polite
linguistic behaviour to be appropriate in a rather limited range of
relationships. It is appropriate to superiors and in the limited
semi-private contexts of social interaction between acquaintances
and people who are friends but not intimates – the 'bulge' area of
ambiguous relationships described by Wolfson's (1988) model. In
general, men appear to feel politeness is dispensable between
intimates in private. They are often reluctant and sometimes
ungracious conversationalists in the home. In some public spheres
too, men seem to regard polite behaviour as unnecessary –
especially between apparent status equals. In many semi-formal
contexts such as debates, meetings and seminars, competition for

the floor is considered more appropriate than polite facilitative turn-taking, for example. And men tend to focus on the referential meaning of interaction, and its potential for enhancing status, rather than on the effects of their language on the feelings of others. Compliments and apologies are kept to a minimum, as are other face supportive speech acts. This is the sphere of the middle-class working man, and it is not a place for unnecessary verbal 'frippery'.

Men's perceptions of politeness

Example 3
Middle-aged man commenting on his wife's complaints that he never expresses appreciation.
I don't see why she needs to be told that she looks good or that the meal was OK. If I don't complain, that implies things are fine.

Redundant verbal frippery seems to be how linguistic politeness is regarded by many men. It is icing on the cake, unnecessary in contexts where 'real' interaction takes place. Polite verbal interaction is based on women's talk, and it has a very limited place in the male public sphere. It is not that men cannot do it. Rather, it seems that most of the time they choose not to. Men seem to have different norms from women concerning situations where polite behaviour is appropriate. In particular, men appear to assess the need for positive politeness quite differently from women, though some men recognise that it is important to most women. The positively polite other-orientated talk that characterises women's interactions is used by men trying to 'pick up' or impress a new woman. It is also used by men who genuinely want to develop, sustain and nurture an intimate relationship.

Example 4
Young man commenting on his girlfriend's parents.
I try to be really polite to her parents. They're so stiff with me and she gets upset if I treat them too casually.

But it is apparently not valued by most men. SNAGs (Sensitive New Age Guys) are still a decided minority and even they tend to confine their sensitivity to a narrow range of contexts. Polite behaviour is acceptable in contexts where nothing important is happening (in men's perception). It has no place when important decisions are to be made.

Politeness in personal relationships

> **Example 5**
> *Claire comments on her son's painting.*
> Claire: He's made a good job of that wall hasn't he.
> Bob: Yes the paint's covered well.

Claire's tag question is affective in intention. It is designed to elicit some praise for their son from her husband, Bob. Bob responds only to the referential content and ignores the invitation to provide a compliment.

Is being polite simply an interpersonal matter then? Whether you treat someone politely or not is likely to influence their perception of you, including their inferences about your education and socialisation. It will also affect your relationship with them. Your politeness behaviour will affect whether you are perceived as being friendly or stand-offish, considerate or over-attentive, respectful or disdainful. Negatively polite behaviour expresses consideration and respect, and may be used to establish a particular degree of social distance. Positive politeness expresses appreciation and good will, and may be used to initiate and maintain a friendship. So the most obvious implications of research on politeness and gender might appear to be in the area of personal relationships, especially between women and men. If women and men use hedges and boosters for somewhat different functions, for instance if they have different preferred politeness strategies, this is likely to result in miscommunication.

> **Example 6**
> *Helen has recently arrived home from work.*
> Helen: what a day/ I never seemed to get a moment to myself/
>   you know//   constant interruptions
> Brian: why don't you get your secretary to protect you/ that's
>   what she's there for isn't it?
> Helen: mm/ well I suppose these people really do need to see me
>   you know // it's just just that there were so many today
> Brian: you should make appointments/ make them make an

appointment/   who do they think they are/ just waltzing
up / expecting you to be available just like that
Helen: no no/ it's not like that love//   anyway it's not really a
problem//   it's just it's just that I don't seem to have got
much done today/ I'm just feeling a bit frustrated/ you
know

Brian focuses on the content or referential meaning of Helen's utterances. He identifies her problem and makes two different suggestions for solving it. He takes a task-orientated approach to the conversation. Helen is seeking sympathy, not advice, as she indicates by her use of the pragmatically appealing use of *you know*. Her focus is the affective meaning of the interaction. She uses attenuating forms like *just* and *a bit* to reduce the force of her complaint, and positive politeness devices such as the address form *love* to appeal to her partner. By contrast, Brian uses directive language such as *you should* and *why don't you*, and a challenging tag *isn't it* to underline the force of his logic. The result is frustrating for both. Brian's attempts to assist do not get the appreciation he feels they deserve. Helen does not get the sympathy and understanding she is seeking. Tannen's book *You Just Don't Understand* (1990a) provides many similar examples.

But while it is true that different interactional norms can result in communication problems in private and intimate interactions, such problems could be considered relatively minor compared to those caused by the overt disvaluing of women's politeness norms in public spheres. It is possible for most interpersonal communication problems between couples to be resolved, as Deborah Tannen (1990a) has argued, with good will and a willingness to learn on both sides. The problem is that such conditions are not always present, and in public contexts they most certainly cannot be assumed. Public contexts are traditionally male contexts and the rules of interaction are male rules. Most men believe that there is no reason for them to play by women's rules.

In this chapter I will argue that there are two major costs involved when society adopts or endorses this view of verbal politeness. First, there is an equity issue. Women are often treated in ways they find uncomfortable and demeaning, and they frequently get a poor deal in terms of access to important and influential forums. Secondly, society is losing out on a valuable interactional resource. What is generally labelled, often rather dismissively, as politeness, has the potential for improving camaraderie, communication and cognition. Linguistic interaction which follows women's norms can result in better working relationships, better understanding of complex issues and better decision-making. What many men dismiss as 'mere' politeness, is in fact a set of valuable interactional skills which can be used very productively in the workplace. And the effects will be beneficial to all on a range of important dimensions.

So there is a great deal of point in extending women's norms for polite behaviour into more public contexts. I will illustrate this by discussing just two contexts in some detail, namely, language in the classroom and peer talk between professionals.

Being polite in class

The benefits of talking time

> Example 7
> Sometimes I feel like saying that I disagree, that there are other ways of looking at it, but where would that get me? My teacher thinks I'm showing off, and the boys jeer. But if I pretend I don't understand, it's very different. The teacher is sympathetic and the boys are helpful. They really respond if they can show YOU how it is done, but there's nothing but 'aggro' if you give any signs of showing THEM how it is done (Kathy, aged sixteen, Inner London comprehensive).
>
> (Spender 1980b: 150)

One of the most obvious reasons for being polite in the classroom is simply to give girls and women a fairer deal. Getting a fair share of the talking time and the teacher's attention is a particular problem for females in mixed-sex classrooms at all levels. But ensuring that your intentions are accurately expressed and interpreted is equally important for both genders, especially in a context such as the classroom where misunderstandings may have serious implications.

Chapter 2 demonstrated that men tend to dominate the talking time in a range of contexts. There is extensive evidence that this pattern can be observed in western classrooms at primary, secondary and tertiary level (e.g. Karp and Yoels 1976; Safilios-Rothschild 1979; Spender 1979, 1980a, 1980b, 1982; Gass and Varonis 1988; de Bie 1987; Stanworth 1987; Weiner and Arnot 1987; Swann 1989, 1992; Madhok 1992). There is also evidence that participants do not perceive this interactional pattern very accurately (Spender 1979, 1982; Edelsky 1981; Whyte 1986; Graddol and Swann 1989). Dale Spender (1982), for instance, notes that teachers who tried to restore the balance by deliberately 'favouring' the girls, were astounded to find that even so they had continued to devote more time to the boys in their classrooms (see also Stanworth 1983). Conversely, Whyte (1986: 196) reports that one male science teacher who managed to create an atmosphere in which girls and boys contributed more equally to discussion, felt that he was devoting 90 per cent of his attention to the girls. Female students are generally not getting their fair share of the talking time. They are too polite. Males dominate mixed-sex classrooms, and male patterns of interaction, interruption and contradiction are consequently pervasive.

But the issue is more than a matter of equity. The organisation of western classrooms is based on the assumption that classroom talk is educationally beneficial to students. Opportunities to answer the teacher's questions and receive evaluative feedback, to ask the teacher for information and clarification, and to discuss material and issues with other students – these are all regarded as important educational strategies, each of which contributes to learning and understanding. If females are denied equal access to these learning resources, they are being educationally disadvantaged. Going further, Michelle Stanworth (1987: 208) points out, on the basis of extensive interviews with teachers and sixth forms students, the ways in which these patterns can lead to negative academic outcomes – for the girls.

> When boys are more outspoken and manifestly confident – and especially when teachers take more notice of boys – pupils tend to see this as evidence that boys are more capable, and more highly valued, than girls.

A vicious circle of lower expectations by both pupils and teachers is all too easily established on the flimsy basis of who talks most in class. There are serious potential consequences of the talking time imbalances which have been documented in so many mixed-sex classrooms.

Second-language learners have additional reason to feel that their progress depends to a considerable extent on access to the floor and to the teacher's attention. Most language teachers believe students benefit from using the second language as often as they can. The classroom is frequently the major context for this practice. In some contexts, the teacher may be the sole source of learners' linguistic input in the second language. But even more commonly the teacher is the only person who can politely and routinely correct learners' errors. So opportunities to practice speaking the second language in the classroom are particularly valuable. Yet research in second-language classrooms reveals the same male-dominated patterns as have been observed in native-speaking contexts. Female language learners are not getting as many opportunities for monitored practice as male learners.

In an Australian study, for instance, adult male learners of English from a range of language and cultural backgrounds answered more of the teachers' questions, made more unsolicited comments, and asked the teachers more questions than the women students (Munro 1986). The teachers reinforced this male-dominated pattern by specifically asking the men more questions. And, in small-group interactions, men took nearly twice as many 'long turns' on average as women, as example 8 illustrates (Munro 1987: Appendix).

Example 8

Small group discussion.

Woman 1: if your mother die she already old/ she got cancer/what
⌈can you do/ understand?
Woman 2: ⌊   mm
Woman 1: you still thinking I don't like my mother die . . .
Man: yes you feel depressed but no in such great –
Woman 1: yeah
Man: you feel depressed but not as you you have cancer or
something like that/ something you know/ you can't do
⌈anything you start to think/ not about yourself
Woman 1: ⌊   mm

```
Man:        ⌈because that's the thing     that's the thing/ . . .
Woman 1:    ⌊                  mm
Man:         you just you think about the family/ about the wife and
            ⌈children/            how they will cope that thing
Woman 1:    ⌊       yes  yes mm
Woman 2:    ⌈ mmh
Woman 1:    ⌊    for the future you see
Man:         that is the thing and need continues for many many days
            ⌈until you die   like I saybefore/maybe
Woman 1:    ⌊           mm
Man:         you don't die from the sickness/ maybe you die from//
Woman 1:    ⌈from the stress
Man:        ⌊            from the stress/ because maybe
            you got cancer you die from from the heart
```

Patterns like these where males dominate the talk suggest female students are being systematically denied opportunities to practice using the second language in the classroom. As a result, it seems likely that their oral skills may suffer. It is also possible that their understanding of complex issues that would benefit from discussion may be impaired (see Holmes 1987, 1989b, 1989c).

The evidence reviewed and presented in Chapter 2 also suggested that men disruptively interrupt other speakers more often than women, and in informal interaction they tend to provide less encouraging positive feedback than women do. Women disagreed 'politely', modifying and qualifying their disagreeing assertions, but men were much more likely to disagree baldly. Bald contradictions and challenges from both women and men certainly occur in lively arguments between native speakers who know each other well, as illustrated in example 9.

Example 9
Three young people who share a flat together talking over dinner.
Tim: I don't see why you have to write your OWN lyrics
Sal: nobody sits down and watches a performer on stage and
        thinks – gee – well he wrote this
Brian: yes they do – yes they do
Sal: you think they DO?
Brian: yeah I think they do
Sal: pardon ME but I don't think they DO

Brian: if a guy gets up on stage or a girl gets up on stage and
they play a song THEY'VE written you know that they
MEAN it
Tim: yes but – but (*unintelligible*)
Sal: oh look – but no look – but that doesn't mean a THING
the other way round / just because a singer hasn't written
that song . . . I think it's the way they PERFORM it
Brian: no – but it's second-hand – it's second-hand would you
rather have a second-hand car or a new car?
Tim: it's not / but they can still MEAN the words of the song
(Stubbe 1978: Appendix)

Throughout this exchange the participants, female and male,
contradict and challenge each other's claims: e.g. 'yes they do –
yes they do', 'pardon ME but I don't think they DO', 'that
doesn't mean a THING' and so on. This style of interaction also
characterises some cultural groups more than others (e.g. Scollon
and Scollon 1981; Tannen 1990a). But such direct disagreement
strategies are not usually appropriate between students in class.
They inhibit some female learners and discourage them from
contributing freely to the discussion.

So it is females who lose out. Their polite way of participating in classroom talk means they are disadvantaged in mixed-
sex classrooms. If there is competition for the floor, interruption
can be an effective strategy for gaining it. The female student
who considers it rude to interrupt another speaker will be less
likely to gain opportunities to contribute. In mixed-sex small
group interaction, she will be providing plenty of encouragement
to others to contribute, but is likely to be receiving less than her
fair share of encouraging feedback in return. Once again the
educational implications are obvious. Most teachers believe that
talk is an important learning strategy, and that discussion aids
students in their attempts to understand and integrate new
material (e.g. Barnes and Todd 1977; Cazden 1987). Interaction
strategies used by males which inhibit these processes are
disadvantaging the females. Boys need to acquire different talk
strategies if girls are not to be disadvantaged in classrooms.

The evidence discussed in Chapter 2 suggested that the
patterns which disadvantage girls were not so evident in the
interactions of younger children, nor in pair interactions, as
opposed to full class and small group discussions between native

speakers (Cheshire and Jenkins 1991; Stubbe 1991). They seem to develop as children approach adolescence. Nor were they so apparent in the science practical classes analysed by Randall (1987), where teachers addressed boys and girls almost equally often, and girls initiated contact with the teacher more often than boys. This suggests that classroom interaction can be a positive experience for both females and males, but it requires some management to achieve this. I will return to this point towards the end of this chapter.

Asking good questions

A similar argument can be made for the value of questions or elicitations in the classroom. In Chapter 2, I discussed evidence first that males tended to ask more questions than females in public contexts, and secondly that men were more likely than women to ask confrontational questions. Similar patterns have been identified in classrooms. Males generally ask more questions than females, and their questions are frequently closed and task-orientated, rather than facilitative and open-ended (Munro 1986; Holmes 1989b; Gilbert 1990, 1991; Jenkins and Cheshire 1990).

Educationists have argued that asking questions gives considerable control over both the structure and the content of an interaction (Barnes et al. 1969; Sinclair and Coulthard 1975; Barnes 1976; Stubbs 1976; Heath 1982). The form and length of responses to questions, for instance, can be influenced by the type of question asked.

Example 10
Primary school classroom.
Teacher: who was the bird that had a big tail that helped him to
       fly
Pupil: uh, oh, a fantail
Teacher: a fantail/ good

The teacher's question restricts the form of the response. The pupils are required to produce a short noun phrase in response. As described in Chapter 2, it is often useful to distinguish between response-restricting and facilitative or supportive questions, according to their function in context. The teacher's question in example 10 is a clear instance of a response-restricting question. The teacher is not inviting pupils to think, or draw on their personal experience, but only to recall facts which have been provided in an earlier lesson. Females tend to use more facilitative or supportive questions than males, opening up discussion and encouraging others to participate. Males use more 'organising' questions or questions that restrict responses to short, factual statements.

The effect of response-restricting questions in the contexts in which they were asked was to close off and stifle discussion. They give the impression that the questioner is not concerned to explore an issue in order to better understand it, but wants a short and very specific answer so that he can proceed to the next stage of the task. A predominance of this type of question will not encourage discussion, and nor will it generate more talk so that language learners can practice using the target language.

Polite interaction strategies in the classroom can benefit all pupils. The strategies which females use most are strategies which encourage others to contribute to the discussion and generate exploratory talk, the kind of talk advocated by educationists as most beneficial to learning (Barnes 1976; Barnes and Todd 1977; Marland 1977; Atkin 1978; Cazden 1987). This no doubt explains, at least in part, the well-attested finding that student participation is generally higher in women teachers' classes (see, for example, Treichler and Kramarae 1983). Exploratory talk is cognitively valuable as a means of coming to grips with new concepts and integrating them with existing knowledge – one obvious function of classroom talk. While males tend to ask more information-specific, closed questions, which do not encourage participants to open up a topic, females tend to ask more questions which invite the addressee to relate material to their own experience. This assists 'engaged learning' and under-standing, since it helps the learner integrate the new material with familiar material (Thorne 1989: 316).

The implications of such patterns in the second-language learning classroom are also obvious. Second-language learners need practice in a wide range of conversational skills, including the ability to ask questions which will generate more talk and assist their understanding. They need to know how to initiate conversations and solicit responses so that the conversational burden is not always on others, as in the following example.

Example 11
Middle-aged woman to overseas visitor at a welcoming social event.

Native speaker:	How long have you been in New Zealand?
Second-language learner:	I here three weeks
Native speaker:	Have you been outside Wellington yet?
Second-language learner:	No
Native speaker:	Have you visited the National Art Gallery.
Second-language learner:	No
Native speaker:	There's a good exhibition on there at the moment. Well worth a visit.
Second-language learner:	Oh. Thank you

This second language learner needs practice in adding comments to his monosyllabic responses in order to develop the conversation. He needs to take some initiatives instead of leaving the burden of the conversation on the native speaker (see Holmes and Brown 1976). The research evidence suggests that females and males do not get equal opportunities to obtain this practice.

Expressing yourself politely in class

Example 12
Teacher: This is going well Beth. You've got some good ideas here.
Beth: Thank you. I found the material you gave us to read very helpful. It was very stimulating.
Teacher: That's good. You could develop this section further I think.

When we consider other aspects of politeness in the classroom context, it is much more difficult to be confident about the precise implications of gender differences. The fact that women tend to express both positive and negative politeness more often and more explicitly than men, no doubt affects teachers' responses to pupils, as well as vice versa. People generally tend to respond well to praise, respect and appreciation, and to polite behaviour as opposed to lack of consideration for their feelings. There is evidence that boys attract both more praise and more blame than girls from teachers (Brophy and Good 1974; Dweck et al. 1978), and it is interesting to speculate on the effects in terms of pupil performance. Teachers no doubt treat pupils better if they are appreciative. Pupils' reactions to each other are doubtless affected by the different politeness norms of females and males. But the precise implications of appreciative, facilitative and positive responses, as opposed to confrontational and challenging behaviour from students in classrooms remain largely unexplored.

The implications of the differential use of hedges and boosters by females and males is another area where further work is needed. If girls use pragmatic particles as ways of expressing positive politeness more often than boys do, while boys use them to express referential epistemic meaning more than girls do, there is abundant scope for misunderstanding and misperception of intentions. Different usage patterns may lead to a perception of one gender as too tentative or too precise, over-simple or over-dogmatic, by teachers of the opposite gender. The gender-based differences in patterns of use of hedges and boosters, which were discussed in Chapter 3, suggest that there is plenty of room for potential misinterpretation between females and males in the classroom. Students obviously need to know the role of qualification and cautious hedging where appropriate. They must be able to recognise when clarity and precision is required in expressing information, as in example 13.

Example 13
Lawyer: And had the heart not been functioning, in other words, had the heart been stopped, there would have been no blood to have come from that region?
Witness B: It may leak down depending on the position of the body after death. But the presence of blood in the alveoli indicates that some active respiratory action had to take place.

(O'Barr and Atkins 1980: 98–9)

In other contexts qualifications are appropriate, together with an indication that nothing can be asserted with great precision.

Example 14
Lawyer: And you saw, you observed what?
Witness C: Well, after I heard – I can't really, I can't definitely state whether the brakes or the lights came first, but I

rotated my head slightly to the right, and looked directly
behind Mr Z, and I saw reflections of lights.

(O'Barr and Atkins 1980: 99)

All these skills involve control of the pragmatic particles which
function as hedges and boosters. Carli's (1990) studies suggest
that in certain contexts mitigation is an effective rhetorical device
in discussion. Female speakers were better able to change male
opinions when they spoke tentatively. Boys may suffer from the
fact that female teachers in particular perceive their politeness
behaviour and their control of pragmatic particles as less
competent, for instance, than that of girls.

If girls generally pay more compliments, give more praise and
take more account of others' feelings than boys, classrooms with
female students are likely to be better learning environments, as
well as pleasanter places to work. Those interacting with female
pupils may feel more appreciated and comfortable, since it seems
likely their face needs will receive more attention. Whether this is
the case, however, is largely unresearched at present.

Teachers' responses to pupils are also likely to be influenced
by gender. The gender of the teacher is the most obvious variable
– one would expect female teachers to provide more praise,
encouraging feedback and agreeing responses than male. But the
gender of the addressee is another factor to consider. Two
small-scale investigations of teacher's responses to pupils in
primary classrooms noted that girls tended to receive more
explicit positive evaluations or compliments on their performance
than the boys, who received more criticism (de Bie 1987; Duijm
1987). Criticism of the girls was only ever implicit while boys
received both implicit and explicit criticism. The implications of
such patterns for students' performance is an obvious area for
further research.

In the second-language classroom there are rather different
implications to be explored. Knowing 'how to do things with
words' (Austin 1962) is an important aspect of learning a
language. Language learners need information on gender-differ-
entiated patterns of language use, so that they can accurately
interpret the social meaning of what they hear, as well as being
able to produce socially appropriate linguistic behaviour if they
so choose (see Holmes 1987, 1989c).

Language learners need to be informed about gender-appropriate ways of using pragmatic particles, and the ways women and men use speech acts such as compliments and apologies. If the data discussed in this book proves generalisable, then there are clear implications for what learners of English need to know about the politeness norms of women and men in English-speaking communities (Holmes 1989c). Women learning English may offend by failing to provide compliments in some contexts. If a woman has her hair cut, for instance, and her friend fails to comment, the absence of a compliment will almost certainly be interpreted as tacit dislike or disapproval of the new style. Men may embarrass others by providing too many compliments, or they may compliment other men inappropriately. A male student, from Micronesia, for instance, who complimented a New Zealand male lecturer on his suit left the lecturer feeling distinctly discomfited. While this student might not wish to alter his behaviour, he has the right to know the likely effect it may induce (see Thomas 1983). Failing to apologise to a woman is likely to cause greater offence than overlooking the need to apologise to a man. And space offences seem to be particularly salient for women, so the absence of an apology for bumping into a woman may be considered very rude or threatening. Apologies between males may be more dispensable. A young Indonesian man who apologised profusely and frequently for his English was regarded as over-doing it by his male New Zealand friends.

Information on gender-based patterns of politeness can assist students acculturate to the speech community whose language they are leaning. Learners need to develop sensitivity to the social norms and values of the target community so that they can make appropriate decisions about the way to use language in the community. Socio-pragmatic information on the way women and men use pragmatic particles and particular speech acts can empower the learner and protect them from unknowingly giving offence. As Thomas (1983: 96) says:

> It is the teacher's job to equip the student to express her/himself in exactly the way s/he chooses to do so – rudely, tactfully, or in an elaborate polite manner. What we want to prevent is her/his being *unintentionally* rude or subservient.

In the educational context, then, there are a variety of implications of the politeness behaviour reviewed in this book. First, there is an equity issue. Female students deserve to be treated more considerately than tends to be the norm in mixed-sex classrooms. Secondly, there are the educational implications of unfair treatment. If learning depends on access to the floor, and on thorough discussion of issues in a supportive environment, then females in mixed-sex classrooms are disadvantaged – with possible cognitive consequences for their grasp of the material. And, thirdly, there is the more specific issue of the importance of providing language learners with information on politeness norms – including gender differentiated patterns of interaction – so that they can draw on this knowledge when they interact with native speakers.

What about interaction in professional contexts? What are the implications of the patterns identified for women and men at work?

Peer interaction in professional contexts

Until relatively recently, women have been largely excluded from public arenas. The public world has been predominantly a male domain; a woman's place was in the home (Hall 1985: 12). As a result, the discourse styles which are felt to be appropriate in public contexts have been established by men (Coates 1993b). The evidence presented in earlier chapters has suggested that male styles are generally referentially or information orientated rather than focused on social or affective meaning. They tend to be concerned with status enhancement rather than with establishing interpersonal relationships, and they are often competitive or adversarial rather than supportive and facilitative.

In Chapter 2, I discussed New Zealand evidence that men tend to dominate the discussion in formal settings such as seminars and lecture presentations. Evidence from elsewhere confirms that this pattern is a widespread one: in seminars (Swacker 1979; Bashiruddin et al. 1990), committee meetings (Eakins and Eakins 1979; Edelsky 1981), mock jury deliberations (Strodtbeck and Mann 1956) and television debates (Franken 1983; Edelsky and Adams 1990), men contribute more often than women, and their contributions are generally longer.

Similarly, the patterns identified in the New Zealand data for interruptions (men tend to disruptively interrupt more than women) and encouraging feedback (women give more than men) have also been noted in the United States of America and Britain. One American study, for instance, compared the regular interactions of female and male managers of comparable status over a fifteen-week period. An analysis of a randomly selected sample of these interactions showed that the male managers interrupted more than the female managers (70 per cent versus 30 per cent), and that the men were generally more aggressive and competitive conversationalists (Schick Case 1988).

These patterns of interaction have obvious implications in the workplace. Of particular relevance are studies which show that these gender-based patterns tend to override status variables, so that even when a woman is in a higher status position or more powerful role, she is likely to be interrupted by a lower status man more often than she interrupts him. As discussed in Chapter 2, it has been found that female doctors were interrupted by their male patients more often than they interrupted them. And subordinate males interrupted higher status females in other work situations more than they did their male counterparts (Woods 1989).

If these patterns are typical, then women in the workplace are not getting a fair deal. They are being treated differently from men of equivalent status and qualifications. One might argue, using a more democratic ideal, that men should be treated with less deference, rather than women with more. But, accepting current norms, it is clear that women in professional jobs which attract respect when men occupy them, are not being treated in ways appropriate to their status. Further evidence comes from a British company which encouraged women into management positions, and which had four women and four men in the eight most highly paid of these positions. But the managing director commented that he had noted how the men were often patronising to the women, and tended to dominate meetings.

> I had a meeting with a [female] sales manager and three of my [male] directors once . . . it took about two hours. She only spoke once and one of my fellow directors cut across her and said 'What A is trying to say Roger . . .' and I think that about sums

it up. He knew better than A what she was trying to say, and she never got anything said.

(Graddol and Swann 1989: 181–2)

These examples refer to women in high status jobs. Most women in the workplace are in subordinate and relatively power-less roles. This suggests that it is most unlikely that they are getting a fair opportunity to contribute to discussion and decision-making. They are unlikely to be getting a fair share of the talking time; they are likely to be interrupted more often than men; and in interactions with a predominantly male group they will get little encouragement to contribute.

The implications of the data on the numbers and types of questions asked by women and men in formal discussions are equally discouraging. Women are not receiving or taking equal opportunities to contribute. But in addition to the equity issue, there is also the loss of valuable and potentially different input to be considered. Women's contributions to discussion are often expressed in ways which encourage others to participate. The devices which characterise women's talk invite others to join in. Women tend to use more qualified statements and participatory linguistic devices such as facilitative questions, supportive elicit-ations and pragmatic particles such as *you know*, than men do. And when they disagree they generally do so politely – in other words, they use a qualified disagreeing utterance rather than a bald contradiction. These are features which generate more exploratory talk of a kind likely to be useful in the discussion of ideas and issues.

Exploratory talk allows people to develop their ideas through the joint negotiation of meaning (Barnes 1976: 28). As mentioned above, this kind of talk is cognitively valuable as a means of coming to grips with new concepts and integrating them with existing knowledge. It is also valuable as a means of thinking through the implications of proposals on which decisions for future action can be based. As such it is the professed goal of many formal and informal meetings in the workplace between colleagues. Because board rooms and workbased meetings among professionals tend to be dominated by male talk, it is generally male ways of interacting which predominate. Challenges, bald disagreements and disruptive interruptions, for instance, are patterns of talk that have been described as typical of males interacting in groups (e.g. Barnes and Todd 1977: 72; Goodwin 1980; Gilbert 1990; Kuiper 1991; Tannen 1990b). How functional are they in meetings aimed at exploring issues and ideas?

Aggressively negative questioning generally leads people to take up entrenched positions – especially in a public debate. Those attacked often respond defensively, and little progress is made in exploring the issues and ideas proposed. Bald disagreements and overt challenges rarely encourage further discussion and exploration of the area of disagreement. Rather, they set up a confrontational structure with the speakers as opponents. Within this kind of framework there is little room for a beneficial exploration of the issues. High-quality exploratory interaction is essentially collaborative, and successful collaboration is based on the use of facilitative devices such as soliciting contributions from others, providing supportive feedback, extending others' contributions and disagreeing in a non-confrontational manner (Barnes and Todd 1977).

There are good grounds then for suggesting that the quality of a discussion is likely to improve when women get a more equal share of the talking time. The interactive strategies which are typically found in the talk of women appear to be the kinds of strategies which encourage high quality exploratory talk, which elicit constructive ideas and encourage the exploration of proposals. Good exploratory talk is characterised by non-threatening, open-ended elicitations which encourage participants to explore the implications of their statements, to support them with explicit argumentation, and to elaborate their reasons for holding a particular position. The issues are more fully explored, arguments are more explicitly justified, and participants' level of understanding of the issues increases. The result will inevitably be a better thought-through outcome.

Interactions which involve women are often more enjoyable too. Staff relations generally benefit when women are involved. Because women encourage others to contribute to the conversation, and respond positively to the contributions of others, participants find them satisfying. Carole Edelsky (1981: 416) noted, for instance, in her analysis of departmental meetings, that the sections of the discussion where women contributed more were those which participants generally found most enjoyable and communicatively satisfying. These were sections Edelsky describes as consisting of a jointly constructed or 'collaborative floor', a 'more informal cooperative venture' than the male-controlled monologues with which they contrasted (1981: 416).

While analysing contributions to formal seminars I too noted evidence that the level of involvement and interest rose as women's participation increased. Two notable instances involved presentations by young women in contexts where women formed a majority of the audience. During the discussion in these seminars exactly the kind of 'shared floor' that Edelsky describes developed, resulting in an enjoyable and intellectually stimulating discussion in both cases. The participants moved from addressing questions to the presenter to responding to each other's comments. The result was a lively and very productive exploration of the topic. And it was fun. Edelsky comments similarly that in the meetings she analysed this type of 'high involvement, synergistic, solidarity building interaction' provided a 'high level of communicative satisfaction' (1981: 416–17), which both men and women enjoyed. So linguistic interaction which follows women's norms can result in better understanding of complex issues, more informed decision-making and better working relationships. By ensuring that all participants are involved, and are given an opportunity to contribute, this kind of interaction makes better use of resources, and it can make work more satisfying and even more fun for all involved.

Politeness strategies in the workplace

If women's positively polite facilitative strategies for interaction can improve the workplace, what effects will their ways of using polite speech acts have? Patterns of politeness developed in more personal interactions and private contexts do not always transfer smoothly to public domains and to interactions in the workplace more generally.

Although they may be effective strategies in private discussion (Carli 1990), hedges, apologies and mitigated directives are often regarded as inappropriate in public speaking. They can give the impression that the speaker is weak and ineffectual. Intensifiers and compliments can lead to a perception of the speaker as over-enthusiastic, over-personal and lacking the distance and dignity appropriate to a formal or public context. In other words, women's patterns of politeness are often dismissed as inappropriate in public formal domains. The evidence reviewed in Chapters 4 and 5 suggested that women pay compliments and offer apologies more often than men do. Such patterns may seem irrelevant in the workplace where the assumption is that social interaction is secondary, and transactional interactions and referential meaning appropriately predominate.

But such assumptions are surely sexist. Showing consideration for the feelings of others in a work context may be regarded as superfluous, or unnecessary and a waste of time by many men, but most women regard verbal politeness as very important. The assumption that affective or social meaning is irrelevant or unimportant in business is also ethnocentric, as those who have compared ways of conducting business in different cultures testify (see Hofstede 1984; Kasper 1990). Other cultures, like many western women, value verbal politeness as a component in business transactions. Women's and men's patterns of exchanging compliments and apologies in the workplace appear to follow the general patterns described in Chapters 4 and 5. In other words, women give and receive more compliments and apologies than men overall, and the fewest compliments and apologies are exchanged between men. When these social exchanges are labelled irrelevant and dismissed as a waste of time, it is apparent that male rather than female norms are dominant. Nelson (1988: 220) quotes a graduate teaching assistant contrasting the male-dominated competitive ethos of the large corporation with the collaborative ethos of the largely female university research teams she had been trained in:

> The corporation emphasises only negative aspects of performance, but we female teachers have been used to stressing the positive first. Our emphasis has always been on what students do right to help students build on what they do well.

It is certainly arguable that business will be conducted more efficiently and successfully if participants feel comfortable and appreciated. And this is far more likely when female politeness norms prevail.

Good social relations are as important in the professional world as in more personal contexts, though this has not always been overtly recognised. Increasingly, however, the fact that cooperative and facilitative discourse styles can be highly functional in a range of professional contexts is gaining recognition. Schick Case (1988: 59) argues, for instance, that both male and female styles of interaction are needed by modern multinational companies. They serve useful and complementary roles in terms of the company's interests.

> The growth of information in our society involves increased inter-action and communication. Having both the feminine and masculine style represented in administrative roles could help increase organizational effectiveness. By including both voices in organizational decision making, problems will be seen in new ways.

The British company mentioned above takes the same view. The company encourages women into management positions because they want to introduce what they call more 'feminine' styles of management alongside the standard masculine approaches (Graddol and Swann 1989: 181). Women's interpersonal skills are increasingly in demand.

There is a growing body of research demonstrating the effectiveness of women's more cooperative styles of discourse in a range of professional domains – medical, care-giving, management, and educational (West 1990; Ainsworth-Vaughn 1992; Coates 1993b; Troemel-Ploetz 1992). These studies show not only that women's interaction strategies are as acceptable as men's in these professional contexts, but also that, measured by the criteria of desirable outcomes, they are often more effective than male strategies. Candace West (1990) demonstrated, for example, that women doctors used more mitigated or hedged directives to their patients while males tended to use 'aggravated' directives (that is directives which explicitly establish status differences). Women doctors tended to negotiate topic changes with patients while male doctors were much more likely to unilaterally change topic (Ainsworth-Vaughn 1992). Interestingly, women doctors were also more likely to receive a compliant response 'with better outcomes for patients', as Coates points out (1993b).

Troemel-Ploetz (1992) identifies a range of discourse strategies used by higher status to lower status females in formal discussion and interviews which reduced inequalities and emphasised solidarity. She describes how high status women attenuate criticisms and avoid reproach, on the one hand, while giving compliments and appreciations on the other (see also Tracy and Eisenberg 1991). They provide support for others' contributions using lots of positive minimal feedback, and they seek areas of agreement rather than conflict. They do not hog the talking time, and they skilfully link their utterances to those of lower status women with joins and repetitions, so giving them conversational support. She suggests these strategies are beneficial in a range of professional contexts such as journalism, management and psychotherapy. Journalists with such skills elicit better quality material in interviews. Managers with these skills avoid confrontation and achieve their goals more quickly and efficiently (Meyerhoff 1992c). Psychotherapists using these politeness strategies enable their clients to better accept and integrate material that is difficult to deal with (Troemel-Ploetz 1992).

Women's interpersonal skills involve decoding and integrating a wide range of disparate types of information. They learn to be sensitive to and respond to both referential and affective meaning, for example. Because of their situation of relative powerlessness in the society as a whole, they have learnt communication skills which have helped them survive. As Dale Spender points out:

> Women have had a greater need for information, a greater need to anticipate danger, to manage situations, to steer hostility, anger, and threats to constructive ends . . . it isn't surprising that they have acquired skills (1992: 552).

She goes on to argue that these kinds of skills are precisely those which will be of value in the 'information revolution' which is currently in progress. 'Women are highly experienced when it comes to the world view that is going to predominate in the information era', she claims (1992: 556). Their ability to manage a range of variables, and to read messages at several levels, to 'juggle multiple realities and forge meaning from them' – these are skills which will stand women in good stead in the technologies of the twenty-first century.

In the light of such research, it is difficult to be convinced by claims that the simple, direct and even confrontational style favoured by many men is the most effective style in many contexts. Schick Case characterised the style of the male managers in her study as 'impersonal authority-oriented speech' using 'competitive and confrontational devices like imperative construction [sic], proof from authority and interruptions to get one's point heard' (1988: 56). They attempted to 'assert status and establish dominance in interpersonal situations. They were more direct, informational, and action-oriented' (Schick Case 1991: 6, cited in Spender 1993). It is hard to believe that such a style will be effective in most interpersonal interactions.

Some men with whom I have debated these issues claim that the combative, challenging, argumentative style associated with men is necessary for intellectual progress. Challenge and criticism, the argument goes, lead a proponent of a theory to further elaborate and develop it. The point is a debatable one. For some – and perhaps especially for some women – a collaborative, cooperative environment may serve this purpose best. Nelson (1988) describes the collaborative interactive patterns of mainly female teacher research teams in Washington, DC. Transcripts of their interactions show not only reciprocity and cooperativeness, but also what Miller (1976) calls 'productive conflict', that is conflict which is beneficial to all participants, as opposed to conflict which results in one winner and many losers. This is consistent with the evidence on the cognitive benefits of exploratory talk which is characterised by a questioning, open-ended, collaborative approach to problem-solving as described above. There is plenty of evidence, then, to suggest that on average females are much better than males at providing a favourable context for the kind of talk which is likely to lead to better understanding and cognitive progress (Nelson 1988; Schick Case 1988; Gilbert 1991) Certainly, Sadker and Sadker (1985) found that classes taught by teachers trained to eliminate bias towards male pupils had a higher level of intellectual discussion. This is one interesting indication of how to proceed if we want to change things.

Strategies for change

I have discussed some of the implications for public and semi-formal contexts, such as classrooms and professional interactions, of the different politeness patterns which tend to characterise female and male behaviour. In this section I will focus on how one might change things. What kinds of strategies could be adopted to ensure that girls in mixed-sex classrooms do not lose out? What steps might be taken to encourage women to participate fully in professional contexts?

Changes will obviously benefit women. In general, women do not get their fair share of the talking time in educational, public and professional contexts. They do not get as much encouragement to contribute to talk in these contexts as men receive from women. In mixed-sex public contexts, women's face needs do not receive as much attention as men's do. This means women have less access to potentially status enhancing talk than men, and they are not encouraged to seek more. It also means the resulting talk does not benefit as much as it could from women's input, and the evidence suggests that such benefits may be considerable.

There are at least three ways of addressing the issue of increasing female participation in mixed-sex classrooms and professional contexts. They differ in the degree of direct control the women involved need to take. First, an attempt can be made to raise the consciousnesses of all those participating. Secondly, teachers and trainers can explicitly teach males the skills they lack – especially in the area of positive politeness – which contribute to women's low involvement in interaction. Thirdly, women can take greater control in public situations and ensure that they and other women get an opportunity to contribute.

Consciousness-raising

Some researchers argue that the reason that women and men use different interaction strategies is that they belong to different cultural groups (Maltz and Borker 1982; Tannen 1987, 1990a). Consciousness raising concerning the different cultural politeness norms of each gender should therefore reduce communication problems. If women and men only understood each other's different rules for speaking, it is argued, all would be well.

There is plenty of evidence that girls and boys develop different ways of interacting and different patterns of linguistic politeness in childhood and adolescence. So it is not surprising that, once they reach adulthood, problems of communication often arise between women and men. Make people more aware of gender differences in ways of communicating, Deborah Tannen suggests (1990a: 297–8), and they will voluntarily change their ways:

> understanding genderlects improves relationships. Once people realize their partners have different conversational styles, they are inclined to accept differences without blaming themselves, their partners, or their relationships. . . . Understanding the other's ways of talking is a giant leap across the communication gap between women and men, and a giant step towards opening lines of communication.

Given some understanding of the different communication patterns which women and men typically use, it seems possible that with mutual tolerance individual private cross-sex miscommunications between couples who are committed to each other's happiness can be resolved. It is an appealing argument, and Tannen illustrates it well with interesting and entertaining anecdotes of success stories. No doubt it describes what is possible for some well-disposed couples, but on the whole I think this solution is probably over-optimistic. Most of the world is not like that.

Many interaction problems are the result of structured inequality in the society. Power is the issue. As Henley and Kramarae say (1991: 27),

> Greater social power gives men the right to pay less attention to, or discount, women's protests, the right to be less adept at interpreting their communications than women are at men's, the right to believe women are inscrutable.

In fact, the problem goes further than this. Women's ways of talking differ from men's because each group has developed interaction strategies which reflect their societal position. The different patterns of interaction into which girls and boys are socialised are not randomly different. Their features are attuned to the requirements of the society. They are determined by the power structure. Women are socialised to be polite: this means being negatively polite in public – not intruding or imposing oneself – and being positively polite in private – taking responsibility for the interaction and ensuring that others are conversationally comfortable.

So if consciousness-raising is to be effective in the wider community, it needs to be backed up by power or authority. Thorne (1989) recommends, for example, that teachers should explicitly focus on inequities in patterns of talk and ways of interacting, and draw them to the attention of the participants. This allows groups to address the problem of providing all participants with an opportunity to express their ideas and contribute to the decisions made. With the backing of the teacher's authority, it has been demonstrated that changes can be achieved (Whyte 1984, 1986; Sadker and Sadker 1985; de Bie 1987; Swann 1992). Graddol and Swann (1989) document strategies for linguistic intervention which have been successfully adopted in Britain in a variety of contexts to redress gender imbalances. One of the case studies they describe was a project developed by a Birmingham schoolteacher, Jackie Hughes, which was aimed at challenging racist and sexist stereotypes. Her aims included 'to facilitate respectful and creative interaction . . . between pupils and staff' (Graddol and Swann 1989: 185). They comment (1989: 186–7):

> Jackie Hughes found that in small discussion groups it was relatively easy to intervene: the composition of groups could be chosen so that they weren't dominated by more talkative pupils; it was also possible to discuss with small groups why some pupils might find it difficult to contribute. Whole class discussion was more difficult to change, but again involving the pupils themselves in a discussion of classroom talk seemed to make them more sensitive and aware of others' needs.

This suggests that consciousness-raising may be effective in encouraging participants to share the talking time, to refrain from disruptively interrupting, and to respond positively and facilitatively to contributions from others, when it is backed up by someone with status and power whom participants have an incentive to please.

Changing the men

Example 15
'I'm waiting for a leader to establish himself so I can go for his throat' said one male participant in the discussion.
(Schick Case 1988: 51)

Because of the way power is distributed in the society, the politeness norms and the patterns of interaction I have described in public formal settings appear to benefit men more than women. It would seem to be most obviously in women's interests rather than men's to initiate change in public settings. But, as I have suggested, this perception is misleading. The benefits to women are mainly in terms of status enhancement, while the potential costs for men and for the relevant group are less thorough understanding of issues, less cognitive progress, and less enjoyment of the interactive process itself. Nevertheless, it may take some time to effectively change these patterns since the costs I have identified are not transparent.

In less formal and public interactions, on the other hand, the evidence I have reviewed suggests that women's patterns of politeness are increasingly being recognised as more effective than men's in terms of the stated objectives of the interaction. In classrooms, small group discussion is often used specifically in order to increase understanding of material, or to encourage pupils to explore an issue thoroughly. In second-language classrooms, practice in using the target language is an obvious goal of classroom talk. In more professional transactions, identifying and meeting the clients' needs is the most obvious objective. The professional must be, above all, other-orientated. In all these situations, the facilitative, supportive, and considerate politeness strategies typical of female talk have been shown to be more effective. How can men be assisted to acquire them?

Since many males appear to lack the ability to use relevant politeness strategies and interactive skills in classrooms and professional transactions, it clearly behoves teachers and trainers to help them acquire these skills, and encourage them to use them in these contexts. Consciousness-raising is one strategy, but, in addition, many males need explicit practice in enhancing their conversational competence so that discussion can be a more effective as well as a pleasanter experience for both the men and their conversational partners.

On the basis of the research reviewed in this book, polite, effective communicators have skills such as the following:

- they are responsive, active listeners, giving support and encouragement to their conversational partners;
- they agree and confirm points made by their partners, elaborating and developing their partner's points from their own experience;
- they disagree in a non-confrontational manner, using modified rather than direct disagreeing assertions;
- they ask facilitative questions which encourage others to contribute to the discussion;
- they use pragmatic particles which make others feel included;
- they compliment others and express appreciation frequently;
- they readily apologise for offences, including interruptions and talking too much;
- they attenuate or mitigate the force of potentially face-threatening acts such as directives, refusals, and criticisms.

Teachers and trainers can use exercises designed to encourage males to practise these skills. There is also a strong case for arguing that this practice should be undertaken initially in all-male groups so that females do not act as guinea pigs to help males acquire skills the females already possess (cf. Johnson and Goldman 1977; Cheshire and Jenkins 1991; Jenkins and Cheshire 1990).

Men will almost certainly find that polite interaction is actually more rewarding. Their understanding of issues will improve. Better decisions will be the outcome of more thorough discussion, and the process will generally be more pleasant for all involved. Nelson (1988: 202) quotes a male teaching assistant who describes how much he enjoyed working in the warm supportive environment provided by his female colleagues. And other men have also reported that they enjoyed small group and one-to-one interactions with women more than with men (e.g. Aries 1976, 1982; Jenkins and Kramer 1978). So, in addition to improvements in their ability to interact effectively in small groups and with clients, males may well find that their inter-actions are more enjoyable.

But there is often no obvious incentive for males to give up highly valued talking time in more formal or public contexts. Why should they encourage others to contribute when there is limited time to make an impact? Why should they respond positively and politely when it is cut-throat tactics which are most admired by others in such contexts? Raised consciousnesses are certainly not enough to alter politeness patterns in contexts where males are in control, and where the rules of interaction are based on male norms. Even well-intentioned males will not succeed in sharing valued talking time without some assistance (or even insistence) from women (Spender 1980b; Coates 1993a) – though a firm chairperson who is concerned to share out speaking turns, can make a difference (Whyte 1984, 1986; Appelman et al. 1987). Until a change occurs, moreover, the potential benefits will not be obvious. So the improved quality of discussion which can result from women's participation cannot act as an incentive for men to change their behaviour until women succeed in obtaining more of the talking time. This can only be a persuasive argument once the current male-dominated interaction patterns change, and more talking time has been effectively claimed and used by women. Consequently, women who want more of this talking time (and some may not) need to devise strategies to ensure they get it.

Taking the initiative

A third way to effect change, then, is for women to take active steps to ensure their politeness norms are taken into account so that women's participation in public contexts increases. There are a number of sources of practical suggestions for increasing women's share of talking time in public formal contexts (Whyte 1984, 1986; Appelman et al. 1987; Thorne 1989; Bashiruddin et al. 1990; Cooks and Hale 1992; Holmes 1992b; Madhok 1992). In general, these suggestions do not involve adopting male strategies, but rather require some preparation in advance, and willingness to take initiatives as opportunities arise.

Strategies for participants

• Women who want to make a contribution in a particular context can cooperate with other women and organise in advance to ensure they get some talking time. So, for example, if a woman knows before a seminar or meeting that she has a point she wishes to contribute, she can tell the chairperson before the meeting starts that she wishes to speak. She can also ensure that other participants know too, so that they can assist in passing the floor to her when she wants it. It is useful to talk in advance with other women to find out whether they also wish to contribute, and to agree on a strategy for passing the speaking rights to another woman once one has spoken.

- Women who wish to contribute during the progress of a discussion should indicate this to the chairperson immediately and very clearly.
- In some cases women will be aware that a colleague or friend could make a useful contribution to a discussion. This is another case where it would be useful to pass the speaking rights to her, giving her a clear indication about the reason for doing so.
- Women can usefully express appreciation for others' points and especially point out the value and implications of good points raised by other women. This will encourage women to contribute more, while modelling for men the use of appropriate positive politeness strategies in more public or formal contexts.
- Women should ensure they do not give up the floor before they have finished their contributions. They can politely point out to potential interrupters that they have not yet completed their point.

Strategies for organisers, chairpersons, trainers and teachers

For those with responsibility for organising public formal talk there are further strategies which can be used to ensure greater access to talking time for females, and better quality discussion.

- Programmes can be organised to ensure women get an equal share of the 'official' talk and that they are used as experts as often as men: chairing sessions, presenting papers, and so on. In addition to being desirable in its own right, this will also encourage women participants to contribute from the floor (Holmes 1988c; Holmes and Stubbe 1992).

- Organisers can actively encourage women to attend meetings and seminars. A larger proportion of women present at a meeting generally leads to greater female participation in the discussion.
- Teachers and seminar organisers can select topics and themes of interest to women and ones where women specialists and experts exist. This too will encourage women to contribute to the discussion.
- It is often useful to provide opportunities for small group discussion as preparation for a full session discussion of issues. This procedure encourages exploratory talk and provides an opportunity for females to gain confidence in expressing their views in a less threatening context. They are then more likely to contribute in the full session.
- A person who is directing or organising activities (teacher, trainer, chairperson) can ensure that females get their fair share of the contributions. It is useful to monitor the behaviour of organisers if they are working towards increasing women's participation and providing females with opportunities to contribute. As mentioned above, impressions can be very misleading in this area.
- It is sometimes possible for a chairperson or director of activities in public or formal contexts to draw participants' attention to strategies that disrupt or inhibit the contributions of females. A disruptive interrupter can be prevented from taking the floor, for example. Bald unsupported disagreements can be politely challenged.
- A chairperson, teacher, trainer or director of activities has the opportunity to comment positively and appreciatively on contributions. This can be used to good effect to encourage female contributors.

The case for more involvement of women in public formal contexts can be made simply on equity grounds. Women are entitled to their fair share of the talking time, and it is reasonable that they should be treated politely in public and formal contexts. The case is strengthened by the fact that participation in such contexts is generally socially valued and has the potential to increase the speaker's standing in the eyes of others. Public talking time increases a person's visibility. Being treated respectfully and considerately in such contexts increases one's mana. Women should be encouraged to participate in forums where their contributions and responses to them may enhance their social status.

Women's polite ways of interacting are undoubtedly experienced positively by both women and men. Most people enjoy talking with a facilitative and encouraging listener far more than being talked at by an aggressive competitive critic. No one likes being interrupted. Most enjoy the opportunity to contribute to a discussion, and people respond well to feedback indicating that others are listening and following what is being said. Most people welcome appreciative remarks, and they can have a positive effect in classrooms and the workplace. While females typically provide this kind of supportive interactional environment for males, they experience it much less often from males, especially in public.

Such equity arguments are fine in principle. In practice, however, those in power are unlikely to change their interaction patterns and adopt more considerate strategies unless they can see some obvious benefits for themselves. It is here that the qualitative benefits of increasing female participation in public and formal speech contexts are relevant. If women's contributions in public forums and meetings are communicatively effective, then such strategies should have the long-term effect of ensuring women's views are sought. In other words, if women's contributions demonstrably improve the quality of the discussion, and people's enjoyment of the interaction, they will be welcomed and encouraged. These benefits should appeal to those concerned with better understanding of issues, fuller exploration of ideas, and better based decision-making. Men who subscribe to such ideals will ensure women get the opportunity to contribute to public discussion. In the meantime, women will almost certainly need to use self-help strategies in order to give men the opportunity to experience those benefits for themselves.

Conclusion

At the end of the first chapter I made the point that the generalisations I would make in this book would be based largely on data collected from middle-class New Zealand women and men who belong to the mainstream culture. The politeness patterns of women from other cultures and social groups cannot be assumed to be the same, though where research elsewhere suggests parallels I have pointed these out. In concluding the book I should add another caveat or two. Those who wish to challenge the claims I have made concerning women's other-orientated approach to interaction may well point to the Margaret Thatchers and Ruth Richardsons (New Zealand's recent Minister of Finance) of this world. The abrasive, challenging, antagonistic speech style adopted by some successful women politicians and business women is certainly not consistent with the patterns outlined in this book. There is no denying that these women have not only adopted masculine styles of public debate, but that they usually equal and often out-do men in challenging, disagreeing with and interrupting their interviewers. They do not conform to female norms. Indeed Margaret Thatcher's interview style has been the focus of linguistic analysis (Beattie 1983). These women are noticeable precisely because they are so different. They are the exceptions. The fact that not all women conform to the patterns outlined in this book does not mean such patterns do not exist.

I am not even suggesting that most women are 'talented, kind, responsible and misunderstood, and are waiting to use their subtle skills for the good of the world' as Dale Spender (1993: 551) so nicely puts it. Nor that all men are unresponsive and taciturn in private, and combative and aggressive in public. There are plenty of individual counter-examples. But the overall patterns are compelling. And, in my view, it is these patterns and their implications which deserve attention.

In considering the implications of politeness research in this chapter, I have focused on more public and formal contexts. These are the contexts where women are most transparently at a disadvantage. This is where we see the effects of limited opportunities for girls in mixed-sex classrooms, and the evidence of systematic discrimination against women in the workplace. It is clearly in the interests of males to define appropriate behaviour in public and formal domains, so that male ways of interacting are accepted as the norm.

But this is not always the case in private interactions. When young people talk at length on the telephone, for example, certain features of the verbal behaviour of some young men more closely resemble the female politeness norms outlined in this book than the male norms. I have observed both my teenage sons now over a period of many years, and I have checked my observations with a range of other middle-class Pakeha parents. These young people spend many happy hours on the telephone to their friends. My teenage son, David, is undoubtedly a very good listener to the young women who call him regularly. He provides lots of encouraging and agreeing responses, and he contributes to their topics with enthusiasm. His older brother, Robbie, has long and intimate conversations (which he refuses to allow me to record!) with his steady girlfriend. As Alice Freed (1992 : 149) points out, these are 'girls and boys talking to each other intimately and with delight and comfort' (usually at their parents' expense, I might add). When a male (even a New Zealand male) is wooing a female, he will adopt strategies which bear a remarkable resemblance to the politeness norms outlined as typical of females in this book. He will listen with attention, seek topics of interest to the woman, encourage her to talk, and even pay her compliments. So some men can certainly be positively polite when they perceive it to be in their interests to do so. I have suggested that it is in everyone's interests that they do so more often, and in a wider range of contexts. I have also suggested some strategies which will help to address the issue in more public and formal contexts.

For it is in these contexts that the social distribution of power generally means that women's polite patterns of interaction are unlikely to predominate. As a result everyone loses out. Women do not get their fair share of talk in contexts which are status enhancing, and so they miss out on the potential social benefits of effective public talk. In some contexts, women's opportunities to explore and talk through the implications of ideas and issues are also reduced. They thus lose out on the opportunity to increase their grasp of a problem or their comprehension of an issue. Discussions which are less antagonistic and confrontational, and more exploratory are generally of better quality and more intellectually beneficial to all involved. So by not adopting women's politeness patterns, others may lose out in this respect too. What has been called 'polite' language in this book, has also proved to be cognitively beneficial language. Linguistic politeness contributes to better understanding, and may assist people to reach better decisions. Finally, interactions which involve the use of positive politeness strategies are generally pleasant and enjoyable experiences. Being polite makes others feel good. There are many sound reasons, then, for recognising the value of polite speech.

References

Ainsworth-Vaughn, Nancy (1992) Topic transitions in physician–patient interviews: power, gender and discourse change. *Language in Society* 21, 3: 409–26.

Allan, Scott (1990) The rise of New Zealand intonation. In Allan Bell and Janet Holmes (eds) *New Zealand Ways of Speaking English*. Clevedon, Avon: Multilingual Matters, pp. 115–28.

Andersen, Elaine Slosberg (1989) *Speaking with Style: the Sociolinguistic Skills of Children*. London: Routledge.

Appelman, Sonja, Anke Heijerman, Monic van Puljenbroek and Karin Schreuder (1987) How to take the floor without being floored. In Dédé Brouwer and Dorian de Haan (eds) *Women's Language, Socialisation and Self-Image*. Dordrecht: Foris, pp. 163–75.

Apte, Mahadev L. (1974) 'Thank you' and South Asian languages: a comparative sociolinguistic study. *Linguistics* 136: 67–89.

Arbini, R. (1969) Tag-questions and tag-imperatives in English. *Journal of Linguistics* 5: 205–14.

Aries, Elizabeth (1976) Interaction patterns and themes of male, female and mixed groups. *Small Group Behaviour* 7, 1:7–18.

Aries, Elizabeth J. (1982) Verbal and non-verbal behaviour in single-sex and mixed-sex groups; are traditional sex roles changing? *Psychological Reports* 51: 127–34.

Aries, Elizabeth J. (1987) Gender and communication. In Phillip Shaver and Clyde Hendrick (eds) *Sex and Gender*. Newbury Park, Cal.: Sage, pp. 149–76.

Armagost, J.L. (1972) English declarative tags, intonation tags and tag questions. *Studies in Linguistics and Language Learning*, Vol. 10. Seattle, Wash.: University of Washington Press, pp. 1–53.

Atkin, J. (1978) Talk in the infant classroom. *English in Education* 12, 2: 10–14.

Atkinson, J. (1984) Wrapped words: poetry and politics among the Wana of Central Sulawesi, Indonesia. In D. Brenneis and F. Myers (eds) *Dangerous Words: Language and Politics in the Pacific*. New York: New York University Press, pp. 33–68.

Austin, J.L. (1961) A plea for excuses. In J.O. Urmson and G.J. Warnock (eds) *Philosophical Papers*, 3rd edn, 1979. Oxford: Oxford University Press, pp. 175–204.

Austin, J.L. (1962) *How to Do Things with Words*. Cambridge, Mass.: Harvard University Press.

Austin, Paddy (1988) The Dark Side of Politeness: a Pragmatic Analysis of Non-Cooperative Communication. Unpublished PhD Dissertation. Christchurch: University of Canterbury.

Austin, Paddy (1990) Politeness revisited: the dark side. In Allan Bell and Janet Holmes (eds) *New Zealand Ways of Speaking English*. Clevedon, Avon: Multilingual Matters, pp. 276–95.

Azman, Azura (1986) Malaysian students' compliment responses. Unpublished terms paper. Wellington: Victoria University of Wellington.

Baird, John E. and Patricia H. Bradley (1979) Styles of management and communication: a comparative study of men and women. *Communication Monographs* 46: 101–11.

Barnes, Douglas (1976) *From Communication to Curriculum*. Harmondsworth: Penguin.

Barnes, Douglas, James Britton and Harold Rosen (1969) (revised edn 1971) *Language the Learner and the School*. Harmondsworth: Penguin.

Barnes, Douglas and Frankie Todd (1977) *Communication and Learning in Small Groups*. London: Routledge and Kegan Paul.

Bashiruddin, Ayesha, Julian Edge and Elizabeth Hughes-Pélégrin (1990) Who speaks in seminars? Status, culture and gender at Durham University. In Romy Clark, Norman Fairclough, Roz Ivanic, Nicki McLeod, Jenny Thomas and Paul Meara (eds) *Language and Power*. London: Centre for Information on Language Teaching, pp. 74–84.

Bassett, Judith, Keith Sinclair and Marcia Stenson (1985) *The Story of New Zealand*. Auckland: Reed Methuen.

Baumann, Marie (1979) Two features of 'women's speech'. In Betty-Lou Dubois and Isobel M. Crouch (eds) *The Sociology of the Languages of American Women*. San Antonio, Tex.: Trinity University Press, pp. 32–40.

Beattie, Geoffrey, W. (1981) Interruption in conversational inter-action and its relation to the sex and status of the interactants. *Linguistics* 19: 15–35.

Beattie, Geoffrey (1983) *Talk: An Analysis of Speech and Non-Verbal Behaviour in Conversation*. Milton Keynes: Open University Press.

Beebe, Leslie and M. Cummings (1985) Speech act performance: a function of the data collection procedure? Paper presented at TESOL '85, New York.

Bell, Allan (1984) Language style as audience design. *Language in Society* 13, 2: 145–204.

Bell, Allan (1990) Audience and referee design in New Zealand media language. In Allan Bell and Janet Holmes (eds) *New Zealand Ways of Speaking English*. Clevedon, Avon: Multilingual Matters, pp. 165–94.

Bernstein, Basil (1962) Social class, linguistic codes and grammatical elements. *Language and Speech* 5: 221–40.

Bilous, Frances R. and Robert M. Krauss (1988) Dominance and accommodation in the conversational behaviours of same- and mixed-gender dyads. *Language and Communication* 8, 3/4: 183–94.

Blum-Kulka, Shoshana and Elite Olshtain (1984) Requests and apologies: a cross-cultural study of speech act realisation patterns (CCSARP). *Applied Linguistics* 5, 3: 196–213.

Blum-Kulka, Shoshana, Brenda Danet and Rimona Gherson (1985) The language of requesting in Israeli society. In Joseph P. Forgas (ed.) *Language and Social Situations*. New York: Springer-Verlag, 113–39.

Boe, S. Kathryn (1987) Language as an expression of caring in women. *Anthropological Linguistics* 29, 3: 271–85.

Braun, Friederike (1988) *Terms of Address: Problems of Patterns and Usage in Various Languages and Cultures*. Berlin: Mouton de Gruyter.

Britain, David (1992) Linguistic change in intonation: the use of High Rising Terminals in New Zealand English. *Language Variation and Change* 4, 1: 77–104.

Brooks, Virginia R. (1982) Sex differences in student dominance behaviour in female and male professors' classrooms. *Sex Roles* 8: 683–90.

Brophy, Jere E. and Good, Thomas L. (1974) *Teacher-Student Relationships: Causes and Consequences*. New York: Holt, Rinehart and Winston.

Brouwer, Dédé (1982) The influence of the addressee's sex on politeness in language use. *Linguistics* 20: 697–711.

Brouwer, Dédé (1989) *Gender Variation in Dutch: A Sociolinguistic Study of Amsterdam Speech*. Dordrecht: Foris.

Brouwer, Dédé, Marinel Gerritsen and Dorian De Haan (1979) Speech differences between women and men: on the wrong track? *Language in Society* 8, 1: 33–50.

Brown, Gillian (1977) *Listening to Spoken English*. London: Longman.

Brown, Penelope (1980) How and why are women more polite: some evidence from a Mayan community. In Sally McConnell-Ginet, Ruth Borker and Nellie Furman (eds) *Women and Language in Literature and Society*. New York: Praeger, pp. 111–36.

Brown, Penelope (1990) Gender, politeness, and confrontation in Tenejapa. *Discourse Processes* 13: 123–41.

Brown, Roger and Marguerite Ford (1961) Address in American English. *Journal of Abnormal and Social Psychology* 62: 375–85.

Brown, Roger and Albert Gilman (1960) The pronouns of power and solidarity. In T. A. Sebeok (ed.) *Style in Language*. Cambridge, Mass.: MIT Press, pp. 253–76.

Brown, Penelope and Stephen Levinson (1987) *Politeness: Some Universals in Language Usage*. Cambridge: Cambridge University Press.

Buffery, A.W.H. and J. Gray (1972) Sex-differences in the development of spatial and linguistic skills. In C. Ounsted and D.C. Taylor (eds) *Gender Differences: their Ontogeny and Significance*. Edinburgh: Churchill Livingstone.

Byrnes, Heidi (1986) Interactional style in German and American conversations. *Text* 6, 2: 189–206.

Cameron, Deborah (1985). *Feminism and Linguistic Theory*. 2nd edn, 1992. London: Macmillan.

Cameron, Deborah, Fiona McAlinden and Kathy O'Leary (1989) Lakoff in context. In Jennifer Coates and Deborah Cameron (eds) *Women in Their Speech Communities*. London: Longman, pp. 74–93.

Carli, Linda L. (1990) Gender, language and influence. *Journal of Personality and Social Psychology* 59, 5: 941–51.

Cattell, Ray (1973) Negative transportation and tag questions. *Language* 49, 3: 612–39.

Cazden, Courtney (1987) Relationships between talking and learning in classroom interaction. In B.K. Das (ed.) *Patterns of Classroom Interaction in Southeast Asia*. Regional English Language Centre Anthology Series, No. 19. Singapore: SEAMEO Regional Language Center.

Chambers, J.C. (1992) Linguistic correlates of gender and sex. *English World-Wide* 13, 2: 173–218.

Cheshire, Jenny (1981) Variation in the use of *ain't* in an urban British English dialect. *Language in Society* 10: 365–81.

Cheshire, Jenny (1982) Linguistic variation and social function. In S. Romaine (ed.) *Sociolinguistic Variation in Speech Communities*. London: Edward Arnold, pp. 153–66.

Cheshire, Jenny (1989) Addressee-oriented features in spoken discourse. *York Papers in Linguistics* 13: 49–63.

Cheshire, Jenny and Nancy Jenkins (1991) Gender issues in the GCSE oral English examination: part 2. *Language and Education* 5, 1: 1–22.

Ching, M. (1982) The question intonation in assertions. *American Speech* 57: 95–107.

Chodorow, Nancy (1974) Family structure and feminine personality. In M.Z. Rosaldo and L. Lamphere (eds) *Woman, Culture and Society.* Stanford: Stanford University Press, pp. 39–59.

Coates, Jennifer (1986) *Women, Men and Language.* London: Longman.

Coates, Jennifer (1987) Epistemic modality and spoken discourse. *Transactions of the Philological Society,* pp. 110–31.

Coates, Jennifer (1989) Gossip revisited: language in all-female groups. In Jennifer Coates and Deborah Cameron (eds) *Women in their Speech Communities.* London: Longman, pp. 94–121.

Coates, Jennifer (1991) Women's cooperative talk: a new kind of conversational duet? In Claus Uhlig and Rüdiger Zimmermann (eds) *Proceedings of the Anglistentag 1990 Marburg.* Tübingen: Max Niermeyer Verlag.

Coates, Jennifer (1993a) *Women, Men and Language.* 2nd edn. London: Longman.

Coates, Jennifer (1993b) The language of the professions: discourse and career. In Julia Evetts (ed.) *Women and Career.* London: Longman.

Coates, Jennifer and Deborah Cameron (eds) (1989) *Women in their Speech Communities.* London: Longman.

Cohen, A. and E. Olshtain (1981) Developing a measure of socio-cultural competence: the case of apology. *Language Learning* 31, 1: 113–34.

Cooks, Leda M. and Claudia L. Hale (1992) A feminist approach to the empowerment of women mediators. *Discourse and Society* 3, 3: 288–300.

Coulmas, Florian (1981) 'Poison to your soul.' Thanks and apologies contrastively viewed. In Florian Coulmas (ed.) *Conversational Routine.* The Hague: Mouton, pp. 69–91.

Crosby, F. and L. Nyquist (1977) The female register: an empirical study of Lakoff's hypotheses. *Language in Society* 6, 3: 313–22.

Cruttenden, A. (1986) *Intonation.* Cambridge: Cambridge University Press.

Crystal, David and Derek Davy (1975) *Advanced Conversational English.* London: Longman.

D'Amico-Reisner, Lynne (1983) An analysis of the surface structure of disapproval exchanges. In Nessa Wolfson and Elliot Judd (eds) *Sociolinguistics and Language Acquisition.* Rowley, Mass.: Newbury House, pp. 103–15.

de Bie, Marloes L.W. (1987) Classroom interaction: survival of the fittest. In Dédé Brouwer and Dorian de Haan (eds) *Women's Language, Socialisation and Self-Image.* Dordrecht: Foris, pp. 76–88.

Deuchar, Margaret (1988) A pragmatic account of women's use of standard speech. In Jennifer Coates and Deborah Cameron (eds) *Women in their Speech Communities.* London: Longman, pp. 27–32.

DeFrancisco, Victoria L. (1991) The sounds of silence: how men silence women in marital relations. *Discourse and Society* 2, 4: 413–23.

Dindia, Kathryn (1987) The effects of sex of subject and sex of partner on interruptions. *Human Communication Research* 13, 3: 345–71.

Dubois, Betty Lou and Isobel Crouch (1975) The question of tag questions in women's speech: they don't really use more of them, do they? *Language in Society* 4: 289–94.

Dundes, Alan, Jerry W. Leach and Bora Özkök (1972) The strategy of Turkish boys' verbal dueling rhymes. In John J. Gumperz and Dell Hymes (eds) *Directions in Sociolinguistics*. New York: Holt Rinehart and Winston, pp. 130–60.

Duijm, Klaartje (1987) Learning to 'be' at school: authority and warmth in the classroom. In Dédé Brouwer and Dorian de Haan (eds) *Women's Language, Socialisation and Self-image*. Dordrecht: Foris, pp. 89–113.

Dweck, Carol S., William Davidson, Sharon Nelson and Bradley Enna (1978) The contingencies of evaluative feedback in the classroom. *Developmental Psychology* 14: 268–76.

Eakins, Barbara and Gene Eakins (1979) Verbal turn-taking and exchanges in faculty dialogue. In Betty-Lou Dubois and Isobel Crouch (eds) *The Sociology of the Languages of American Women*. San Antonio, Tex.: Trinity University, pp. 53–62.

Eckert, Penelope (1989) The whole woman: sex and gender differences in variation. *Language Variation and Change* 1: 245–68.

Eckert, Penelope (1990) Cooperative competition in adolescent 'girl talk'. *Discourse Processes* 13: 91–122.

Edelsky, Carole (1981) Who's got the floor? *Language in Society* 10: 383–421.

Edelsky, Carole and Adams, Karen (1990) Creating inequality: breaking the rules in debates. *Journal of Language and Social Psychology* 9, 3: 171–90.

Eder, Donna (1990) Serious and playful disputes: variation in conflict talk among female adolescents. In Allen D. Grimshaw (ed.) *Conflict Talk: Sociolinguistics Investigations of Arguments in Conversations*. Cambridge: Cambridge University Press, pp. 67–84.

Edmondson W.J. (1981) On saying you're sorry. In Florian Coulmas (ed.) *Conversational Routine*. The Hague: Mouton, pp. 273–88

Ervin-Tripp, Susan, Mary Catherine O'Connor and Jarrett Rosenberg (1984) Language and power in the family. In Cheris Kramarae, Muriel Schulz and William O'Barr (eds) *Language and Power*. New York: Sage, pp. 116–35.

Fishman, Pamela M. (1978) Interaction: the work women do. *Social Problems* 25, 4: 397–406. Revised version in Barrie Thorne, Cheris

Kramarae and Nancy Henley (eds) (1983) *Language, Gender and Society.* Rowley, Mass.: Newbury House, pp. 89–101.

Fishman, Pamela M. (1980) Conversational insecurity. In Howard Giles, W. Peter Robinson and Philip M. Smith (eds) *Language: Social Psychological Perspectives.* Oxford: Pergamon, pp. 127–32.

Fishman, Pamela M. (1983) Interaction: the work women do. In Barrie Thorne, Cheris Kramarae and Nancy Henley (eds) *Language, Gender and Society.* Rowley, Mass.: Newbury House, pp. 89–101.

Franken, Margaret (1983) Interviewers' strategies: how questions are modified. Unpublished terms paper. Wellington: Victoria University.

Fraser, Bruce (1981) On apologising. In Florian Coulmas (ed.) *Conversational Routine.* The Hague: Mouton, pp. 259–71.

Freed, Alice F. (1992) We understand perfectly: a critique of Tannen's view of cross-sex communication. In Kira Hall, Mary Bucholtz and Birch Moonwomon (eds) *Locating Power.* Proceedings of the Second Berkeley Women and Language Conference, 4 and 5 April 1992, Vol. 1. Berkeley, Cal.: Berkeley Women and Language Group, University of California, pp. 197–206.

Galbraith, J.K. (1983) *The Anatomy of Power.* Boston, Mass.: Houghton Mifflin.

García, Carmen (1989) Apologizing in English: politeness strategies used by native and non-native speakers. *Multilingua* 8, 1: 3–20.

Gass, Susan M. and E. M. Varonis (1988) Sex differences in Non-native speaker/non-native speaker interactions. In R.R. Day (ed.) *Talking to Learn: Conversations in Second Language Acquisition.* Rowley, Mass.: Newbury House.

Geertz, Clifford (1960) *The Religion of Java.* Glencoe, Ill.: The Free Press.

Gibson, Deborah Jean (1976) A thesis on *eh*. Unpublished MA paper. University of British Columbia. Department of Linguistics.

Gilbert, Jane (1990) Secondary School Students Talking about Science: Language Functions, Gender and Interactions in Small Group Discussions. MA thesis. Wellington: Victoria University.

Gilbert, Jane (1991) Achieving equity in small discussion groups. *Working Papers in Language, Gender and Sexism 2, 2:* 55–74.

Gilligan, Carol (1982) *In a Different Voice.* London: Harvard University Press.

Goffman, Erving (1967) *Interaction Ritual.* New York: Anchor Books.

Goffman, Erving (1971) *Relations in Public.* New York: Basic Books.

Goodwin, Marjorie H. (1980) Directive-response speech sequences in girls' and boys' task activities. In Sally McConnell-Ginet, Ruth Borker and Nelly Furman (eds) *Women and Language in Literature and Society.* New York: Praeger, pp. 157–73.

Goodwin, Marjorie H. and Goodwin, Charles (1987) Children's arguing. In Susan U. Philips, Susan Steele and Christine Tanz (eds) *Language, Gender and Sex in Comparative Perspective*. Cambridge: Cambridge University Press, pp. 200–48.

Gottman, J.M. and R.L. Levenson (1988) The social psychophysiology of marriage. In P. Noller and M.A. Fitzpatrick (eds) *Perspectives on Marital Interaction*. Clevedon and Philadelphia, Pa.: Multilingual Matters, pp. 182–202.

Graddol, David and Joan Swann (1989) *Gender Voices*. Oxford: Blackwell.

Greif, Esther B. and Jean B. Gleason (1980) Hi, Thanks and Goodbye: more routine information. *Language and Society* 9, 2: 159–66.

Gumperz, John J. (1978) The conversational analysis of interethnic communication. In E. Lamar Ross (ed.) *Interethnic Communication: Proceedings of the Southern Anthropological Society*. Athens, Georgia: University of Georgia Press, pp. 13–31.

Guy, Gregory and Julia Vonwiller (1984) The meaning of an intonation in Australian English. *Australian Journal of Linguistics* 4, 1: 1–17.

Guy, Gregory, Barbara Horvath, Julia Vonwiller, Elaine Daisley and Inge Rogers (1986) An intonational change in progress in Australian English. *Language in Society* 15, 1: 23–52

Haas, Adelaide (1979) The acquisition of genderlect. In Judith Orasanu, Mariam K. Slater and Leonore Loeb Adler (eds) *Annals of the New York Academy of Sciences: Language, Sex and Gender*, 327: 101–13.

Hall, Catherine (1985) Private person versus public someones: class, gender and politics in England, 1780–1850. In Carolyn Steedman, Cathy Urwin and Valerie Walkerdine (eds) *Language, Gender and Childhood*. Routledge, London, pp. 10–33.

Hartman, Maryann (1979) A descriptive study of the language of men and women born in Maine around 1900. In Betty-Lou Dubois and Isobel Crouch (eds) *The Sociology of the Languages of American Women*. San Antonio, Tex.: Trinity University, pp. 81–90.

Heath, Shirley B. (1982) Questioning at home and at school: a comparative study. In G. Spindler (ed.) *Doing the Ethnography of Schooling: Educational Anthropology in Action*. New York: Holt, Rinehart and Winston, pp. 102–31.

Henley, Nancy M. and Cheris Kramarae (1991) Gender, power and miscommunication. In Nikolas Coupland, Howard Giles and John W. Wiemann (eds) *'Miscommunication' and Problematic Talk*. London: Sage, pp. 18–43.

Herbert, Robert K. (1989) The ethnography of English compliments and compliment responses: a contrastive sketch. In Wieslaw Olesky (ed.) *Contrastive Pragmatics*. Amsterdam: John Benjamins, pp. 3–35.

Herbert, Robert K. (1990) Sex-based differences in compliment behaviour. *Language in Society* 19: 201–24.

Hiller, U. (1985) Some sex-related differences in the use of spontaneous speech. *Linguistic Agency University of Duisburg (previously Trier) Papers,* Series B, p. 140.

Hirschman, Lynette (1974) Analysis of supportive and assertive behaviour in conversations. Paper given at meeting of the Linguistic Society of America, San Francisco, California.

Hofstede, G. (1984) Motivation, leadership and organization: do American theories apply abroad? In D. Kolb, I. Rubin and J. McIntyre (eds) *Organizational Psychology.* Englewood Cliffs, NJ: Prentice-Hall, pp. 309–30.

Holmes, Janet (1982a) Expressing doubt and certainty in English. *RELC Journal* 13, 2: 9–28.

Holmes, Janet (1982b) The functions of tag questions. *English Language Research Journal* 3: 40–65.

Holmes, Janet (1984a) 'Women's language': a functional approach. *General Linguistics* 24, 3: 149–78.

Holmes, Janet (1984b) Hedging your bets and sitting on the fence: some evidence for hedges as support structures. *Te Reo* 27: 47–62.

Holmes, Janet (1984c) Modifying illocutionary force. *Journal of Pragmatics* 8, 345–65.

Holmes, Janet (1985) Sex differences and miscommunication: some data from New Zealand. In J.B. Pride (ed.) *Cross-cultural Encounters: Communication and Miscommunication.* Melbourne: River Seine, pp. 24–43.

Holmes, Janet (1986a) Functions of *you know* in women's and men's speech. *Language in Society* 15, 1: 1–22.

Holmes, Janet (1986b) Compliments and compliment responses in New Zealand English. *Anthropological Linguistics* 28, 4: 485–508.

Holmes, Janet (1987) Sex differences and language use in the ESL classroom. In Bikram K. Das (ed.) *Communication and Learning in the Classroom Community.* Anthology Series 19. Singapore: SEAMEO Regional Language Centre, pp. 5–36.

Holmes, Janet (1988a) *Of course*: a pragmatic particle in New Zealand women's and men's speech. *Australian Journal of Linguistics* 8, 1: 49–74.

Holmes, Janet (1988b) Paying compliments: a sex-preferential positive politeness strategy. *Journal of Pragmatics* 12, 3: 445–65.

Holmes, Janet (1988c) Sex differences in seminar contributions. *BAAL Newsletter* 31: 33–41.

Holmes, Janet (1989a) *Sort of* in New Zealand women's and men's speech. *Studia Linguistica* 42, 2: 85–121.

Holmes, Janet (1989b) Stirring up the dust: the importance of sex as a variable in the ESL classroom. *Proceedings of the ATESOL 6th Summer School, Sydney*. Vol. 1, pp. 4–39.

Holmes, Janet (1989c) Sex differences and interaction: problems for the language learner. In Paul Meara (ed.) *Beyond Words. British Studies in Applied Linguistics 4*. London: British Association of Applied Linguistics in association with CILT, pp. 38–57.

Holmes, Janet (1989d) Sex differences and apologies: one aspect of communicative competence. *Applied Linguistics* 10, 2: 194–213.

Holmes, Janet (1990a) Politeness strategies in New Zealand women's speech. In Allan Bell and Janet Holmes (eds) *New Zealand Ways of Speaking English*. Clevedon, Avon: Multilingual Matters, pp. 252–76.

Holmes, Janet (1990b) Apologies in New Zealand English. *Language in Society* 19, 2: 155–99.

Holmes, Janet (1991) Language and gender. *Language Teaching* 24, 4: 207–20.

Holmes, Janet (1992a) *An Introduction to Sociolinguistics*. London: Longman.

Holmes, Janet (1992b) Women's talk in public contexts. *Discourse and Society* 3, 2: 131–50.

Holmes, Janet (1993) New Zealand women are good to talk to: an analysis of politeness strategies in interaction. *Journal of Pragmatics* 20, 2: 91–116.

Holmes, Janet, Allan Bell and Mary Boyce (1991) *Variation and Change in New Zealand English: a Social Dialect Investigation*. Project Report to the Social Sciences Committee of the Foundation for Research, Science and Technology. Wellington: Victoria University.

Holmes, Janet and Dorothy Brown (1976) Developing sociolinguistic competence in a second language. *TESOL Quarterly* 10, 4: 423–31.

Holmes, Janet and Maria Stubbe (1992) Women and men talking: gender-based patterns of interaction. In Suzann Olsson (ed.) *The Gender Factor: Women in New Zealand Organizations*. Palmerston North: Dunmore Press, pp. 149–63.

Horvath, Barbara (1985) *Variation in Australian English: the Sociolects of Sydney*. Cambridge: Cambridge University Press.

House, Juliane and Gabriele Kasper (1981) Politeness markers in English and German. In Florian Coulmas (ed.) *Conversational Routine*. The Hague: Mouton, pp. 157–85.

Huddleston, R. (1970) Two approaches to the analysis of tags. *Journal of Linguistics* 6: 215–21.

Hudson, R.A. (1975) The meaning of questions. *Language* 51, 1: 1–31.

Hughes, Susan E. (1992) Expletives of lower working class women. *Language in Society* 21, 2: 291–303.

Hymes, Dell (1962) The ethnography of speaking. In T. Gladwin and W. Sturtevant (eds) *Anthropogy and Human Behaviour*. Washington. DC: Anthropological Society of Washington, pp. 15–53.

Hymes, Dell (1972) On communicative competence. In J.B. Pride and Janet Holmes (eds) *Sociolinguistics*. Harmondsworth: Penguin, pp. 269–93.

Hymes, D. (1974) Ways of speaking. In R. Baumann and J. Sherzer (eds) *Explorations in the Ethnography of Speaking*. Cambridge: Cambridge University Press, pp. 433–51.

Hyndman, Christine (1985) Gender and language differences: a small study. Unpublished terms paper. Wellington: Victoria University.

Ide, Sachiko (1982) Japanese sociolinguistics: politeness and women's language. *Lingua* 57: 357–85.

Ide, Sachiko (1990) How and why do women speak more politely in Japanese. In Sachiko, Ide and Naomi Hanaoka McGloin (eds) *Aspects of Japanese Women's Language*. Tokyo: Kurosio, pp. 63–79.

Ide, Sachiko, Motoko Hori, Akiko Kawasaki, Shoko Ikuta and Hitomi Haga (1986) Sex differences and politeness in Japanese. *International Journal of the Sociology of Language* 58: 25–36.

Inoue, Kyoko (1979) Japanese: a story of language and people. In Shopen, Timothy (ed.) *Languages and their Speakers*. Cambridge, Mass.: Winthrop.

James, A.R. (1983) Compromisers in English: a cross-disciplinary approach to their interpersonal significance. *Journal of Pragmatics* 7: 191–206.

James, Bev and Kay Saville-Smith (1989) *Gender, Culture and Power*. Auckland: Oxford University Press.

James, Deborah and Sandra Clarke (1992) Interruptions, gender and power: a critical review of the literature. In Kira Hall, Mary Bucholtz and Birch Moonwomon (eds) *Locating Power*. Proceedings of the Second Berkeley Women and Language Conference, 4 and 5 April 1992, Vol. 2. Berkeley, Cal.: Berkeley Women and Language Group, University of California, pp. 286–99.

James, E., C. Mahut and G. Latkiewicz (1989) The investigation of an apparently new intonation pattern in Toronto English. *Information Communication* 19: 11–17.

Jenkins, Lee and Cheris Kramer (1978) Small group process: learning from women. *Women's Studies International Quarterly* 1: 67–84.

Jenkins, Nancy and Jenny Cheshire (1990) Gender issues in the GCSE oral English examination: part 1. *Language and Education* 4: 261–92.

Johnson, Donna M. and Duane H. Roen (1992) Complimenting and involvement in peer reviews: gender variation. *Language in Society* 21, 1: 27–57.

Johnson, Fern L. and Lynda Goldman (1977) Communication education for women: a case for separatism. *Communication Education* 26: 319–26.

Johnson, Janet L. (1980) Questions and role responsibility in four professional meetings. *Anthropological Linguistics* 22: 66–76.

Jones, Deborah (1975) Male and female language and the expression of uncertainty. Unpublished terms paper. Wellington: Victoria University.

Kalcik, Susan (1975) '... like Ann's gynaecologist or the time I was almost raped' – personal narratives in women's rape groups. *Journal of American Folklore* 88: 3–11.

Karp, David A. and William C. Yoels (1976) The college classroom: some observations on the meanings of student participation. *Sociology and Social Research* 60: 421–39.

Kasper, Gabriele (1990) Linguistic politeness: current research issues. *Journal of Pragmatics* 14: 193–218.

Kissling, Elizabeth Arveda (1991) Street harassment: the language of sexual terrorism. *Discourse and Society* 2, 4: 451–60.

Kissling, Elizabeth Arveda and Cheris Kramarae (1991) 'Stranger compliments': the interpretation of street remarks. *Women's Studies in Communication* Spring: 77–95.

Knapp, Mark L., Robert Hopper and Robert A. Bell (1984) Compliments: a descriptive taxonomy. *Journal of Communication* 34, 4: 12–31.

Kramer, Cheris (1975) Sex-related differences in address systems. *Anthropological Linguistics* 17, 5: 198–210.

Kuiper, Koenraad (1991) Sporting formulae in New Zealand English; two models of male solidarity. In Jenny Cheshire (ed.) *English around the World: Sociolinguistic Perspectives*. Cambridge: Cambridge University Press, pp. 200–9.

Labov, William (1972) Rules for ritual insults. In T. Kochman (ed.) *Rappin' and Stylin' Out*. Chicago, Ill.: University of Illinois Press, pp. 265–314.

Labov, William (1990) The intersection of sex and social class in the course of linguistic change. *Language Variation and Change* 2: 205–54.

Lakoff, Robin (1973) Language and woman's place. *Language in Society* 2: 45–79.

Lakoff, Robin (1975) *Language and Woman's Place*. New York: Harper and Row.

Lane, Chris (1990) The sociolinguistics of questioning in district court trials. In Allan Bell and Janet Holmes (eds) *New Zealand Ways of Speaking English*. Clevedon, Avon: Multilingual Matters, pp. 221–51.

Lapadat, J. and Seesahai, M. (1977) Male versus female codes in informal contexts. *Sociolinguistics Newsletter* 8, 3: 7–8.

Laver, John (1981) Linguistic routines and politeness in greeting and parting. In Florian Coulmas (ed.) *Conversational Routine*. The Hague: Mouton, pp. 289–304.

Leech, Geoffrey N. (1983) *Principles of Pragmatics*. London: Longman.

Leet-Pellegrini, H.M. (1980) Conversational dominance as a function of gender and expertise. In Howard Giles, Peter Robinson and Philip Smith (eds) *Language: Social Psychological Perspectives*. Pergamon Press: Oxford, pp. 97–104.

Lehtonen, Jaakko and Kari Sajavaara (1985) The silent Finn. In Deborah Tannen and Muriel Saville-Troike (eds) *Perspectives on Silence*. Norwood, NJ: Ablex, pp. 193–201.

Lewandowska-Tomaszczyk, Barbara (1989) Praising and complimenting. In Wieslaw Olesky (ed.) *Contrastive Pragmatics*. Amsterdam: John Benjamins, pp. 73–100.

Loban, W. (1966) *Problems in Oral English*. Research Report No. 5. Urbana Ill.: National Council of Teachers of English.

Maccoby, Eleanor, E. and Carol N. Jacklin (1974) *The Psychology of Sex Differences*. Stanford, Cal.: Stanford University Press.

Madhok, Jacqueline (1992) The effect of gender composition on group interaction. In Kira Hall, Mary Bucholtz and Birch Moonwomon (eds) *Locating Power*. Proceedings of the Second Berkeley Women and Language Conference, 4 and 5 April 1992, Vol. 2. Berkeley, Cal.: Berkeley Women and Language Group, University of California, pp. 371–85.

Maltz, Daniel N. and Borker, Ruth A. (1982) A cultural approach to male-female miscommunication. In John J. Gumperz (ed.) *Language and Social Identity*. Cambridge: Cambridge University Press, pp. 196–216.

Manes, Joan (1983) Compliments: a mirror of cultural values. In Nessa Wolfson and Elliot Judd (eds) *Sociolinguistics and Language Acquisition*. Rowley, Mass.: Newbury House, pp. 96–102.

Manes, Joan and Nessa Wolfson (1981) The compliment formula. In Florian Coulmas (ed.) *Conversational Routine*. The Hague: Mouton, pp. 115–32.

Marland, M. (1977) *Language Across the Curriculum*. London: Heinemann.

McGlone, J. (1980) Sex differences in human brain asymmetry: a critical survey. *Behavioural and Brain Sciences* 3: 215–63.

McKeever, Walter F. (1987) Cerebral organization and sex: interesting but complex. In Susan U. Philips, Susan Steele and Christine Tanz (eds) (1987) *Language Gender and Sex in Comparative Perspective*. Cambridge: Cambridge University Press, pp. 268–77.

McLemore, Cynthia (1991) The interpretation of L*H in English. *Texas Linguistic Forum 32: Discourse*, pp. 175–96.

McMillan, J.R., A.K. Clifton, D. McGrath and W.S. Gale (1977) Woman's language: uncertainty or interpersonal sensitivity and emotionality? *Sex Roles* 3, 6: 545–59.

Meyerhoff, Miriam (1986) The kind of women who put '-ish' behind everything and 'sort of' in front of it – a study of sex differences in New Zealand English. Unpublished MA thesis. Wellington: Victoria University.

Meyerhoff, Miriam (1992a) 'We've all got to go one day, eh': power-lessness and solidarity in the functions of a New Zealand tag. In Kira Hall, Mary Bucholtz and Birch Moonwomon (eds) *Locating Power*. Proceedings of the Second Berkeley Women and Language Conference, 4 and 5 April 1992, Vol. 2. Berkeley, Cal.: Berkeley Women and Language Group, University of California, pp. 409–19.

Meyerhoff, Miriam (1992b) 'A sort of something': hedging strategies on nouns. *Working Papers in Language Gender and Sexism* 3: 59–73.

Meyerhoff, Miriam (1992c) Review of Deborah Tannen *You Just Don't Understand*. *Australian Journal of Linguistics* 12: 236–41.

Millar, M. and K. Brown (1979) Tag questions in Edinburgh speech. *Linguistische Berichte* 60: 24–45.

Miller, Jean Baker (1976) *Toward a New Psychology of Women*. Boston, Mass.: Beacon Press.

Mulac, Anthony, John M. Wiemann, Sally J. Widenmann, and Toni W. Gibson (1988) Male/female language differences and effects in same sex and mixed-sex dyads: the gender-linked language effect. *Communication Monographs* 55, 4: 315–35.

Munro, Fran (1986) Sex and language use in the ESL classroom. Unpublished terms paper. Graduate Diploma in TESOL. Sydney: Sydney College of Advanced Education.

Munro, Fran (1987) Female and male participation in small-group interaction in the ESOL classroom. Unpublished terms project. Graduate Diploma in TESOL. Sydney: Sydney College of Advanced Education.

Murray, Stephen O. and Lucille H. Covelli (1988) Women and men speaking at the same time. *Journal of Pragmatics* 12, 103–11.

Nässlin, S. (1984) The English Tag Question. *Stockholm Studies in English*. Stockholm: Almqvist and Wiksell.

Natale, M., Entin, E. and J. Jaffe (1979) Vocal interruptions in dyadic communication as a function of speech and social anxiety. *Journal of Personality and Social Psychology* 37: 865–78.

Nelson, Marie Wilson (1988) Women's ways: interactive patterns in predominantly female research teams. In Barbara Bate and Anita

Taylor (eds) *Women Communicating: Studies of Women's Talk.* Ablex: New Jersey, pp. 199–232.

Ng, Sik Hung and James J. Bradac (1993) *Power in Language.* London: Sage.

Ngan-Woo. F.E. (1985) *Fa'asamoa: The World of Samoans.* Auckland: Office of the Race Relations Conciliator.

Noller, Patricia (1993) Gender and emotional communication in marriage: different cultures or differential social power? *Journal of Language and Social Psychology* 12, 1/2: 132–52.

O'Barr, W.M. and B.K. Atkins (1980) 'Women's language' or 'powerless language'. In Sally McConnell-Ginet, Ruth Borker and Nellie Furman (eds) *Women and Language in Literature and Society.* New York: Praeger, pp. 93–110.

Ochs, Elinor (1987) The impact of stratification and socialization on men's and women's speech in Western Samoa. In Susan U. Philips, Susan Steele and Christine Tanz (eds) *Language, Gender and Sex in Comparative Perspective.* Cambridge: Cambridge University Press, pp. 50–70.

Octigan, Mary and Sharon Niederman (1979) Male dominance in conversations. *Frontiers* 4, 1: 50–4.

Oleksy, W. (1977) Tags in English and equivalent constructions in Polish. *Poznan Studies in Contrastive Linguistics* 7: 95–109.

Olshtain E. and A.D. Cohen (1983) Apology: a speech act set. In Nessa Wolfson and Elliot Judd (eds) *Sociolinguistics and Language Acquisition.* Mass.: Newbury House, pp. 18–35.

Östman, J.-O. (1981) *'You know': A Discourse-Functional Approach.* Amsterdam: John Benjamins B.V.

Owen, Marion (1983) *Apologies and Remedial Interchanges: A Study of Language Use in Social Interaction.* Berlin: Mouton, Walter de Gruyter.

Philips, Susan U., Susan Steele and Christine Tanz (eds) (1987) *Language, Gender and Sex in Comparative Perspective.* Cambridge: Cambridge University Press.

Piliavin, Jane A. and Rachel R. Martin (1978) The effects of the sex composition of groups on style of social interaction. *Sex Roles* 4: 281–96.

Pilkington, Jane (1992) 'Don't try to make out that I'm nice!' The different strategies women and men use when gossiping. *Wellington Working Papers in Linguistics* 5: 37–60.

Pomerantz, Anita (1978) Compliment responses: notes on the co-operation of multiple constraints. In J. Schenkein (ed.) *Studies in the Organisation of Conversational Interaction.* New York: Academic Press, pp. 79–112.

Poynton, Cate (1985) *Language and Gender: Making the Difference.* Victoria: Deakin University

Poynton, Cate (1989) Terms of address in Australian English. In Peter Collins and David Blair (eds) *Australian English.* St Lucia: University of Queensland, pp. 55–69.

Preisler, Bent (1986) *Linguistic Sex Roles in Conversation.* Berlin: Mouton de Gruyter.

Quirk, R., S. Greenbaum, G. Leech and J. Svartvik (1985) *A Comprehensive Grammar of the English Language.* London: Longman.

Randall, Gay J. (1987) Gender differences in pupil–teacher interaction in workshops and laboratories. In Gaby Weiner and Madeline Arnot (eds) *Gender Under Scrutiny: New Enquiries in Education.* London: Hutchinson, pp. 163–72.

Roberts, Celia, Evelyn Davies and Tom Jupp (1992) *Language and Discrimination.* London: Longman.

Roger, Derek (1989) Experimental studies of dyadic turn-taking behaviour. In Derek Roger and Peter Bull (eds) *Conversation: an Interdisciplinary Perspective.* Clevedon: Multilingual Matters, pp. 75–95.

Rubin, Donald R. and Marie Wilson Nelson (1983) Multiple determinants of a stigmatised speech style: women's language, powerless language or everyone's language? *Language and Speech* 26, 3: 273–90.

Sadker, M. and D. Sadker (1985) Sexism in the schoolroom of the '80s. *Psychology Today* March 1985: 54–7.

Safilios-Rothschild, Constantina (1979) *Sex Role, Socialisation and Sex Discrimination: a Synthesis and Critique of the Literature.* Washington, DC: National Institute of Education.

Schick Case, Susan (1988) Cultural differences, not deficiencies: an analysis of managerial women's language. In Suzanna Rose and Laurie Larwood (eds) *Women's Careers: Pathways and Pitfalls.* New York: Praeger, pp. 41–63.

Schiffrin, Deborah (1987) *Discourse Markers.* Cambridge: Cambridge University Press.

Schourup, L.C. (1985) *Common Discourse Particles in English Conversation.* New York: Garland.

Scollon, Ron and Suzanne B. K. Scollon (1981) *Narrative, Literacy and Face in Interethnic Communication.* Norwood, NJ: Ablex.

Sheldon, Amy (1990) Pickle fights: gendered talk in preschool disputes. *Discourse Processes* 13: 5–31.

Sheldon, Amy (1992a) Conflict talk: sociolinguistic challenges to self-assertion and how young girls meet them. *Merrill-Palmer Quarterly* 38, 1: 95–117.

Sheldon, Amy (1992b) Preschool girls' discourse competence: managing conflict. In Kira Hall, Mary Bucholtz and Birch Moonwomon (eds) *Locating Power*. Proceedings of the Second Berkeley Women and Language Conference, 4 and 5 April 1992, Vol. 2. Berkeley, Cal.: Berkeley Women and Language Group, University of California, pp. 528–39.

Shimanoff, Susan B. (1977) Investigating politeness. In E.O. Keenan and T.L. Bennett (eds) *Discourse across Time and Space*. Southern California Occasional Papers in Linguistics. No. 5, pp. 213–41.

Sifianou, Maria (1992) *Politeness Phenomena in England and Greece: a Cross-Cultural Perspective*. Oxford: Clarendon Press.

Sinclair, John McH. and R. Malcolm Coulthard (1975) *Towards an Analysis of Discourse*. London: Oxford University Press.

Smith, Janet S. (1992) Women in charge: politeness and directives in the speech of Japanese women. *Language in Society* 21, 1: 59–82.

Smith, Philip (1985) *Language, the Sexes and Society*. Oxford: Blackwell.

Smith-Hefner, Nancy J. (1988) Women and politeness: the Javanese example. *Language in Society* 17, 4: 535–54.

Soskin, William F. and Vera. P. John (1963) The study of spontaneous talk. In Roger Barker (ed.) *The Stream of Behaviour*. New York: Appleton-Century Crofts, pp. 228–87.

Spender, Dale (1979) Language and sex differences. *Osna Brücker Beiträge Zur Sprach-Theorie: Spräche und Geschlecht* II: 38–59.

Spender, Dale (1980a) *Man Made Language*. London: Routledge and Kegan Paul.

Spender, Dale (1980b) Talking in class. In Dale Spender and Elizabeth Sarah (eds) *Learning to Lose*. London: The Women's Press. pp. 148–54.

Spender, Dale (1982) *Invisible Women*. London: The Women's Press.

Spender, Dale (1992) Information management: women's language strengths. In Kira Hall, Mary Bucholtz and Birch Moonwomon (eds) *Locating Power*. Proceedings of the Second Berkeley Women and Language Conference, 4 and 5 April 1992, Vol. 2. Berkeley, Cal.: Berkeley Women and Language Group, University of California, pp. 549–59.

Stanworth, Michelle (1983) *Gender and Schooling*. London: Hutchinson.

Stanworth, Michelle (1987) Girls on the margins: a study of gender divisions in the classroom. In Gaby Weiner and Madeleine Arnot (eds) *Gender Under Scrutiny*. London: Hutchinson.

Strodtbeck, Fred L. and Richard D. Mann (1956) Sex role differentiation in jury deliberations. *Sociometry* 19: 3–11.

Stubbe, Maria (1978) Sex roles in conversation: a study of small group interaction. Unpublished term paper. Wellington: Victoria University.

Stubbe, Maria (1991) Talking at cross-purposes: the effect of gender on New Zealand primary schoolchildren's interaction strategies in pair discussions. MA thesis. Wellington: Victoria University.

Stubbs, Michael (1976) *Language, Schools and Classroom*, 2nd edn 1983. London: Methuen.

Swacker, Marjorie (1979) Women's verbal behaviour at learned and professional conferences. In Betty-Lou Dubois and Isobel Crouch (eds) *The Sociology of the Languages of American Women*. San Antonio, Tex.: Trinity University, pp. 155–60.

Swann, Joan (1989) Talk control: an illustration from the classroom of problems in analysing male dominance of conversation. In Jennifer Coates and Deborah Cameron (eds) *Women in their Speech Communities*. London: Longman, pp. 122–40.

Swann, Joan (1992) *Girls, Boys and Language*. Oxford: Blackwell.

Tannen, Deborah (1984) *Conversational Style: Analyzing Talk Among Friends*. Norwood, NJ: Ablex.

Tannen, Deborah (1986) Introduction. *Text* 6, 2: 143–51.

Tannen, Deborah (1987) *That's Not What I Meant! How Conversational Style Makes or Breaks Relationships*. New York: Ballantine.

Tannen, Deborah (1990a) *You Just Don't Understand: Women and Men in Conversation*. New York: William Morrow.

Tannen, Deborah (1990b) Gender differences in topical coherence: creating involvement in best friends' talk. *Discourse Processes* 13: 73–90.

Thomas, Jenny (1983) Cross-cultural pragmatic failure. *Applied Linguistics* 4, 2: 91–112.

Thomas, Jenny (1985) Complex illocutionary acts and the analysis of discourse. *Lancaster Papers in Linguistics 11*. Lancaster: University of Lancaster.

Thomas, Jenny (1989) Discourse control in confrontational interaction. In Leo Hickey (ed.) *The Pragmatics of Style*. London: Croom Helm, pp. 133–56.

Thorne, Barrie (1989) Rethinking the ways we teach. In Carol S. Pearson, Donna L. Shavlik and Judith G. Touchton (eds) *Educating the Majority: Women Challenge Tradition in Higher Education*. New York: Collier Macmillan, pp. 311–25.

Thorne, Barrie, Cheris Kramarae and Nancy Henley (eds) (1983) *Language, Gender and Society*. Rowley, Mass.: Newbury House.

Torrance, Nancy and David R. Olson (1984) Oral language and the acquisition of literacy. In Anthony D. Pellegrini and Thomas D. Yawkey (eds) *The Development of Oral and Written Language: Readings in Developmental and Applied Psycholinguistics*. Norwood, NJ: Ablex, pp. 167–81.

Tracy, Karen and Eric Eisenberg (1991) Giving criticism: a multiple goals case study. *Research on Language and Social Interaction* 24: 37–70.

Treichler, Paula A. and Cheris Kramarae (1983) Women's talk in the ivory tower. *Communication Quarterly* 31: 118– 32.

Troemel-Ploetz, Senta (1992) The construction of conversational equality by women. In Kira Hall, Mary Bucholtz and Birch Moonwomon (eds) *Locating Power*. Proceedings of the Second Berkeley Women and Language Conference, 4 and 5 April 1992, Vol. 2. Berkeley, Cal.: Berkeley Women and Language Group, University of California, pp. 581–9.

Trosborg, A. (1987) Apology strategies in natives/non-natives. *Journal of Pragmatics* 11: 147–67.

Turner, L.J. and R.E. Pickvance (1972) Social class differences in the expression of uncertainty in five-year-old children. *Language and Speech* 15: 303–25.

Uchida, Aki (1992) When 'difference' is 'dominance': a critique of the 'anti-power-based' cultural approach to sex differences. *Language in Society* 21, 4: 547–68.

Valdés, Guadalupe and Cecilia Pino (1981) Muy a tus órdenes: compliment responses among Mexican-American bilinguals. *Language in Society* 10, 1: 53–72.

van Alphen, Ingrid (1987) Learning from your peers: the acquisition of gender-specific speech styles. In Dédé Brouwer and Dorian De Haan (eds) *Women's Language, Socialisation and Self-image*. Dordrecht: Foris, pp. 58–75.

Weiner, Gaby and Madeline Arnot (eds) (1987) *Gender Under Scrutiny: New Enquiries in Education*. London: Hutchinson.

West, Candace (1984) When the doctor is a lady. *Symbolic Interaction* 7, 1: 87–106.

West, Candace (1990) Not just 'doctors' orders: directive response sequences in patients' visits to women and men physicians. *Discourse and Society* 1, 1: 85–112.

West, Candace and A. García (1988) Conversational shift work: a study of topical transitions between women and men. *Social Problems* 35, 5: 551–75.

West, Candace and Don Zimmerman (1977) Women's place in everyday talk: reflections on parent-child interaction. *Social Problems* 24: 521–9.

West, Candace and Don H. Zimmerman (1983) Small insults: a study of interruptions in cross-sex conversations between unacquainted persons. In Barrie Thorne, Cheris Kramarae and Nancy Henley (eds) *Language, Gender and Society*. Rowley, Mass.: Newbury House, pp. 102–17.

West, Candace and Don H. Zimmerman (1987) Doing gender. *Gender and Society* 1, 2: 125–51.

Wetzel, Patricia J. (1988) Are 'powerless' communication strategies the Japanese norm? *Language in Society* 17, 4: 555–64. Reprinted in Sachiko Ide and Naomi McGloin (eds) (1991) *Aspects of Japanese Women's Language*. Tokyo: Kurosia, pp. 115–26.

Whyte, J. (1984) Observing sex sterotypes and interactions in the school lab and workshop. *Educational Review* 36: 75–86.

Whyte, J. (1986) *Girls into Science and Technology: the Story of a Project*. London: Routledge and Kegan Paul.

Wierzbicka, Anna (1985) Different cultures, different languages, different speech acts. *Journal of Pragmatics* 9: 145–61.

Wierzbicka, Anna (1987) *English Speech Act Verbs: A Semantic Dictionary*. New York: Academic Press.

Wolfson, Nessa (1981a) Compliments in cross-cultural perspective. *TESOL Quarterly* 15, 2: 117–24.

Wolfson, Nessa (1981b) Invitations, compliments and the competence of the native speaker. *International Journal of Psycholinguistics* 24: 7–22.

Wolfson, Nessa (1983) An empirically based analysis of complimenting in American English. In Nessa Wolfson and Elliot Judd (eds) *Sociolinguistics and Language Acquisition*. Rowley, Mass.: Newbury House, pp. 82–95.

Wolfson, Nessa (1984) 'Pretty is as pretty does': a speech act view of sex roles. *Applied Linguistics* 5, 3: 236–44.

Wolfson, Nessa (1988) The bulge: a theory of speech behaviour and social distance. In J. Fine (ed.) *Second Language Discourse: A Textbook of Current Research*. Norwood, N.J.: Ablex, pp. 21–38.

Wolfson, Nessa and Joan Manes (1980) Don't 'Dear' me! In Sally McConnell-Ginet, Ruth Borker and Nelly Furman (eds) *Women and Language in Literature and Society*. New York: Praeger, pp. 79–92.

Wolfson, Nessa, Lynne D'Amico-Reisner and Lisa Huber (1983) How to arrange for social commitments in American English: the invitation. In Nessa Wolfson and Elliot Judd (eds) *Sociolinguistics and Language Acquisition*. Rowley, Mass.: Newbury House, pp. 116–28.

Woods, Nicola (1989) Talking shop: sex and status as determinants of floor apportionment in a work setting. In Jennifer Coates and Deborah Cameron (eds) *Women in Their Speech Communities*. London: Longman, pp. 141–57.

Woods, Nicola (1992) 'It's not what she says it's the way that she says it': the influence of speaker sex on pitch and intonational linguistic features. Paper given at Sociolinguistics Symposium 9. University of Reading, April 1992.

Zimin, Susan (1981) Sex and politeness: factors in first- and second-language use. *International Journal of the Sociology of Language* 27: 35–58.

Zimmerman, D.H. and C. West (1975) Sex roles, interruptions and silences in conversation. In Barrie Thorne and Nancy Henley (eds) *Language and Sex: Difference and Dominance*. Rowley, Mass.: Newbury House, pp. 105–29.

Author index

General index